RACHAEL RAY
2,4,6,8

RACHAEL RAY

2, 4, 6, 8

GREAT MEALS FOR COUPLES OR CROWDS

CLARKSON POTTER/PUBLISHERS

NEW YORK

Copyright © 2006 by Rachael Ray
Photographs copyright © 2006 by Ben Fink

Published in the United States by Clarkson Potter/Publishers, an imprint of the
Crown Publishing Group, a division of Random House, Inc., New York.
www.crownpublishing.com
www.clarksonpotter.com

Clarkson N. Potter is a trademark and Potter and colophon are registered
trademarks of Random House, Inc.

Library of Congress Cataloging-in-Publication Data is available upon request

ISBN-13: 978-1-4000-8256-8
ISBN-10: 1-4000-8256-0

Printed in the United States of America

Design by Jennifer K. Beal

10   9   8   7   6   5   4   3   2   1

First Edition

2,4,6,8, WHO DO I APPRECIATE?

This book is dedicated to cheerleaders everywhere! Not the girls in short skirts with pom-poms but the *real* cheerleaders out there: moms, dads, good neighbors who watch our pets and water our plants, people who work two jobs and can still smile at strangers, doctors who know how nervous they make us, firemen who still climb trees to rescue kittens. Thanks for keeping us all going!
Rah! Rah! Yay, you!

CONTENTS

04 MEALS FOR 4

9

CONTENTS

08 MEALS FOR 8

INTRODUCTION

2, 4, 6, 8 gives you flexibility with your 30-minute meals. Most recipes are written in base 4, right? But even if your family is exactly that size, whenever it's just-the-two-of-you at home for dinner or if a couple of couples come over to join you for a meal, you have to do some math to get the servings right. This book offers up easy-to-make meals by the number you'll be serving, whether you are planning a date night or a dinner party.

And it's not only the yields that vary from section to section. In the section for two, for example, some of the recipes include ingredients that are pricier and more precious for special nights. Hey, when it's just the two of you, go for it! It's not like you're searing scallops for eight or buying tenderloin steaks for the whole neighborhood—indulge! There are some easy, fun menus for two, too, for when you are home alone (you may want seconds) and are just too pooped to pop!

I went a little heavy on the section for four because we all cook for that number most often, right? Even when it's just me and the hubby at home I'm cooking for four because we have big appetites and a pit bull to feed. The recipes in this section cover a broad range of tastes to satisfy even the pickiest eaters and the ingredients are largely made up of on-hand basic nuts-and-bolts fine dining for four!

If your need to feed goes beyond the average you won't have to sweat the math multiplying your teaspoons and tablespoons; just turn the page to the sections for serving six and eight. Here you'll find hearty casseroles, platters of pasta, and other crowd-pleasing meals that won't have you chopping and prepping for hours—I've even thrown in some really easy desserts so you'll look like a hero and never break a sweat. (I love a good fake-out! Your guests will think you've been slaving all day!)

No matter how many are at the table, 2, 4, 6, or 8, the meal will taste great and it won't take more than 30 minutes—unless you get into the wine first! Enjoy a really delish dish, tonight!

RECIPES

02

02 04

I NEVER COOK FOR ONE, EVEN WHEN I AM ALONE. IT'S TOO DEPRESSING TO SEE SUCH SMALL AMOUNTS. BESIDES, ALL THE WOMEN IN MY FAMILY CAN OUTEAT ANY MAN I'VE EVER MET, SO I USUALLY GO BACK FOR SECONDS. WHEN IT COMES TO 30-MINUTE MEALS, THOUGH, THESE ARE AS SMALL AS THEY'LL GET. IF YOU ARE A PARTY OF TWO AND YOU'RE DINING WITH YOUR HONEY OR A BUDDY, NO WORRIES. I DON'T SKIMP ON PORTION SIZE, EITHER.

- Make the vinai-
  grette and salad
  but don't combine.

- Make the
  sandwiches.

- Stir up the
  cocktails and toss
  the salad.

BISTRO BRUNCH OR MIDNIGHT SUPPER FOR TWO

- **Vodka Still Works Cocktails**
- **Croque Madame (Ham and Cheese Sandwiches with Béchamel and Egg)**
- **Green Salad with Strawberry Balsamic Vinaigrette**

I love lazy Sunday brunch and sexy late-night suppers. A bistro favorite is a *croque monsieur*, a toasted ham and cheese sandwich, made into a *croque madame* with the addition of an egg on top. Strawberries and balsamic vinegar make a fruitful pairing to dress the salad alongside this French classic. As for the cocktail, I first had this drink on my honeymoon at the Singhita safari lodge in South Africa. The staff insisted my husband and I enjoy our first night as man and wife at their lodge in our rooms. They served these cocktails before a four-course meal in our suite. Wow! Talk about love at first sip! This cocktail makes a great first impression on any mate, whether you are single or married!

VODKA STILL WORKS COCKTAIL

1   teaspoon **Angostura bitters**
2   shots chilled **vodka**
6   to 8 ounces **ginger ale**

Place the bitters in a tall glass and combine them with the vodka, using a cocktail spoon. Add ice to the glass, then fill it with ginger ale and stir again. Serve this with a straw.

1 SERVING

CROQUE MADAME

- 6 tablespoons ($^3/_4$ stick) **butter**
- 1 rounded tablespoon all-purpose **flour**
- 1 cup **milk**

  Salt and **black pepper**
- $^1/_8$ teaspoon freshly grated or ground **nutmeg** (eyeball it)
- 2 teaspoons **Dijon mustard**
- 2 large **eggs**
- 4 slices **white bread**
- 4 deli slices **ham** (look for a low-moisture ham rather than boiled)
- 4 deli slices **Swiss cheese** (look for Emmentaler)

  Chopped fresh flat-leaf parsley, chives, or thyme, for garnish (choose from any or all on hand)

Place a small sauce pot over medium-low heat and melt 2 tablespoons of the butter in it. Whisk in the flour and cook for 1 minute or so. Whisk in the milk and bring it to a bubble, then drop the heat to low. Season the sauce with salt, pepper, nutmeg, and the Dijon.

When the béchamel sauce coats the back of a spoon, turn off the heat.

Heat 1 tablespoon of the butter in a medium nonstick skillet over medium-low heat. When the butter melts, crack in the eggs, keeping the whites separate from each other. Cook them to desired doneness, sunnyside up to over hard. While the eggs cook, generously butter the bread with the remaining 3 tablespoons of butter. Keep the buttered sides facing out and build ham and cheese sandwiches, spreading béchamel on the insides of the bread and using 2 slices of ham and cheese for each sandwich. Heat a second skillet over medium heat. Cook the sandwiches until golden, 3 to 4 minutes, then turn. Cook them for 2 minutes more, then transfer them to plates and top with eggs and more sauce, garnish with the chopped herb of choice, and serve with a fork and knife.

2 SERVINGS

GREEN SALAD WITH STRAWBERRY BALSAMIC VINAIGRETTE

2 teaspoons **strawberry jam**

1 tablespoon **balsamic vinegar**

3 tablespoons **EVOO** (extra-virgin olive oil; eyeball it)

Salt and **black pepper**

6 **strawberries**, sliced

4 cups chopped **romaine** or mixed greens of any kind

Place the jam in a medium bowl and whisk in the vinegar and then EVOO. Season the dressing with salt and pepper. Add the strawberries and greens to the bowl and toss to coat evenly in the dressing.

2 SERVINGS

■ ● ■

- Assemble the sandwiches.

- Start the salad and make the dressing.

- Coat and fry the sandwiches.

- Toss the salad.

THE COUNT OF MONTE CRISTO SUMMERS IN PORTOFINO

- Mozzarella and Ham in Carrozza
- Potato and Dandelion Salad with Pancetta

A Monte Cristo sandwich is an old diner favorite of mine—a sandwich of ham, turkey, and cheese, dipped in egg, and cooked on the griddle until golden. This is a twist on *mozzarella in carrozza*, "mozzarella in a carriage," a specialty in Campania, Italy. I add ham—yum-o! Alongside: a simple, hearty salad of potatoes and dark greens.

MOZZARELLA AND HAM IN CARROZZA

- 4 slices good-quality **Italian bread**
- 2 slices **fresh mozzarella** cheese, $^3/_4$ inch thick
- 4 slices **rosemary roast ham** (look for Rosmarino by Citterio in the packaged deli meats case) or $^1/_4$ pound prosciutto cotto (cooked Italian ham)
- 3 tablespoons **EVOO** (extra-virgin olive oil)
- $^1/_2$ cup all-purpose **flour**, for dredging
  Pinch of freshly grated or ground **nutmeg**
  Pinch of **cayenne pepper**
  Salt
- 2 **eggs**
  Splash of **milk** or half-and-half

Make sandwiches using 2 slices of bread, 1 slice of mozzarella, and 2 slices of ham for each. Heat the EVOO in a skillet over medium heat. Pour the flour onto a plate and season it with nutmeg, cayenne, and salt. In a shallow dish, beat the eggs with milk or half-and-half. Dredge the sandwiches in the flour, then coat them in the eggs. Fry the sandwiches for 2 minutes on each side, halve, and serve.

2 SERVINGS

POTATO AND DANDELION SALAD WITH PANCETTA

4 small **red potatoes**, thinly sliced

Salt

1/4 pound **green beans**, stem ends trimmed, cut into thirds

2 tablespoons **red wine vinegar** (eyeball it)

3 tablespoons **EVOO** (extra-virgin olive oil), plus a bit for drizzling

2 to 3 fresh **thyme** sprigs, leaves stripped from the stems and chopped

4 slices **pancetta**, chopped

1 large **shallot**, thinly sliced

1 bunch of **dandelion greens**, stems removed, chopped

Pinch of freshly grated or ground **nutmeg**

Black pepper

Place the potatoes in a pot with water to cover. Bring the water to a boil and salt it. Cook the potatoes for 5 minutes, then add the green beans and cook for 2 minutes more.

While the potatoes and beans cook, whisk together the vinegar, EVOO, and thyme. Heat a skillet over medium-high heat. Add a drizzle of oil and the pancetta. Cook the pancetta until brown, 4 to 5 minutes, then add the shallots and cook for a minute or two more.

Drain the potatoes and beans and add them to the pan with the shallots and pancetta. Add the dressing to the pan and toss to coat. Arrange the greens in a shallow serving bowl and toss them with the potatoes and beans. Season the salad with nutmeg, salt, and pepper and serve.

2 SERVINGS

■ ■ ■

GAME PLAN

• Make the salad while the eggs bake.

BRUNCH, LUNCH, OR LINNER, FOR TWO

• Baked Eggs Florentine
• Bacon and Tomato Salad with Garlic Croutons

I love eggs; they're delicious and inexpensive. I eat them for B, L, or D—which is breakfast, lunch, or dinner. This menu has the potential for an all-day egg affair for you and your buddy.

BAKED EGGS FLORENTINE

1   10-ounce box frozen **spinach**
2   tablespoons **EVOO** (extra-virgin olive oil; eyeball it)
1   tablespoon **butter**
1   small **onion**, finely chopped
1   large **garlic clove**, chopped
4   fresh **thyme** sprigs, leaves stripped and chopped
     Salt and **black pepper**
$^3/_4$ cup **chicken stock** (eyeball it)
$^1/_2$ cup **heavy cream** or half-and-half (eyeball it)
     Freshly grated or ground **nutmeg**
4   **eggs**
$^1/_2$ cup shredded or grated **Gruyère cheese** (a couple overflowing handfuls)

Preheat the oven to 450° F.

Place the spinach on a plate and microwave on High for 6 minutes to defrost. Heat a medium skillet over medium-high heat with the EVOO and the butter. Once the butter melts, add the onions, garlic, thyme, salt, and pepper and cook, stirring frequently, for 4 to 5 minutes.

continued

While the onions are cooking, place the defrosted spinach in a clean kitchen towel and squeeze out the excess liquid. Add the spinach to the onions, break it up with a spoon, then add the chicken stock, heavy cream, and a little nutmeg. Bring it up to a simmer and cook until it's creamy and thick, a couple of minutes. Transfer the spinach mixture to a small baking dish; I like to use my 8 by 11-inch oval baking dish. With the back of a spoon, create 4 divots in the spinach. Crack one egg at a time into a shallow cup or ramekin, then gently slide an egg into each divot in the spinach. Season the eggs with a little salt and pepper, sprinkle with the Gruyère cheese, and bake for 10 minutes for runny yolks and about 15 minutes for a really super-firm egg.

Serve the baked eggs Florentine along with the Bacon and Tomato Salad with Garlic Croutons.

2 SERVINGS

BACON AND TOMATO SALAD WITH GARLIC CROUTONS

- 3 tablespoons **EVOO** (extra-virgin olive oil; eyeball it)
- 4 **bacon** slices
- 4 thick slices **crusty bread**
- 1 **garlic clove**, peeled and cut in half
  Softened **butter**, for the toast
- 2 large **shallots**, thinly sliced
- 1 pint **red cherry tomatoes**, halved
- 1 pint **yellow cherry tomatoes**, halved
- 1/4 cup fresh **flat-leaf parsley** leaves, a generous handful, chopped
- 10 fresh **basil** leaves, chopped
- 2 tablespoons **balsamic vinegar** (eyeball it)
  Freshly ground black pepper

Preheat a medium skillet with about 1 tablespoon of the EVOO (once around the pan), add the bacon, and cook until crisp. While the bacon is getting crispy, put the bread in the toaster or under the broiler and toast until golden. Rub the toasted bread with the cut side of the garlic clove, then spread it with butter. Cut the toasts into large bite-size croutons. Transfer the bacon to a paper-towel-lined plate to drain. Add the shallots to the skillet and cook, stirring every now and then, for 3 to 4 minutes.

While the shallots are cooking, in a bowl, combine the tomatoes, parsley, basil, and garlic croutons. Chop or crumple up the crispy bacon and add it to the tomatoes. To the skillet with the shallots, add the balsamic vinegar and lots of black pepper. Turn the heat off and whisk in the remaining EVOO. Pour the dressing over the tomatoes, toss to coat the salad, then serve.

2 SERVINGS

■ ■ ■

ANOTHER BRUNCH OR LINNER

• **Poached Eggs on Potato, Spinach, and Smoked Salmon Salad with Creamy Caper Dressing**

I know, I know: breakfast is the most important meal of the day and I have permanently damaged my health and well being because I only have coffee for breakfast. The exception is Saturday and Sunday, when I *do* eat breakfast—albeit, at noon and with plenty of champagne or a Bloody Mary to wash it down.

POACHED EGGS ON POTATO, SPINACH, AND SMOKED SALMON SALAD WITH CREAMY CAPER DRESSING

1 pound small **red potatoes**, cut into quarters
  Salt
4 large handfuls of **baby spinach**
  Zest and juice of 1 lemon
1/4 cup pitted **kalamata olives**, coarsely chopped
  Black pepper
1 tablespoon **Dijon mustard** (eyeball it)
3 tablespoons **mayonnaise** (eyeball it)
2 tablespoons **capers** (eyeball it), drained and chopped
2 tablespoons chopped fresh **dill**
1 tablespoon **white vinegar** (eyeball it)
4 **eggs**
3 or 4 slices **smoked salmon**, cut into strips

Place the potatoes in a sauce pot, cover them with water, place the pot over high heat, and bring the water to a boil. Once it is boiling, add some salt and cook until the potatoes are tender, 12 to 15 minutes. Drain the potatoes and spread out on a cookie sheet to cool, about 5 minutes.

When cool, transfer the potatoes to a bowl. Add the spinach, lemon zest, and olives and season them with salt and pepper.

In a bowl, combine the mustard, mayonnaise, capers, dill, lemon juice, and a little splash of cold water to loosen up the dressing—just enough to make it drizzle-able.

Fill a medium skillet with about 2 inches of water. Bring the water to a gentle simmer over high heat. Once the water is at a bubble, turn the heat down to medium low; you need a gentle simmer for poaching eggs. Pour the vinegar into the simmering water. Crack an egg into a small bowl, then gently slide the egg into the simmering water. Repeat this with the remaining 3 eggs. Cook the eggs for about 2 minutes for runny yolks, or about 4 minutes for solid yolks. Do not allow the water to boil. Use a slotted spoon to remove the eggs to a towel-lined plate to drain.

Add the salmon to the potato mixture, and toss to combine and then divide between two plates. Top each serving of salad with two poached eggs and then liberally drizzle each with the caper dressing.

2 SERVINGS

■ ■ ■

BOLLYWOOD NIGHT

- Get the soup going.

- While the onions cook, mix and form the patties.

- Add the stock to the soup and cook the patties while the soup simmers.

- **Indian-Spiced Chickpea and Fire-Roasted Tomato Soup**
- **Spiced Lamb or Chicken Patties in a Pita**
- **Store-bought chips, such as Terra Spiced Taro variety**

One of my favorite restaurants in New York City is Tamarind, my personal Mecca for savory Indian delights, whether I eat there or order take-out. When I am at home in the country, though, there's no Tamarind to dial up, so I make my *own* take-out. This is my latest *Passage to India* menu. Enjoy it with a great Indian flick. My rental pick? *Monsoon Wedding.*

INDIAN-SPICED CHICKPEA AND FIRE-ROASTED TOMATO SOUP

1/4	cup **EVOO** (extra-virgin olive oil)
2	**garlic cloves**, chopped
1	15-ounce can **chickpeas**, drained
1/2	small **onion**, coarsely chopped
1	teaspoon ground **cumin**, 1/3 palmful
1/2	teaspoon ground **cardamom**
1/2	teaspoon ground **turmeric**
	Salt and **black pepper**
1	cup **chicken or vegetable stock**
1	28-ounce can **fire-roasted tomatoes**
1/4	cup **plain yogurt**

Heat the EVOO in a medium pot over medium heat. Add the garlic and cook for 2 to 3 minutes. Combine the chickpeas and onions in a food processor and process until finely chopped. Add them to the pot and cook for 5 minutes to sweeten the onions. Season the chickpeas with the cumin, cardamom, turmeric, salt, and pepper. Stir in the stock, then the tomatoes, and simmer the soup for 5 to 10 minutes to combine the flavors. Serve it with a dollop of yogurt on top.

2 SERVINGS

SPICED LAMB OR CHICKEN PATTIES IN A PITA

- 1 pound **ground lamb or chicken**
  Salt and **black pepper**
- 1 teaspoon ground **cumin**, $^1/_3$ palmful
- 1 teaspoon ground **coriander**, $^1/_3$ palmful
- 1 teaspoon **sweet paprika**, $^1/_3$ palmful
- 2 **garlic cloves**, minced
- 2 tablespoons chopped fresh **mint**
- 2 tablespoons chopped fresh **cilantro**
- 2 tablespoons **plain yogurt**
- 2 tablespoons **EVOO** (twice around the pan), plus some for drizzling
- $^1/_4$ **seedless cucumber**, thinly sliced
- 1 **plum tomato**, thinly sliced
- $^1/_4$ small **onion**, thinly sliced
- 1 small **romaine heart**, shredded
  Juice of $^1/_2$ lemon
- 2 **pitas**, warmed

Combine the meat and spices, garlic, herbs, and yogurt and form 4 very thin patties, $^1/_4$ to $^1/_2$ inch thick. Heat the 2 tablespoons of EVOO in a nonstick skillet over medium-high heat. Cook the patties until they are golden and cooked through, 3 to 4 minutes on each side.

Dress the sliced veggies and lettuce with lemon juice, a liberal drizzle of EVOO, and salt and pepper. Slice the tops off of the pitas to open up the pockets. Layer 2 patties and half of the veggies into each pita and serve.

2 SERVINGS

■ ■ ■

STEAK NIGHT, TABLE FOR TWO, PLEASE

- T-bone Steaks with Arugula and Tomatoes
- Garlic and Parsley Potatoes with Red and Black Pepper
- Charred Asparagus Tips

My husband, John, and I have date night most nights of the week because we love to cook and we're pretty fond of each other, too. Cooking together is fun and relaxing for us and sorta sexy. The flavors in this menu are best developed on a grill. We made this just the other night; I did the prep and John ran the grill. Preheat your grill to high before you begin cooking and you'll be sitting down with your date quicker than you'd get an appetizer at your nearest steak house.

GARLIC AND PARSLEY POTATOES WITH RED AND BLACK PEPPER

1 pound **fingerling, small white, or Yukon Gold potatoes**
4 **garlic cloves,** crushed
3 tablespoons **EVOO** (extra-virgin olive oil; eyeball it)
$1/2$ to 1 teaspoon **red pepper flakes**
   A generous handful of fresh **flat-leaf parsley** leaves, chopped
   Coarse salt and **coarse black pepper**

Preheat the outdoor grill to high or the oven to 500° F.

Rip off a couple of sheets of foil about 18 inches long and stack the 2 sheets together. Cut the potatoes into wedges and pile them up in the center of the foil. Combine the garlic with the potatoes and dress them with the EVOO, red pepper flakes, parsley, and lots of salt and pepper. Pull the ends of the foil together and fold them over, then close up the opposite sides to form a packet. Keep the potatoes as flat as possible and centered in the packet. Cook for 20 minutes, turning once. On a grill, keep the packet off to the side of the heat so you do not scorch the potatoes. Keep the grill lid down for the first 10 minutes. In the oven, place the packet just below the center of the oven and turn it once.

2 SERVINGS

T-BONE STEAKS WITH ARUGULA AND TOMATOES

T-bones are thin-cut porterhouse steaks. (Porterhouse steaks also have a larger cut of tenderloin.) If you use porterhouse steaks instead of the T-bones, have them cut 1 inch thick.

2   large **T-bone steaks**, 1 inch thick
2   tablespoons **EVOO** (extra-virgin olive oil), plus more for coating the meat
2   tablespoons fresh **rosemary** leaves, from about 4 sprigs, finely chopped
    Salt and **black pepper**
2   **Roma tomatoes**, seeded and thinly sliced
4   to 5 cups **arugula leaves**, cut into $^1/_2$-inch strips
    Juice of 1 lemon

Preheat an outdoor grill or indoor grill pan to high.

Use a pastry brush to coat the meat lightly on both sides with EVOO. Rub the meat with rosemary and season it with salt and pepper. Let the meat rest at room temperature for 15 minutes. Cook it for 4 minutes on each side for medium rare. Let the meat rest for 5 minutes before cutting it. Dress the tomatoes and arugula with lemon juice, the 2 tablespoons of EVOO, and salt and pepper. Top the meat with lots of tomatoes and arugula and serve.

2 SERVINGS

CHARRED ASPARAGUS TIPS

3/4 pound to 1 pound **asparagus**, 1 bundle
  EVOO (extra-virgin olive oil), for liberal drizzling
  Salt and **black pepper**

Preheat an outdoor grill to high or the oven to 500° F.

Hold a spear of asparagus at both ends, then snap it. Where the asparagus breaks naturally can be your guide to trim the bundle of spears. Save the tough ends to make soup, if you like. Dress the spears with EVOO, salt, and pepper. Place them directly on the grill and char them on all sides, for 3 to 4 minutes. For oven preparation, scatter the spears on a thin pizza pan or baking sheet and roast them for 5 to 6 minutes, or until they are charred at the edges.

2 SERVINGS

■ ■ ■

SMOKEHOUSE SPECIAL

- **Smoky Chicken Tortilla Soup with Chipotle and Fire-Roasted Tomatoes**
- **Garden Salad with Smoked Almond–Cilantro Dressing**

People that come from the mountains, like me, *love* smoke. We have fireplaces inside and fire pits in our yards, and smoked foods are all favorites in our cooking. In addition to bacon, this menu uses smoked jalapeños (chipotles), fire-roasted tomatoes, and smoked almonds to satisfy my smoky cravings.

GARDEN SALAD WITH SMOKED ALMOND–CILANTRO DRESSING

5 to 6 cups chopped **romaine lettuce**

1/2 cup shredded **carrots**

2 **scallions**, cut into 3-inch lengths then sliced into thin sticks

2 to 3 **baby zucchini**, cut into matchsticks

1/2 **red bell pepper**, cut into matchsticks

1 small **garlic clove**

1/2 cup **smoked almonds**

4 soft **sun-dried tomatoes**, chopped

Handful of fresh **cilantro** leaves

Handful of fresh **mint** leaves

3 tablespoons **red wine vinegar** (eyeball it)

1/3 cup **EVOO** (extra-virgin olive oil; eyeball it)

Black pepper

Place the lettuce on a large platter and scatter the veggies on top. Place the garlic, almonds, sun-dried tomatoes, cilantro, mint, and vinegar in a food processor and turn it on; if you have trouble getting the dressing going, add a splash of water (about 2 tablespoons), then stream in the EVOO. Process the dressing, then season it with black pepper. Pour it evenly over the salad and serve.

SMOKY CHICKEN TORTILLA SOUP WITH CHIPOTLE AND FIRE-ROASTED TOMATOES

3 cups **chicken stock**

1 pound **chicken tenders**

1 **bay leaf**, fresh if available

1 tablespoon **EVOO** (extra-virgin olive oil)

4 slices thick, smoky, center-cut **bacon**, chopped

1 **onion**, finely chopped

4 **garlic cloves**, chopped

2 **chipotles in adobo**, chopped, plus 2 tablespoons adobo sauce

1 28-ounce can crushed **fire-roasted tomatoes**

   Salt

3 to 4 cups **corn tortilla chips**, lightly crushed

2 cups shredded fresh **smoked mozzarella** or smoked sharp white cheddar cheese (3/4 pound)

1 **lime**, cut into wedges

1/2 **red onion**, chopped

   Chopped **fresh cilantro**, for garnish

Bring the stock to a simmer and add the chicken tenders and bay leaf. Poach the chicken for 6 to 7 minutes.

While the chicken poaches, heat the EVOO in a medium soup pot or deep skillet over medium-high heat. Add the bacon and cook it until crisp, then remove it to a paper-towel-lined plate with a slotted spoon. Drain off the excess fat, leaving 2 to 3 tablespoons in the pan. Add the onions and garlic to the skillet and cook them for 5 minutes, then stir in the chipotles and adobo sauce and the tomatoes.

Remove the chicken from the stock, dice it, then add it to the tomato mixture in the skillet. Pass the poaching stock through a strainer, then add it to the soup. Season to taste with salt.

Place a pile of crushed tortilla chips in the bottom of each soup bowl. Cover the chips liberally with smoked cheese, then ladle the hot soup down over the top. Pass bowls of lime, red onions, cilantro, and the reserved bacon at the table to finish the soup.

2 SERVINGS, WITH SOME SECONDS

BURGER NIGHT

• **BLT Turkey Burger Clubs**

• **Giuseppe's Cheesy Tots**

This is a tricky one: there's not only BLT flavors *in* these turkey burgers (in the form of bacon, leeks, and sun-dried tomatoes) they also get sandwiched between bread slices and *topped* with a BLT. Giuseppe's Cheesy Tots are potato tots made even better (yes, it *is* possible).

Heads up: if you have to buy the turkey in a pre-measured package, you will have some raw meat left over. Wrap and freeze the remainder, then defrost and crumble it into risotto or soup another night.

GIUSEPPE'S CHEESY TOTS

3 cups **frozen potato tots** (eyeball it)

1 cup shredded **Asiago cheese**

1 teaspoon **dried thyme**

$1/2$ teaspoon **dried oregano**

$1/4$ teaspoon **red pepper flakes**

Preheat the oven to 425° F.

Scatter the potato tots on a small cookie sheet and place it in the oven. Bake for 12 minutes or according to the package instructions.

In the last 2 to 3 minutes of cooking time, remove the potato tots from the oven and scatter the cheese, thyme, oregano, and red pepper flakes over them. Return them to the oven just long enough to set and brown the cheese then remove the tots, cover them loosely with foil, and switch on the broiler.

2 SERVINGS

BLT TURKEY BURGER CLUBS

2 tablespoons **EVOO** (extra-virgin olive oil), plus some for drizzling

5 slices **smoky bacon**

1 small **leek**

3/4 pound **ground turkey breast**

1 tablespoon **grill seasoning**, such as McCormick's Montreal Steak Seasoning

6 to 8 soft **sun-dried tomatoes**, chopped (available in pouches or bulk bins in the produce department)

1 **vine-ripe tomato**, thinly sliced

Salt

6 slices **white sandwich bread**

1/2 cup **herbed cheese** such as Alouette or Boursin

1/4 cup **cream** or half-and-half

Black pepper

4 leaves **green leaf or Bibb lettuce**

Heat a medium nonstick skillet with a drizzle of EVOO over medium to medium-high heat. Chop one slice of the bacon and add it to the pan. While the bacon cooks, trim the tough green tops from the leek, halve the leek lengthwise, and thinly slice it into half-moons. Place the slices in a colander and rinse vigorously with running water, separating the layers to release the grit. Dry the leeks on a clean kitchen towel and add them to the browned chopped bacon. Wilt the leeks for 2 or 3 minutes, then transfer them and the bacon pieces to a plate to cool. Return the skillet to the stove over low heat and add the 2 tablespoons of EVOO.

Place the turkey in a bowl and add the grill seasoning, sun-dried tomatoes, and cooled-to-handle leeks and bacon. Mix the meat and other ingredients, then form 2 very large patties no thicker than 1 inch. The patties will hang just off the sides of the bread once cooked.

Raise the heat under the EVOO and add the burgers. Cook them for 6 minutes on each side.

Heat a second skillet over medium-high heat and add the remaining 4 slices of bacon. Cook the bacon until it is crisp and transfer it to a paper-towel-lined plate to drain. (Don't pour the fat down the drain; it'll cause a clog. Cool the fat and discard it in the garbage.)

Season the sliced tomatoes with salt.

Place the sliced bread under the broiler and toast for 1 minute on each side.

In a blender or food processor, combine the herbed cheese, cream or half-and-half, and pepper.

Assemble the clubs: bread, burger, herbed-cheese sauce, bread, bacon, lettuce, tomatoes, herbed-cheese sauce, and bread. Serve the cheesy tots alongside.

2 SERVINGS

■ ■ ■

SPICY SEAFOOD GRILL

• Sea Bass with Puttanesca and Potatoes

These simple foil packets are a roasted alternative to fish in parchment, steamy paper pouches of fish and veggies. The flavor produced by this method is pronounced; you'll be surprised at how much great grill flavor you can get even though the meal is cooked in a foil packet. Puttanesca is a classic Italian sauce named for ladies of the night: spicy, fast, easy, and bold! With vegetable, starch, and protein piled together, this is a one-pouch meal with NO CLEANUP! Made on the grill, this is sure to become a three-season favorite.

SEA BASS WITH PUTTANESCA AND POTATOES

1 tablespoon **anchovy paste**
Juice of $1/2$ lemon
$1/4$ cup **EVOO** (extra-virgin olive oil), plus more for liberal drizzling
1 pound **fingerling, small white, or Yukon Gold potatoes**
4 **garlic cloves**, crushed
16 to 20 **cherry tomatoes**
A generous handful of fresh **flat-leaf parsley** leaves, chopped
$1/4$ cup pitted **kalamata olives**, chopped
4 tablespoons **capers**, drained
$1/2$ to 1 teaspoon **red pepper flakes**
$1/2$ cup **white vermouth** or dry white wine
2 **sea bass fillets**, 6 to 8 ounces each
Salt and **black pepper**

Preheat a grill to medium temperature, about 375° F.

Rip off 4 pieces of foil, each 18 inches long, and make 2 double-thick stacks. In a bowl, combine the anchovy paste with the lemon juice, then stream in the $^1/_4$ cup of EVOO. Cut the potatoes into wedges and add them to a second bowl with the garlic. Halve most of the tomatoes and add them to the bowl. (You can leave small, grape-size tomatoes whole; they'll burst on their own during cooking.)

Add the parsley, olives, capers, and red pepper flakes to the potatoes; drizzle with the anchovy and oil dressing; and toss to combine. Divide the potatoes and tomatoes evenly between the two foil slabs. Bend the edges of the foil up a bit and douse each packet with $^1/_4$ cup of white vermouth or wine. Drizzle some oil over the fish and season with salt and pepper. Place the fish atop the potatoes and tomatoes and seal the packets up. Grill them for 20 minutes, turning once. Open the packets carefully and serve.

2 SERVINGS

ADAPTATION

To prepare this recipe in the oven, seal the ingredients in parchment-paper pouches and bake at 400° F for 20 minutes without turning, or until the fish is opaque. (Omit the vermouth or wine entirely as this method, essentially steaming the fish, produces more liquids in the packet.) The color and texture will be softer using this method, but the potent flavor of the sauce still hits its spicy mark on your palate.

DINNER FOR DIVINE OR DEVILISH DUOS

- **Chicken Marvalasala and Pappardelle with Rosemary Gravy**
- **Devilish Angel Cake with Drunken Berries**

People often ask me how I continue to come up with new ideas for 30-Minute Meals. One trick I use is to revisit classics and take them to a new level, raising the bar a bit; that's why I call this chicken Marvalasala—it's Chicken Marsala taken to divine new heights. The wide ribbon pasta I serve along with the chicken in this menu is topped with my version of a wonderful, rich gravy created by chef Emeril Lagasse; he uses it to drown shrimp.

CHICKEN MARVALASALA AND PAPPARDELLE WITH ROSEMARY GRAVY

Salt

$3/4$ pound **pappardelle** pasta (you can substitute fettuccine)

4 large, thin boneless, skinless **chicken breast cutlets**

Black pepper

4 tablespoons **EVOO** (extra-virgin olive oil)

2 large **garlic cloves**, crushed

2 **portobello mushroom caps**, sliced

12 **shiitake mushrooms**, stemmed and sliced

4 tablespoons ($1/2$ stick) **butter**

2 tablespoons **tomato paste** (the kind in a tube stores easily in the refrigerator)

2 tablespoons minced fresh **rosemary** (a couple of sprigs)

2 tablespoons all-purpose **flour**

$1^1/2$ cups **chicken stock** (eyeball it)

1 tablespoon **Worcestershire sauce** (eyeball it)

2 tablespoons **capers**, drained

$1/2$ cup **Marsala wine**

Grated **Pecorino Romano** cheese
A couple handfuls of **arugula** or baby spinach leaves, thinly sliced,
for garnish

Put a large covered pot of water on to boil for the pasta. When it comes up to a boil, salt the water, drop in the pasta, and cook to al dente.

While the pasta is working, season the chicken with salt and pepper. Heat a large nonstick skillet with 2 tablespoons of the EVOO, 2 times around the pan, over medium to medium-high heat. Add the chicken to the pan and brown it lightly on both sides, then remove it to a platter and cover it with foil to hold in the heat. To the same skillet, add the remaining 2 tablespoons of EVOO and 1 clove of the garlic. Cook the garlic for a minute or so, then remove it and add the mushrooms. Cook until the mushrooms brown evenly and become tender, 8 to 10 minutes.

While the mushrooms work, start the gravy for the pasta. In a deep medium skillet, melt 2 tablespoons of the butter into the tomato paste over medium heat. Add the remaining garlic clove and cook it for a couple of minutes, then remove. Add the rosemary, cook for 1 minute, then add the flour and whisk it into the garlic-infused tomato butter. Cook the flour for a minute, then whisk in the stock and Worcestershire sauce. Simmer to thicken, 5 minutes. Season the sauce with salt and pepper to your taste.

To the cooked mushrooms, add the capers and Marsala and reduce for a minute or so. Add the remaining 2 tablespoons of butter in small bits to finish the sauce, and shake the pan to incorporate it. Slide the chicken back into the sauce and warm it through.

Drain the pasta and toss it with the rosemary gravy and a handful of cheese. Serve the pasta alongside the Chicken Marvalasala, and scatter arugula or spinach across both the chicken and pasta to garnish.

2 SERVINGS

DEVILISH ANGEL CAKE WITH DRUNKEN BERRIES

$1/3$ cup **dry Italian red wine**

3 tablespoons **sugar**

A few grinds of **black pepper**

$1/2$ pint **strawberries**, sliced

$1/2$ pint **blackberries**

1 store-bought **angel food cake**

Whipped cream, from a canister (in the dairy case)

Finely chopped fresh **mint** or orange zest, for garnish

Combine the wine, sugar, and pepper in a medium bowl. Add the berries, toss to combine, and set aside for 20 minutes. Cut the cake into thick slices and douse the wedges with wine-soaked berries. Garnish each serving with whipped cream and fresh mint or orange zest.

4 SERVINGS (YOU CAN HAVE SECONDS ON A DATE NIGHT)

■ ■ ■

SANDWICH NIGHT

• **Italian Tuna Melts with White Beans and Provolone**

I love tuna salad, but I always hold the mayo! In my family, EVOO was used to dress or cook almost any food, so I still make my tuna salads with lemon and oil, rather than mayo. This one is especially hearty.

ITALIAN TUNA MELTS WITH WHITE BEANS AND PROVOLONE

- 1 15-ounce can **white beans**, rinsed and drained
- 1 can **tuna in water or oil**, drained and flaked
- 1/4 **red onion**, chopped
- 2 tablespoons **capers**, drained
- 2 **celery ribs**, finely chopped
  Handful of pitted **kalamata olives**, chopped
- 2 to 3 fresh **rosemary** sprigs, finely chopped
  Juice of 1 lemon
- 2 1-inch-thick slices of **crusty bread**
- 1 **garlic clove**, peeled and halved
- 3 tablespoons **EVOO** (extra-virgin olive oil), plus more for drizzling
- 1 cup **arugula**, chopped
  Salt and **black pepper**
- 4 deli slices mild or sharp **Provolone cheese**

Preheat the broiler.

Place half of the beans in a mixing bowl and mash them with a fork. Add the rest of the beans to the bowl along with the tuna, onions, capers, celery, olives, rosemary, and lemon juice. Char the bread on both sides under the broiler, rub it with the cut garlic, and drizzle with EVOO. Dress the arugula with the 3 tablespoons of EVOO, then mix and season with salt and pepper. Pile the arugula on the bread, divide the tuna between the two slices, and top each with a couple pieces of cheese. Melt the cheese under the broiler until bubbly.

MEALS FOR 2

ANYTIME IS SPRINGTIME SUPPER

• Bibb Lettuce Salad with Sesame-Shallot Dressing
• Shrimp Primavera Pasta with Asparagus, Peas, and Leeks
• Fruit Sorbet and Berries (store-bought)

Anytime is springtime. As the title suggests, this menu can transform the lousiest days and worst weather into a perfect spring evening. The light, bright flavors make for an easy, elegant menu any time of the year.

SHRIMP PRIMAVERA PASTA WITH ASPARAGUS, PEAS, AND LEEKS

Salt

1/2 pound **spaghetti**

1 **leek**

2 tablespoons **EVOO** (extra-virgin olive oil)

2 **garlic cloves**, thinly sliced

1/2 pound **shiitake mushrooms**, stemmed and sliced

1 cup **chicken or vegetable stock**

2 teaspoons **lemon zest**

1/2 pound medium to large **shrimp**, peeled and deveined

3/4 to 1 pound **asparagus** (1 bundle), trimmed to 4 inches then cut into thirds

1 cup **frozen peas**

2 tablespoons **butter**, cut into small pieces

Black pepper

1 cup shaved or grated **Romano cheese**

Handful of fresh **flat-leaf parsley** leaves, chopped

Place a large covered pot of water on the stove and bring it up to a boil for the pasta. Salt the water and cook the spaghetti to al dente.

While the pasta is working, trim the tough green tops and the roots from the leek. Halve the leek lengthwise and dice it thin. Place the leeks in a colander and rinse them vigorously to release any grit. Drain the leeks well.

Heat the EVOO in a large, deep skillet over medium heat, add the garlic, and cook for a minute. Add the leeks and shiitakes and cook until they are tender, 3 to 4 minutes. Add the stock, raise the heat a little, and bring it up to a bubble. Once the stock bubbles, add the zest and the shrimp and cook it for 2 minutes, then add the asparagus and peas to the pan and cook them for 2 minutes more.

Melt the butter into the sauce, add the drained pasta to the pan, and toss to combine the shrimp and vegetables with the spaghetti. Season with a little pepper, adjust the salt to taste, and garnish with the cheese and parsley.

2 SERVINGS

BIBB LETTUCE SALAD WITH SESAME-SHALLOT DRESSING

- 2 tablespoons **sesame seeds**
- 1 tablespoon finely chopped **shallot**
- 2 tablespoons **red wine vinegar**
- 1/4 cup **EVOO** (extra-virgin olive oil; eyeball it)
  Salt and **black pepper**
- 1 head **Bibb lettuce**, cleaned and separated
- 4 **radishes**, thinly sliced
- 1/4 **seedless cucumber**, thinly sliced

Place the sesame seeds in a small pan and toast them over low heat until fragrant. Place the shallots and vinegar in a bowl and let them stand for 10 minutes. Add the sesame seeds to the bowl, then stream in the EVOO as you whisk the dressing. Season with salt and pepper.

Arrange the lettuce, radishes, and cucumbers on 2 plates and pour the dressing evenly over the salads.

2 SERVINGS

- Bring the water to a boil for the pasta.

- While the water heats, make the salad, but don't add the warm ingredients to the greens.

- Make the pasta and sauce; toss the salad.

PASTA FOR YOU AND ME

- **Warm Fennel and Orange Salad**
- **Prosciutto and Spinach Bucatini**

Pasta makes me happy and nothing ends a tough day better than a big, fat bowl of bucatini. Bucatini is spaghetti's husky cousin with a hole in the middle: fun, loveable, and delicious. If you can't locate bucatini, perciatelli is very similar. Otherwise, just use the thickest spaghetti you can get.

WARM FENNEL AND ORANGE SALAD

2	tablespoons **EVOO** (extra-virgin olive oil), plus some for drizzling
1	**fennel bulb**
	Salt and **black pepper**
1	small head of **radicchio**, cored and sliced
1/4	cup fresh **flat-leaf parsley** leaves, a generous handful, chopped
	Zest and juice of 1 orange
1	tablespoon **red wine vinegar** (eyeball it)

Place a medium skillet over medium-high heat with the 2 table-spoons of EVOO (twice around the pan). While the pan is heating up, cut the fennel bulb into quarters lengthwise; remove the core and then thinly slice the quarters. Add the sliced fennel to the hot skillet and season it with salt and pepper. Cook, stirring frequently, for about 2 minutes; you want to warm it and cook it a little bit but it should still be nice and crunchy. While the fennel is cooking, arrange the radicchio and parsley in a salad bowl. Add the orange zest and juice to the fennel, stir, and turn the heat off. Transfer the warm fennel to the bowl with the radicchio and parsley, then add the red wine vinegar and a drizzle of EVOO. Toss, taste, and adjust the salt and pepper.

2 SERVINGS

PROSCIUTTO AND SPINACH BUCATINI

Salt

$^1/_2$ pound **bucatini** pasta

3 tablespoons **EVOO** (extra-virgin olive oil; eyeball it)

3 large **garlic cloves**, thinly sliced

1 teaspoon **red pepper flakes**

1 pound **fresh spinach**, stems removed, shredded

6 slices **prosciutto**, cut into thin strips

Zest and juice of 1 lemon

Black pepper

$^1/_2$ cup grated **Parmigiano-Reggiano**, a couple of generous handfuls, plus more to pass at the table

Place a large covered pot of water over high heat and bring it up to a boil to cook the pasta. Once the water boils, add some salt and the pasta and cook to al dente. Heads up: you'll need to reserve a couple of ladles of the cooking water just before you drain the pasta.

While the pasta cooks, heat a large skillet over medium-high heat with the EVOO. Add the sliced garlic and cook it until it's golden, about 1 minute. Add the red pepper flakes and a couple of ladles of the starchy pasta cooking water. Stand back: it will really bubble up! Add the drained pasta to the skillet and toss it around until the pasta has soaked up about three fourths of the liquid. Turn the heat off and add the spinach, prosciutto strips, lemon zest, and lemon juice, and season with a little salt and pepper. Toss to wilt the spinach and distribute the prosciutto. Sprinkle the pasta liberally with the Parmigiano, toss to coat the pasta, and serve.

2 SERVINGS

■ ■ ■

CHOP HOUSE SUPPER

• Make the caramelized onion sauce.

• While the sauce simmers, start the chops.

• Get the couscous going while the chops cook on the first side.

• **Pork or Veal Chops with Caramelized Onion Sauce**

• **Mushroom Cherry Couscous**

This might sound like a fancy-pants menu but don't let it fool you. It eats like a stick-to-your-ribs, Monday-to-Friday supper. If cherries aren't your thing, then substitute any dried fruit in the couscous. While we're talking substitutes, chicken breasts will do if chops aren't what you're into tonight.

PORK OR VEAL CHOPS WITH CARAMELIZED ONION SAUCE

4 tablespoons **EVOO** (extra-virgin olive oil; eyeball it)

1 large **onion** or 2 medium onions, chopped

5 or 6 **fresh thyme** sprigs

Salt and **black pepper**

2 large **garlic cloves**, chopped

3 tablespoons **balsamic vinegar** (eyeball it)

1 cup **chicken stock** (eyeball it)

2 tablespoons **butter**

1/4 cup **parsley**, a handful

2 bone-in **veal rib chops** or bone-in loin pork chops, 1 to 1 1/2 inches thick

TIDBIT

If you are using veal chops, you can reduce the cooking time slightly if you prefer them a bit pink inside. For chicken breasts, cook for 6 minutes on each side.

For the caramelized onion sauce, preheat a large skillet over medium heat with 2 tablespoons of the EVOO. Add the onions and thyme sprigs, then season them with salt and pepper. Cook, stirring every now and then, for 10 to 12 minutes, or until golden brown. Add the garlic and continue to cook for 1 minute, then add the vinegar and chicken stock. Bring to a simmer over high heat and cook until the liquids have reduced by half, 3 to 4 minutes more. Turn the heat off, remove the thyme twigs (all the flavorful leaves will have fallen off by now), and add the butter and parsley. Stir until the butter melts.

Once the onions are on their way, preheat a second skillet over medium-high heat with the remaining 2 tablespoons of EVOO. Season the chops liberally with salt and pepper and add them to the hot skillet. Cook the chops for 5 minutes on the first side. Resist the temptation to move the chops around in the pan, as it will slow down the browning. Flip the chops and reduce the heat to medium. Cook them on the second side for 8 to 10 minutes, or the desired doneness. Transfer them to a plate and cover loosely with aluminum foil to rest for a couple of minutes. Serve the chops topped with some of the caramelized onion sauce.

2 SERVINGS

MUSHROOM CHERRY COUSCOUS

3 tablespoons **EVOO** (extra-virgin olive oil; eyeball it)
3 **portobello mushroom caps**, thinly sliced
5 to 6 fresh **sage** leaves, chopped
2 large **garlic cloves**, chopped
  A couple pinches of **red pepper flakes**
  Salt and **black pepper**
1 cup **chicken stock**
$^1/_4$ cup **dried cherries**, a generous handful
1 cup **couscous**

Heat the EVOO in a skillet with a tight-fitting lid over medium-high heat. Add the sliced mushrooms and spread them out in the skillet. Cook them without stirring for about 3 minutes; they'll get nice and brown if you don't touch them. Next, add the sage, garlic, red pepper flakes, and salt and pepper, and continue to cook, stirring every now and then, for about 5 minutes. Add the chicken stock and dried cherries and raise the heat. When the stock is boiling add the couscous, shake the skillet to settle it into the liquid. Turn the heat off, cover the skillet, and let it sit for 5 minutes. Fluff the couscous with a fork and serve.

2 SERVINGS

LIKE GRANDMA SHOULD HAVE MADE

- **Mega Meat-Stuffed Shells**
- **Celery and Mushroom Salad**

My grandpa Emmanuel was the head cook in his house. My mama was the eldest of ten, so she got to help out a lot. This is the kind of supper I envision the kids having back in the day, made a little easier with shortcuts like chopped frozen spinach.

MEGA MEAT-STUFFED SHELLS

1 10-ounce box **chopped frozen spinach**
   Salt
8 **jumbo pasta shells**
2 tablespoons **EVOO** (extra-virgin olive oil), plus some for drizzling
1 pound **meat loaf mix** (ground beef, pork, and veal)
3 **garlic cloves**, 2 chopped, 1 crushed and halved
1 small **onion**, finely chopped
   Black pepper
$1/8$ teaspoon freshly grated or ground **nutmeg** (eyeball it)
1 **egg**, beaten
$1/4$ cup **Italian-style bread crumbs** (a handful)
$1/2$ cup grated **Romano or Parmigiano-Reggiano cheese** (2 handfuls)
$1/4$ teaspoon **red pepper flakes**
1 8-ounce can **tomato sauce**
   A few fresh **basil** leaves, torn

Place the frozen spinach on a plate and defrost it in the microwave on high for 6 minutes. Wring the spinach dry in a clean towel.

While the spinach is in the microwave, preheat the oven to 425° F and, in a large covered pot, bring the water to a boil for the shells. Salt the boiling water and cook the shells for 6 to 7 minutes; they should still be firm at the center. Drizzle them with EVOO and set aside in a shallow baking dish.

While the pasta is working, brown the meat over medium to medium-high heat in 1 tablespoon of the EVOO (once around the pan). Add the chopped garlic and onions to the meat; season them with salt, pepper, and nutmeg; and cook the mixture for 5 minutes more. Transfer the meat to a bowl. Add the spinach and mix them together. Add the egg, bread crumbs, and half the cheese and combine. Fill the shells with the meat mixture and sprinkle the rest of the cheese on top, then bake for 11 to 12 minutes to set the filling in the shells and crisp the pasta at the edges.

While the shells bake, heat the remaining tablespoon of EVOO in a small pot over low heat with the halved garlic clove and cook for 3 to 4 minutes. Remove the garlic, add the red pepper flakes, and cook for a minute more, then stir in the tomato sauce and simmer for 5 minutes. Stir in the basil.

Pour $1/2$ cup of sauce on each dinner plate and top it with 4 shells. Yum-o!

2 SERVINGS

CELERY AND MUSHROOM SALAD

4 **celery ribs**, with leafy tops, wiped clean and thinly sliced on an angle

2 **portobello mushroom caps**, wiped clean with a damp towel

Handful of fresh **flat-leaf parsley** leaves, chopped

$^1/_2$ cup **arugula leaves**, chopped

$^1/_2$ cup **basil leaves**, about 10 leaves, torn or shredded

Juice of $^1/_2$ lemon

EVOO (extra-virgin olive oil), for drizzling

Salt and **black pepper**

A chunk of **Parmigiano-Reggiano**, to make shavings from

Combine the salad ingredients and dress them with the lemon juice and EVOO. Season with salt and pepper and top the salad with shavings of the cheese made with a vegetable peeler.

2 SERVINGS

■ ■ ■

GAME PLAN

- **Get the soup going.**

- **While the soup simmers, get the frittata into the oven.**

- **Make the tea while the frittata bakes.**

SICK DAY

- **Ginger Honey Tea**
- **Olive Frittata**
- **My Mom's 15-Minute Tomato and Bean Stoup**

I called my mom one rainy day from the road. I told her I was on my way home, I was getting a cold, and I really wanted soup for supper. She said she didn't know what she had around to make it with, but she'd come up with something. This is what she made and it was just what the doctor ordered. You don't have to be sick to enjoy it, but this is what I make when I am. The eggs and olives are always in my fridge and the frittata turns the stoup into a real meal. You have to keep your strength up, right?

GINGER HONEY TEA

1-inch piece of **fresh ginger**, peeled

1 large strip of **lemon zest**

6 cups **water**

1/3 cup **honey** (eyeball it)

Juice of 1 lemon

4 **chamomille or other tea bags**

In a small pot, combine the ginger, lemon zest, honey, and 6 cups water and bring to a boil. Add the lemon juice and transfer the mixture to a teapot. Add the tea bags to the pot and steep. Remove the bags and serve.

2 BIG MUGFULS

MEALS FOR 2

OLIVE FRITTATA

- 3 tablespoons **EVOO** (extra-virgin olive oil)
- 1 **onion**, thinly sliced
- 1 **roasted red pepper**, drained, patted dry, and diced
- 1/2 to 2/3 cup drained chopped **Spanish green olives** with pimiento
- 6 **eggs**
  A generous splash of **half-and-half** or milk
  Salt and **black pepper**

Preheat the oven to 400° F.

Heat the EVOO (three times around the pan) in a small 6- to 8-inch skillet over medium heat; choose one that can be transferred to the oven (no rubber on the handles). Add the onions to the hot oil and cook until soft and tender but not caramelized—don't let the onions color. Add the roasted peppers and the olives and combine. Beat the eggs with the half-and-half or milk and season them with salt and pepper. (Go easy on the salt because of the olives.) Pour the eggs into the skillet and keep settling them to the bottom of the pan as you would an omelet. When the eggs are firm on the bottom and set, transfer the pan to the oven for about 10 minutes, until the top is golden brown. Cut and serve from the skillet or invert the frittata onto a serving plate.

2 SERVINGS

MY MOM'S 15-MINUTE TOMATO AND BEAN STOUP

2 tablespoons **EVOO** (extra-virgin olive oil)

3 **garlic cloves**, chopped

1/2 teaspoon **red pepper flakes**

1 medium **onion**, chopped

2 **carrots**, peeled and thinly sliced

2 **celery ribs**, chopped

1 small **zucchini**, sliced

2 cups **vegetable or chicken stock**

1 15-ounce can **diced tomatoes**

1 15-ounce can **tomato sauce**

1 15-ounce can **small white beans** or cannellini beans

1 10-ounce box frozen cut **green beans**

  Salt and **black pepper**

1 cup fresh **basil leaves**, torn or shredded

  Grated **Parmigiano-Reggiano or Romano cheese**, for topping

  Crusty bread, for mopping

Add the EVOO to a large pot. Add the garlic and red pepper flakes, stir, then add the onions, carrots, celery, and zucchini. Cook for 10 minutes, then add the stock, tomatoes, tomato sauce, and both kinds of beans. Bring the stoup up to a bubble and season it with salt and pepper to taste. Simmer for 5 minutes. Turn off the heat and wilt the basil into the stoup. Ladle up the stoup and serve it with lots of grated cheese and bread.

4 SOULFUL BOWLFULS, 2 SERVINGS WITH SECONDS, OR ENOUGH FOR 1 STAY-IN-BED DAY

■ ■ ■

SPANISH-MEXICAN FIESTA

• **Garlicky Guacamole and Chips**
• **Serrano-Wrapped Halibut with Tortillas**
• **Savoy Cabbage with Cumin, Coriander, and Lime**
• **Warm Cinnamon-Chipotle Tomato Salsa**
• **Saffron and Olive Rice**

There is a hideaway called El Parador on East Thirty-fourth Street in Manhattan that serves what many call their favorite Mexican food in the city. The menu is a perfect marriage and balance of classic Spanish technique and flavor with Mexican tradition and soul. This menu reminds me of my friends Manny and Alex, the father and son who own El Parador and will greet you at the door. Perhaps one night I'll have the honor to prepare it for them.

SAFFRON AND OLIVE RICE

$1/2$ tablespoon **EVOO** (extra-virgin olive oil)

1 cup **white rice**

2 cups **chicken stock**

Pinch of **saffron threads** or 1 individual packet of saffron powder

1 tablespoon **butter**, cut into small pieces

$1/4$ cup chopped **Spanish green olives** with pimiento

Handful of fresh **flat-leaf parsley** leaves, finely chopped

Heat a medium pot over medium heat with the EVOO. Add the rice and toast for a minute or two, then add the chicken stock and bring it to a simmer. Stir in the saffron and cover the pot; reduce the heat to low. Cook the rice until tender, about 18 minutes. Stir in the butter, olives, and parsley and fluff the rice with a fork.

2 SERVINGS WITH SECONDS

RACHAEL RAY 2, 4, 6, 8

SERRANO-WRAPPED HALIBUT WITH TORTILLAS, SAVOY CABBAGE, AND WARM CINNAMON-CHIPOTLE TOMATO SALSA

- 8 small, **soft flour tortillas**
- 3 tablespoons **EVOO** (extra-virgin olive oil)
- $^1/_2$ head **Savoy cabbage**, shredded
- $^3/_4$ small **onion**, thinly sliced
  Salt
- 1 teaspoon ground **coriander**, $^1/_3$ palmful
- $^1/_2$ tablepoon ground **cumin**, $^1/_2$ palmful
- 1 teaspoon **lime zest**
- 2 6-ounce **halibut fillets**
  Black pepper
- $^1/_2$ teaspoon **smoked sweet paprika**
- 4 very thin slices **Serrano ham** or proscuitto
- $^1/_4$ cup all-purpose **flour**, for dredging
- 1 or 2 **chipotles in adobo**, medium to extra-hot, finely chopped, plus 2 tablespoons of the adobo sauce
- 2 pinches ground **cinnamon**
- 1 15-ounce can crushed **fire-roasted tomatoes**
- 2 tablespoons **butter**
  Juice of 1 lime

Preheat the oven to 250° F. Dampen a clean kitchen towel and stack the tortillas in the center. Wrap the tortillas in the towel and place into a small pie or cake pan of a similar size, cover the dish with foil, and heat the tortillas for 20 minutes.

Heat a tablespoon of the EVOO (once around the pan) in a medium skillet over medium-high heat and add the cabbage and onions. Season the cabbage with salt, the coriander, cumin, and lime zest. Cook the cabbage for 10 minutes, turning frequently.

continued

Season the fish fillets with salt, pepper, and the smoked paprika. Overlap 2 slices of Serrano to measure the length of the fillet. Place the fish on top. Wrap the sides up and over the fillet to enclose it completely. Repeat with the remaining ham and halibut. Spread a little flour on a cutting board or plate and dredge the ham-covered fish. Discard the remaining flour.

In a small sauce pot over medium heat, combine the chipotles, adobo sauce, cinnamon, and fire-roasted tomatoes. When the salsa bubbles, reduce the heat to low.

Heat the remaining 2 tablespoons of EVOO in a medium nonstick skillet over medium-high heat. Add the fish to the pan and cook for 2 to 3 minutes, then turn the fillets and reduce the heat to medium low. Cook the fish a minute or so, add the butter, and as it melts, begin basting the fish with it. Turn off the heat and let the fish stand for 1 minute more. Slice each fish fillet into $1/2$-inch slices and fan them out on 2 dinner plates. Squeeze some lime juice over the cabbage and pile it alongside the fish. Pour the salsa into small cups or ramekins and serve it with the fish. Place the tortillas on a trivet in the towel and hot dish to keep them soft. As you dine, wrap the fish, cabbage, and sauce in tortillas and eat.

2 SERVINGS

GARLICKY GUACAMOLE AND CHIPS

1 ripe Haas **avocado**
1 small **jalapeño**, seeded and finely chopped
1/4 small **onion**, finely chopped
1 **garlic clove**, cracked
1 teaspoon coarse **salt**
Juice of 1 lemon
Tortilla chips, any variety

Halve the avocado and discard the pit. Scoop the flesh into a small bowl and add the jalapeños and onions. On a cutting board, chop the garlic then sprinkle it with salt. Using the side of your knife and applying pressure with the heel of your hand, mash the garlic and salt into a paste. Add the salty garlic paste and lemon juice to the avocado and mash the guacamole with a fork until it's fairly smooth. Scoop it into a serving dish and surround it with a few handfuls of good-quality tortilla chips.

2 SERVINGS

■ ■ ■

WHERE'S THAT BOLERO CD? MENU

• **Chorizo-Stuffed Bread Bites**
• **Warm Mushroom and Sherry Vinegar Salad**

The first recipe in this menu tells the story of a dinner roll who met a calzone he liked and they went to Spain for a vacation. They had a blast in Barcelona and came home tastier for the experience. Ah, foreign exchange can be such a romantic experience.

CHORIZO-STUFFED BREAD BITES

7 to 8 ounces precooked **chorizo**, finely chopped

1/2 small **onion**, chopped

1 **roasted red pepper**, chopped

1 8-ounce package refrigerator **crescent rolls**, such as Pillsbury

6 ounces **manchego cheese**, grated (if not available, use shredded mozzarella)
Freshly ground black pepper

Preheat the oven according to the directions on the crescent roll package.

Preheat a medium skillet over medium-high heat; add the chorizo and onions and cook, stirring every now and then, for about 4 minutes. (There is no need for any oil as the chorizo will render enough fat to deal with the onions.) Transfer the chorizo mixture to a bowl and add the roasted red peppers; stir to combine. Unwrap the refrigerator dough and separate into triangles. Arrange on a cookie sheet. Place about a tablespoon of the chorizo mixture toward the wide end of a triangle and top that with about a tablespoon of the cheese. Roll the filled dough toward the pointed end. Don't worry if some of the chorizo sneaks out as you're rolling it; you're way too busy to worry about something as boring as a little chorizo peeking out.

Repeat with the remaining filling and dough. Sprinkle the rolls with a little freshly ground black pepper. Bake according to the package directions, anywhere from 11 to 13 minutes. Remove the bread bites from the oven and let them cool for a minute or two before serving.

2 SERVINGS

WARM MUSHROOM AND SHERRY VINEGAR SALAD

  5 tablespoons **EVOO** (extra-virgin olive oil; eyeball it)
  1 pound **button mushrooms**, stems trimmed, halved
  1 large **garlic clove**, chopped
  $^1/_2$ **onion**, chopped
   Salt and **black pepper**
  6 cups **chopped sturdy greens,** such as escarole, radicchio, and frisée
  $^1/_2$ pint **grape tomatoes**, halved
  2 **celery ribs**, thinly sliced
  $^1/_4$ cup fresh **flat-leaf parsley** leaves, a generous handful, chopped
  3 tablespoons **sherry vinegar** (eyeball it)
  2 teaspoons **Dijon mustard** (eyeball it)

Place a large skillet over medium-high heat with about 2 tablespoons of the EVOO, twice around the pan. Add the mushrooms and brown them without stirring for 3 to 4 minutes, then stir; add the garlic, onions, salt, and pepper; and continue to cook for about 5 minutes.

While the mushrooms are cooking, combine the mixed greens, grape tomatoes, celery, parsley, and a little salt and pepper in a bowl. Remove the mushrooms from the heat and add the sherry vinegar, a splash of water, the mustard, and some pepper. Whisk in the remaining 3 tablespoons EVOO and then pour the mushrooms and dressing over the greens and veggies. Toss to combine and serve immediately.

2 SERVINGS

■ ■ ■

TAKE-OUT NIGHT TAKES ON BURGER NIGHT

- **Soy, Garlic, and Ginger Chicken Burgers with Chowchow**
- **Cold Sesame Noodle Salad**

Some nights at my house, we can't decide between burgers and take-out. This menu seals the deal and solves the argument with a meal that is at once healthful Make-Your-Own-Take-Out food *and* a better-for-you burger.

Heads up: you can make the chowchow in a double batch and save it in the fridge for a couple of weeks to use on sammies or dogs.

CHICKEN BURGERS WITH CHOWCHOW AND COLD SESAME NOODLE SALAD

Salt

1/2 pound **perciatelli** or spaghetti

1/2 pound **Savoy cabbage**, half coarsely chopped, half shredded

1/2 **red onion**, chopped

1 **celery rib**, chopped

1 small **red bell pepper**, chopped

1 large **unripe or green tomato**, chopped

1/4 cup **cider vinegar**

1/4 cup **sugar**

1/2 teaspoon **five-spice powder** (eyeball it)

1/2 teaspoon **cayenne pepper**

1/2 teaspoon ground **turmeric**

Black pepper

3/4 pound **ground chicken**

2 **garlic cloves**, chopped

2 tablespoons peeled and grated **fresh ginger**

> **TIDBIT**
>
> You'll have some raw ground chicken left over if you have to buy it pre-packaged at the market. Place it in a food storage bag and freeze it. Then, next time you are making a veggie soup, remove it from the freezer, defrost, and crumble it in.

2 tablespoons finely chopped fresh **cilantro** or flat-leaf parsley leaves

1/4 cup plus 2 tablespoons **tamari**

2 tablespoons **vegetable oil** (eyeball it)

1/4 cup **smooth peanut butter**

1 teaspoon **dark sesame oil** (eyeball it)

4 **scallions,** cut into thirds then shredded into grass-like threads

2 tablespoons **toasted sesame seeds**

2 crusty **cornmeal kaiser rolls**, split

4 pieces of **leaf or Bibb lettuce**

Bring a large covered pot of water to a boil. Add salt and the pasta and cook to al dente. Drain the pasta and run it under cold running water until it's cool.

While the water is coming to a boil, place the chopped cabbage in a food processor. Pulse the processor to finely chop the cabbage, then transfer to a medium sauce pot. Add the red onions, celery, red bell peppers, and tomatoes to the processor and pulse to finely chop. Add the veggies to the pot with the cabbage, then add the vinegar, sugar, five-spice powder, 1/4 teaspoon of the cayenne pepper, the turmeric, salt, and pepper. Bring the relish to a boil, then cook over medium heat for 10 to 12 minutes. Adjust the seasonings.

While the chowchow works, mix the meat with the garlic, ginger, cilantro, 2 tablespoons of the tamari, a little salt, and lots of black pepper. Form 2 large, inch-thick patties—they'll hang off the bun! Add the oil to a skillet and get it screaming hot over medium-high heat. Add the patties and cook them for 5 to 6 minutes on each side.

In a small pot, melt the peanut butter over low heat and whisk in the remaining 1/4 cup tamari, the sesame oil, and the remaining 1/4 teaspoon cayenne pepper. Pour the sauce over the cold noodles and toss them with the shredded Savoy cabbage, the scallions, and sesame seeds.

Place the burgers on the rolls and top them with lots of chowchow and lettuce, set the roll tops in place, and serve with the noodle salad.

2 SERVINGS

AREN'T WE FANCY? SUPPER

- **Cognac-Sauced Pepper Steaks**
- **Caramelized Onion–Dressed Salad with Toasted Hazelnuts**

You'll be hooked at first bite on these Cognac-Sauced Pepper Steaks. To prepare the sauce, I recommend picking up a nip (small two-ounce bottle) of cognac, sold in most liquor stores. Ah, the little nip: not just small and cute but very practical for those of you out there who don't want to commit to an entire bottle of something like cognac. (That's right. *I've* got your back.) Nips: they're not just for airplanes or mini bars anymore!

COGNAC-SAUCED PEPPER STEAKS

2   10- to 12-ounce **shell steaks** (sirloin), 1 to 1$^{1}/_{2}$ inches thick
    Salt
1   heaping tablespoon **coarsely ground black pepper**, a palmful
2   tablespoons **EVOO** (extra-virgin olive oil), plus more if needed
$^{1}/_{2}$ small **onion**, chopped
1   large **garlic clove**, chopped
1   nip of **cognac** or 2 healthy shots
$^{3}/_{4}$ cup **beef or chicken stock** (eyeball it)
$^{1}/_{4}$ cup **heavy cream** (eyeball it)
2   tablespoons fresh **flat-leaf parsley** leaves, a small handful, chopped

Season the steaks with some salt, then sprinkle one side of the steaks with the coarsely ground pepper and press it in with your fingers.

Preheat a large skillet over medium-high heat with 2 tablespoons of EVOO, twice around the pan. Add the steaks peppered side down, cook them for 4 minutes, then turn and cook for 3 minutes more for medium rare. (Go a minute longer on each side if you like your steak medium to medium-well done.) Remove the steaks to a plate and cover them loosely with a piece of aluminum foil to keep them warm while they rest. Return the skillet to the heat with a drizzle more EVOO if necessary and add the onions and garlic. Season with a little salt and cook, stirring frequently, for 3 to 4 minutes. Remove the skillet from the heat and add the cognac, then return it to the burner and let it flame up. (Be careful to stand back from the stove.) Once the flames die down, add the beef stock and the cream and turn the heat up to high; cook until the sauce is slightly thickened. Add the parsley to the sauce, then pour it over the steaks and serve.

2 SERVINGS

CARAMELIZED ONION–DRESSED SALAD WITH TOASTED HAZELNUTS

$1/2$ cup **whole peeled hazelnuts**
  6 tablespoons **EVOO** (extra-virgin olive oil)
  1 large **onion**, finely chopped
    Salt and **black pepper**
  3 tablespoons **balsamic vinegar** (eyeball it)
$1/2$ tablespoon **Dijon mustard**
  3 **plum tomatoes**, sliced
  4 large cups **baby spinach** or arugula or another green
    of your choice
$1/4$ cup **crumbled blue cheese**

Preheat the oven to 325° F. Place the hazelnuts on a baking sheet and toast them in the oven for 10 to 12 minutes; your nose will know when they are done. Remove them from the oven and transfer to a cutting board. When cool, run your knife through them once to coarsely chop them.

continued

While the nuts are toasting up, place a large skillet over medium-high heat with 2 tablespoons of the EVOO, twice around the pan. Add the onions, season with a little salt and pepper, and cook, stirring frequently, for 10 minutes. Add 1 tablespoon of the balsamic vinegar and a big splash of water. Continue to cook for about 1 minute, using a wooden spoon to scrape up any bits on the bottom of the pan. Remove the onions from the skillet and transfer to a bowl; stir in the remaining vinegar and the mustard. In a slow, steady stream, whisk the remaining 4 tablespoons EVOO into the onion dressing.

In a salad bowl, combine the tomatoes, baby spinach, chopped hazelnuts, and the blue cheese crumbles. Pour the caramelized onion dressing over the salad and toss to combine. Adjust the salt and pepper to taste.

2 SERVINGS

■ ■ ■

GAME PLAN

• Make the mustard sauce.

• Mix and form the crab cakes.

• Get the crab cakes going, then make the spinach.

APPETIZER-AS-ENTREE MENU

• **Crab Cakes with a Creamy, Grainy Mustard Sauce**
• **Wilted Spinach with Tomatoes**

Crab cakes are one of the most popular starters but they also make a great dinner, any night of the week. Also, thanks to ever-improving supermarket fish departments, great-quality lump crab meat is available any time of the year. Crab cakes are easy enough to make that you shouldn't save them for special occasions. Treat yourself to a rich supper of these cakes every now and then and it'll be even more fun to share them in their mini version next time you're having the gang over.

CRAB CAKES WITH A CREAMY, GRAINY MUSTARD SAUCE

  4 tablespoons **EVOO** (extra-virgin olive oil; eyeball it)

$^1/_2$ small **onion**, finely chopped

  1 **garlic clove**, chopped

    Salt and **black pepper**

  2 heaping tablespoons **grainy mustard**

$^3/_4$ cup **chicken stock** (eyeball it)

$^1/_4$ cup **heavy cream** or half-and-half (eyeball it)

  7 slices **white sandwich bread**

$^1/_2$ cup **mayonnaise**, a couple of heaping tablespoons

  4 **scallions**, finely chopped

$^1/_4$ cup fresh **flat-leaf parsley** leaves, a generous handful, chopped

  1 teaspoon **hot sauce** (eyeball it)

$^1/_2$ small **red bell pepper**, finely chopped

  1 pound **fresh lump crab meat**, available in tubs at the fish counter

  2 tablespoons **butter**

continued

Preheat a small sauté pan or sauce pot over medium-high heat with 1 tablespoon of the EVOO, once around the pan. Add the onions and garlic and season with salt and pepper. Cook, stirring frequently, for 3 to 4 minutes. Add the grainy mustard, chicken stock, and cream and bring the sauce up to a simmer. Cook until thick, 2 to 3 minutes. Turn the sauce off and reheat it when you're ready to serve. If it thickens up too much, add a splash more of the chicken stock or water to loosen it up.

TIDBIT

Fresh crab meat is a better value than the canned stuff, because canned crab meat is packed with lots of water.

Place the bread in a food processor and use the pulse button to break it up, then let 'er rip and make fine bread crumbs.

In a bowl, combine the mayonnaise, scallions, parsley, hot sauce, red bell peppers, salt, and pepper. Gently run your fingers through the crab meat, feeling for any shells or cartilage while trying not to break up the meat too much. Add the crab meat to the mayonnaise mixture with a quarter of the fresh bread crumbs and gently fold the mixture to combine. Place the remaining bread crumbs on a plate; divide the crab mixture into 4 equal portions. Transfer the 4 crab portions to the plate with the bread crumbs and coat each one, gently pressing to adhere the bread crumbs and forming 1- to 1$^{1}/_{2}$-inch-thick cakes.

Preheat a medium nonstick skillet over medium heat with the remaining EVOO, 3 times around the pan, and the butter. Once the butter melts, add the crab cakes and cook them for about 4 minutes on each side or until they are golden brown and heated through.

Divide the sauce between 2 plates, top with the crab cakes, and serve.

2 SERVINGS

WILTED SPINACH WITH TOMATOES

    2   tablespoons **EVOO** (extra-virgin olive oil; eyeball it)
  $^1\!/_2$ pint **grape tomatoes**
    2   **garlic cloves**, chopped
        Salt and **black pepper**
    1   pound **spinach**, triple washed, stemmed and coarsely chopped

Preheat a large skillet over medium-high heat with the EVOO, twice around the pan. Add the grape tomatoes and cook until they start to burst, 4 to 5 minutes. Add the garlic, season the tomatoes with salt and pepper, and cook for 2 more minutes. Add the spinach, turning it until it is partially wilted. Adjust the salt and pepper, then serve immediately.

2 SERVINGS

■ ■ ■

STEAK OUT

• **Sliced Steak with Green Olive and Tomato Sauce**

• **Sautéed Artichokes and Mushrooms**

When you are in the mood, nothing hits the spot like a juicy steak. This sliced steak has it good: it's slathered with a groovy green olive and tomato sauce. Sexy!

SLICED STEAK WITH GREEN OLIVE AND TOMATO SAUCE

2 tablespoons **Worcestershire sauce** (eyeball it)

2 teaspoons **hot sauce** (eyeball it)

2 tablespoons **EVOO** (extra-virgin olive oil), plus some for drizzling
   Salt and **black pepper**

1 1/2 pounds **boneless shoulder steak** or top round steak (often labeled London broil in the meat case)

1 medium **red onion**, chopped

2 large **garlic cloves**, chopped

1 cup **chicken stock** (eyeball it)

1/2 cup large **pitted green olives**, chopped

1/4 cup fresh **flat-leaf parsley** leaves, a generous handful, chopped
   Juice of 1 lemon

3 **plum tomatoes**, seeded and chopped

3 tablespoons cold **butter,** cut into pieces

Preheat the broiler on high.

Combine the Worcestershire sauce, hot sauce, a liberal drizzle of EVOO, salt, and pepper and smear this mixture all over the steak. Put the steak on a broiler pan and situate the pan on the rack closest to the flame. Broil it for 6 minutes per side. Remove it from the broiler and allow the meat to rest for 5 minutes, loosely covered with a piece of aluminum foil.

While the steak is broiling, make the green olive and tomato sauce. Preheat a medium skillet over medium-high heat with the 2 tablespoons of EVOO, twice around the pan. Add the onions and garlic and season with salt and pepper. Cook, stirring frequently, for 5 minutes; let the onions take on a little color. Add the chicken stock and cook until it has reduced by half. Add the olives, parsley, lemon juice, and tomatoes. Stir them to combine, turn off the heat, and add the cold butter, stirring until it is completely melted and incorporated.

Slice the rested steak very thin against the grain and on a slight angle. Serve the sliced steak with some of the green olive and tomato sauce.

2 SERVINGS

SAUTÉED ARTICHOKES AND MUSHROOMS

- 2 tablespoons **EVOO** (extra-virgin olive oil)
- 1/2 pound **cremini mushrooms**, quartered
- 3 **garlic cloves**, chopped
  Salt and **black pepper**
- 1 15-ounce can **quartered artichoke hearts**, drained
- 1/2 cup **chicken stock** (eyeball it)
- 1/4 cup fresh **flat-leaf parsley** leaves, a generous handful, chopped

Preheat a large skillet over medium-high heat with the EVOO. Add the mushrooms and cook, stirring occasionally, for about 5 minutes, or until they take on a little color. Add the garlic and season the darkened mushrooms with salt and pepper, cook them for 2 minutes more, then add the artichokes and chicken stock to the skillet and cook them together to heat through. Add the parsley to the skillet, toss to combine, and serve.

2 SERVINGS

THE DEAL WITH VEAL

- **Thin and Crispy Veal Topped with Prosciutto and Fontina**
- **A Green Triple Threat: Green Olive–Dressed Green Apple and Arugula Salad**

If you tell me dinner is going to be breaded and skillet-fried, you're looking at me with a big, veal-eatin' grin on! If you then follow up on the breaded-fried information and promise me some prosciutto and melted fontina on top, well, that smile may be fixed on me until tomorrow night's supper comes along. Are we a lot alike?

THIN AND CRISPY VEAL TOPPED WITH PROSCIUTTO AND FONTINA

2 boneless **veal shoulder chops**, no more than 1 inch thick

Salt and **black pepper**

$1/2$ cup all-purpose **flour**

2 **eggs,** beaten

1 cup **plain bread crumbs**

$1/2$ cup grated **Parmigiano-Reggiano**, 2 generous handfuls

$1/2$ teaspoon grated or ground **nutmeg**

6 to 8 fresh **sage leaves**, chopped

Olive oil, for frying

4 thin slices **prosciutto di Parma**

4 thin slices **fontina cheese**

Pound the veal chops to $1/4$-inch thickness between sheets of wax paper or plastic wrap using a small, heavy skillet. They should be about 10 inches wide. Season the chops with salt and pepper. Set up an assembly line with a dish with the flour, a shallow dish with the beaten eggs, and a plate with the bread crumbs combined with the Parmigiano, nutmeg, and chopped sage. Coat one chop in the flour and shake off the excess, then dip it into the eggs and coat thoroughly. Lastly, coat it in the bread crumbs, making sure every inch is covered. Repeat with the second chop.

Heat a thin layer of olive oil in a very large skillet over medium to medium-high heat. When the oil is hot, add the 2 breaded chops. Cook until they are golden brown, about 3 minutes. Flip the chops and top each with 2 slices of prosciutto and then 2 slices of fontina cheese. Cook for about 2 minutes, then loosely cover the skillet with a piece of aluminum foil to melt the cheese. Once the second side is brown and the cheese has melted, about 1 more minute, remove the veal from the skillet and serve.

2 SERVINGS

A GREEN TRIPLE THREAT: GREEN OLIVE–DRESSED GREEN APPLE AND ARUGULA SALAD

10 to 12 large **pitted green olives**, finely chopped
$^1/_2$ tablespoon **Dijon mustard** (eyeball it)
 2 tablespoons **white wine vinegar** (eyeball it)
   Salt and **black pepper**
$^1/_4$ cup **EVOO** (extra-virgin olive oil; eyeball it)
 1 **green apple**, such as Granny Smith, cored and thinly sliced
 5 to 6 cups **arugula**, coarsely chopped

In a salad bowl, combine the green olives, mustard, white wine vinegar, and a little salt and pepper. In a slow, steady stream, whisk in the EVOO. Add the apples and arugula and toss to coat. Serve.

2 SERVINGS

GAME PLAN

• Start the soup.

• Assemble the sammies while the soup simmers.

• Blend the soup and reheat it while the sammies toast.

SOUP AND SAMMY NIGHT

• Creamy Sweet Pea and Pancetta Soup
• Fontina, Olive, and Roasted Red Pepper Paninis

This menu is a really rich, satisfying way to end a day or perk up a midday lunch. I'm crazy for the paninis. I used to pile cheese and peppers on olive bread and press them, but once when the bakery counter was sold out of the bread, I had to come up with a makeshift substitute. It worked out so well that now, even when the bread is at the market waiting for me, I am torn as to which method to use. One thing I'm *not* torn up about is how good a hot panini is when dunked into a steaming bowl of soup. Yum-o!

CREAMY SWEET PEA AND PANCETTA SOUP

1 tablespoon **EVOO** (extra-virgin olive oil; eyeball it)
4 thick slices **pancetta**, chopped
1 small **onion**, chopped
1 **garlic clove**, chopped
   Leaves from 3 to 4 fresh **thyme** sprigs
2 cups **chicken stock** (eyeball it)
1 10-ounce box **frozen peas**
1/4 cup **mascarpone cheese**
   Salt and **black pepper**

TIDBIT

Always be careful when blending a hot liquid, as its volume can expand dramatically; to be super safe, leave the top vent hole open and cover with a kitchen towel as you blend.

Heat a medium sauce pot over medium-high heat with the EVOO, once around the pan. Add the pancetta and cook it until it's crisp, 3 to 4 minutes. Remove the pancetta and drain it on a paper towel. Return the pot to the stove over medium heat, then add the onions, garlic, and thyme leaves and cook, stirring frequently, for 5 minutes. Add the chicken stock and turn the heat up to high. When the stock boils, reduce it to a simmer and cook for 5 minutes more. Add the peas and cook for another 2 minutes. Transfer the soup to a blender or food processor along with the mascarpone and purée until it is smooth. Do this in 2 batches in order to avoid any messy mishaps.

Return the soup to the pot. To thicken it, turn the heat back on and reduce to the desired consistency, 3 to 5 minutes. Season the soup with salt and pepper. Serve the soup topped with the crispy pancetta.

2 SERVINGS

FONTINA, OLIVE, AND ROASTED RED PEPPER PANINIS

 1 **roasted red pepper**
$^1/_4$ cup **pitted kalamata olives**
A small handful of fresh **flat-leaf parsley** leaves
A couple pinches of **red pepper flakes**
 4 slices **fontina cheese**, 4 to 6 ounces total
 4 slices good-quality **crusty bread**

Preheat a panini press, medium skillet, or grill pan over medium heat.

Slice the roasted red pepper into strips, then pile them together on a cutting board with the olives and parsley leaves. Run your knife through the mixture to coarsely chop them together. Season the mixture with some red pepper flakes.

Place a slice of fontina cheese on each of 2 bread slices, then top each sandwich with an equal amount of the red pepper and olive mixture. Cover with a second slice of cheese and top with the remaining bread slices.

If you are using a sandwich press, place the sammies in the machine and press. For the skillet or grill-pan method, add the paninis to the pan, place a piece of foil on top of the sandwiches, and press with a full tea kettle, another pan weighted with cans, or a garden brick. Brown and crust the sandwiches, about 2 minutes on each side; cut and serve.

2 SERVINGS

■ ■ ■

MEALS FOR 2

- Start the ravioli going and make the dessert sauce as they fry.

- Make the steaks, sauce, and asparagus.

- Assemble the dessert just before serving.

SCENES FROM AN ITALIAN RESTAURANT

- Toasted Ravioli
- Pepper-Crusted Tenderloins with Mushroom Marsala Cream
- Roasted Asparagus
- Wine-Soaked Peaches with Ice Cream

This menu is for a special night: Congratulations! Happy Anniversary! I'm sorry. I love you. Thank you for everything. Take your pick and say it with food.

TOASTED RAVIOLI

2 **eggs**

A splash of **milk** or half-and-half

Salt and **black pepper**

1$^1/_2$ cups **Italian-style bread crumbs** (eyeball it)

$^1/_2$ cup grated **Parmigiano-Reggiano cheese**, 2 generous handfuls

A handful of finely chopped fresh **flat-leaf parsley** leaves

12 large fresh **spinach and cheese ravioli** (1 package, about $^3/_4$ pound)

5 tablespoons **EVOO** (extra-virgin olive oil)

3 **garlic cloves**, finely chopped

A couple pinches of **red pepper flakes**

2 **roasted red peppers**, drained

1 14-ounce can **crushed tomatoes**

A handful of fresh **basil** leaves, thinly sliced

Beat the eggs and the splash of milk in a shallow dish and season with salt and pepper. Combine the bread crumbs with the cheese and parsley in a second dish. Dip the fresh ravioli in the eggs, then coat with the bread crumbs. Heat 3 tablespoons of the EVOO over medium heat in a large skillet, then toast the ravioli until deep golden, 3 to 4 minutes on each side.

In a small sauce pot, heat the remaining 2 tablespoons of EVOO with the garlic and red pepper flakes over medium-low heat. Grind the roasted peppers in a food processor and add them to the garlic after it has cooked for a couple of minutes. Stir in the tomatoes and season the sauce with salt and pepper. Heat through, then wilt in the basil and transfer the sauce to a small bowl. Surround the sauce with the toasted ravioli for dipping and serve as an appetizer.

2 SERVINGS

PEPPER-CRUSTED TENDERLOINS WITH MUSHROOM MARSALA CREAM AND ROASTED ASPARAGUS

- 4   1-inch-thick **beef tenderloin steaks**, 3 to 4 inches round, about 1 pound total
- 3/4   pound **asparagus**, ends trimmed (fat stems should be peeled down a bit as well)
- 2   tablespoons **EVOO** (extra-virgin olive oil), plus extra for liberal drizzling **Salt** and **black pepper**
- 4   teaspoons **coarse black pepper**, a rounded palmful
- 2   tablespoons **butter**
- 6   **white mushroom caps**, very thinly sliced
- 1/3   cup **Marsala** (eyeball it)
- 2/3   cup **heavy cream** (eyeball it) Chopped fresh **flat-leaf parsley** or chives, for garnish

Preheat the oven to 425° F. Set the meat on the counter to take the chill off. Spread the asparagus on a small baking sheet, dress it with a liberal drizzle of EVOO, and season it with salt. Roast the spears until they are tender and the ends are crisp and slightly brown at the edges, 10 to 12 minutes. The asparagus should remain bright green.

continued

Pour the coarse black pepper onto a small plate. Heat the 2 table-spoons of EVOO in a nonstick skillet over medium-high to high heat. When the oil smokes, press each steak into the pepper to coat it on one side, then place the peppered side of the meat down in the skillet. Sear and caramelize the meat for 3 to 4 minutes, then turn and cook for 2 minutes on the second side for rare, 3 minutes for pink.

While the meat cooks, heat a small skillet over a medium flame and melt the butter. Add the mushrooms and lightly sauté them for 4 to 5 minutes. Season the mushrooms with salt and pepper and add the Marsala to the pan. Reduce the liquid by half (a minute or so), cooking off the alcohol and concentrating the flavor, then stir in the cream and warm it through. Reduce the heat a bit and let the sauce thicken for 2 to 3 minutes.

Spoon the sauce over the meat and serve with the asparagus.

2 SERVINGS

WINE-SOAKED PEACHES WITH ICE CREAM

1 1/2 cups **red wine**
1/2 cup **sugar**
1 **cinnamon stick**
2 or 3 **whole peppercorns**
1 or 2 **strips of lemon zest**
2 large **ripe peaches,** halved and pitted
1 pint **vanilla bean ice cream**

Combine the wine, sugar, cinnamon, peppercorns, and zest in a sauce pot and reduce over medium-high heat to a syrup, 12 to 15 minutes. Remove the cinnamon, peppercorns, and zest with a slotted spoon and discard. Add the peach halves and turn to coat in the wine sauce. Spoon the winey peaches into dishes and top them with ice cream.

2 SERVINGS

SPANISH-MEXICAN FIESTA
Garlicky Guacamole and Chips
Serrano-Wrapped Halibut with Tortillas
Cinnamon-Chipotle Tomato Salsa
Savoy Cabbage with Cumin, Coriander,
  and Lime
Saffron and Olive Rice

SCENES FROM AN ITALIAN RESTAURANT
Toasted Ravioli
Pepper-Crusted Tenderloins
with Mushroom
Marsala Cream
Roasted Asparagus
Wine-Soaked Peaches

HALLOWEEN HOOPLA
Pumpkin-Peanut Curry Noodles
5-Spice Seared Scallops
**   and Shrimp**
Looking for Mr. Goodbar Sundaes

04

SPORTS AND SAMMY NIGHT
Grilled Kielbasa Reubens with
**   Mustard-Caraway Sauerkraut**
Smoked Paprika O-Rings
Root Beer Floats (store bought)

09

NASCAR MENU
Caution-Flag Chili
Flat-Tire Corn and Black
   Bean Toppers
Fired-Up Peaches and Cream

RICH FLAVOR, SMALL PRICES
**Hearty Sausage and Mushroom Stew
over Polenta
Caramelized Cayenne Pear and
Blue Cheese Salad
Flourless Chocolate Cake
with Whipped Cream
and Raspberries
(store bought)**

MARCO "POLLO" MENU
Italian Chicken Pot Pie from the Boot
Boozy Berries and Biscuits

88

BURGER NIGHT HITS THE ROAD TO MOROCCO
Grilled Moroccan-Spiced Turkey Burgers with Mango Chutney Slaw
Veggie Chickpea and Couscous Salad with Yogurt Dressing

THIS IS MY MAGIC NUMBER. MOST NIGHTS JOHN AND I COOK AND WE COOK FOUR PORTIONS. IT'S THE NORM. WE ARE BOTH SOLID EATERS BUT, IF THERE ARE LEFTOVERS, JOHN IS ALREADY CRAFTING THEM INTO A SANDWICH IN HIS MIND'S EYE BEFORE THEY HIT THE FRIDGE. MOST BOOKS ARE WRITTEN IN "BASE 4" SERVINGS, AS WELL. BUT, NOT THIS ONE! IF YOUR NEED WHEN YOU FEED GOES BEYOND FOUR, CHECK OUT THE GREAT MEALS IN CHAPTERS "6" AND "8." YOU DON'T HAVE TO SWEAT THE MATH MULTIPLYING YOUR TEASPOONS AND TABLESPOONS; JUST KEEP TURNING THE PAGES.

SHOW-STOPPER PRE-THEATER DOUBLE DATE

• Italian Club Finger Sandwiches
• Seared Scallops with Lemon-Scented Bread Crumbs
• Fettuccine with Asparagus and Saffron Cream Sauce

Going out to a show can be pretty pricey even without paying for dinner in the theater district. Make this lovely pre-theater dinner at home and skip going out for dinner. Instead, treat yourself to dessert and a night cap after the show.

ITALIAN CLUB FINGER SANDWICHES

- 6 thin slices **white bread**, such as Pepperidge Farm Thin White Sandwich Bread
- 1 cup soft, **spreadable herb cheese**, such as Alouette
- 8 slices **prosciutto di Parma**
- 12 fresh **arugula or basil leaves** (spicy vs. sweet flavor)
- 2 **plum tomatoes**, thinly sliced
  Salt
- 2 **radishes**
  Toothpicks

Trim the crusts from the bread, if you want to. Spread 4 slices with the soft herbed cheese. Top each cheese-covered slice with 2 slices of prosciutto, 3 arugula leaves, and top with a few tomato slices seasoned with a pinch of salt. Stack two of the completed layers one atop the other, making 2 stacks, each 2 layers high. Top each stack with a third bread slice to make 2 triple-decker sandwiches.

Thinly slice and salt the radishes. Spear a couple radish slices onto each toothpick as you place 4 toothpicks in each sandwich. Cut each sandwich into 4 equal parts. The yield will be 8 triple-decker, square mini "club" sandwiches, 2 per person.

4 SERVINGS

SEARED SCALLOPS WITH LEMON-SCENTED BREAD CRUMBS AND FETTUCCINE WITH ASPARAGUS AND SAFFRON CREAM SAUCE

Salt
1 pound **asparagus tips**
1 pound **fettuccine**
2 tablespoons **EVOO** (extra-virgin olive oil), plus some for drizzling
2 **garlic cloves**, chopped
1 **shallot**, thinly sliced
$^1/_2$ cup **dry white wine** (eyeball it)
$^1/_2$ cup **chicken stock** (eyeball it)
1 14-ounce can **crushed tomatoes**
Pinch of **saffron** or 1 packet saffron powder (available in many markets on the spice aisle)
$^1/_4$ cup **heavy cream** (eyeball it)
Black pepper
2 tablespoons **butter**
1 cup **bread crumbs** (3 overflowing handfuls)
Zest of 1 lemon
Handful of fresh **flat-leaf parsley** leaves, finely chopped
16 **sea scallops**, trimmed

Bring an inch of water to a boil in a large skillet and bring a large covered pot of water to a boil for the pasta. When the water in the skillet comes to a boil, add salt and the asparagus and blanch for 2 minutes. Drain the asparagus and reserve. When the pasta water comes to a boil, salt it and cook the fettuccine to al dente.

continued

In the pan that you blanched the asparagus in, heat the 2 tablespoons of EVOO, twice around the pan, over medium heat. Add the garlic and shallots and sauté for 4 to 5 minutes. Deglaze the pan with the wine, then cook for 30 seconds to reduce it slightly. Add the stock, tomatoes, and saffron and simmer for 10 minutes. Stir in the cream, then season the sauce with salt and pepper.

While the sauce cooks, heat a skillet over medium-low heat. Add the butter and when it melts, add the bread crumbs and toast them. Stir in salt and pepper, the lemon zest, and parsley, then scrape the mixture into a bowl. Wipe the pan clean and return the skillet to medium-high heat and preheat until it's very hot. Drizzle the scallops with EVOO and add them to the hot pan to brown and caramelize on each side, 3 minutes on the first side and 2 minutes on the second.

Chop the asparagus on an angle into 1-inch pieces and add to the sauce. Drain the pasta and toss it with the asparagus and sauce. Serve the pasta with the seared scallops, 4 per person, alongside, and top the scallops with the lemon-scented bread crumbs.

4 SERVINGS

■ ■ ■

LEAN MEAN GUMBO MACHINE

- Dandelion Green Gumbo
- Good Thyme Rice
- Meatless Muffaletta Panini

MEATLESS MUFFALETTA PANINI

2 handfuls of good-quality **pitted green and black olives**

1 cup **giardiniera** (pickled cauliflower, carrot, and hot pepper mix), drained

4 sesame or cornmeal **kaiser rolls**, split

8 deli slices sharp **Provolone cheese**

1 15-ounce can **artichoke hearts in water**, drained and thinly sliced

2 **roasted red peppers**, drained and thinly sliced

Preheat a griddle or a grill pan over medium-high heat, or prepare a panini press.

Place the olives and pickled veggies in a food processor and pulse or chop them into a relish. Divide the relish among the bottom halves of the sandwich rolls and top it with a single slice of cheese. Layer the sliced artichokes and peppers onto the cheese, then add another slice of Provolone to each sandwich and press the tops in place.

Place the sandwiches on the griddle or grill pan and press them with a heavy skillet weighted down with cans, or place them in the panini press. Press the sammies for a few minutes on each side, then cut into halves and serve.

4 SERVINGS

DANDELION GREEN GUMBO WITH GOOD THYME RICE

- 4 tablespoons **EVOO** (extra-virgin olive oil)
- 1 cup **long-grain white rice**
- 6 cups **chicken or vegetable stock**
- 4 to 5 fresh **thyme** sprigs
- 2 tablespoons **butter**
- 4 **garlic cloves**, finely chopped
- 3 to 4 **celery ribs** from the heart, with greens, chopped
- 1 **red bell pepper**, chopped
- 1 large **yellow onion**, chopped
- **Salt** and **black pepper**
- 1 teaspoon **sweet paprika**, 1/3 palmful
- 1 **bay leaf**, fresh or dried
- 3 tablespoons all-purpose **flour**
- 1 12-ounce bottle **pale beer**
- 1 to 2 tablespoons **hot sauce**, such as Frank's Red Hot, medium to spicy
- 1 tablespoon **Worcestershire sauce** (eyeball it)
- 1 15-ounce can **petite diced, crushed, or stewed tomatoes**
- 4 to 5 cups **dandelion greens**, from 2 bundles, stemmed and chopped
- 1/4 teaspoon freshly grated or ground **nutmeg**
- 2 teaspoons **lemon zest**
- 2 **scallions**, finely chopped

Heat a sauce pot over medium heat. Add 2 tablespoons of the EVOO and the rice. Toast the rice for 2 minutes, add 2 cups of the stock and the thyme sprigs, and bring to a boil. Cover the pot, reduce the heat to a simmer, and cook for 18 minutes, or until tender.

While the rice cooks, heat a soup pot over medium to medium-high heat. Add the remaining 2 tablespoons of EVOO and the butter. When the butter melts into the oil, add the garlic, celery, bell peppers, and onions and season them with salt, pepper, and the paprika. Cook to soften the veggies, 5 minutes, then add the bay leaf and flour and cook for another minute. Stir in the beer and reduce the liquid by half, a minute or so. Add the hot sauce, Worcestershire, tomatoes, and greens. Season the greens with nutmeg and stir them into the pot. Add the remaining 4 cups of stock to the pot, raise the heat to bring it to a quick boil, then simmer for 15 minutes, or until the greens are no longer bitter. Adjust the seasonings to taste.

Uncover the rice and add the lemon zest and scallions. Remove the thyme stems and fluff the rice with a fork. Remove the bay leaf from the gumbo. Serve the gumbo topped with scoops of rice.

4 SERVINGS

MEXICAN SURF AND TURF

- Sliced Chili-Rubbed Flank Steak
- Spicy Rice with Shrimp
- Guacamole Stacks
- Lemon and Lime Sorbet (store-bought)

We are breaking down two misconceptions here: that Mexican food has to be heavy and unhealthy and that surf and turf has to be expensive to make. This is a well-balanced menu that pairs thinly sliced steak with inexpensive shrimp, rice, and lots of fresh veggies. It's a reason to throw a fiesta.

SLICED CHILI-RUBBED FLANK STEAK ON SPICY RICE WITH SHRIMP AND GUACAMOLE STACKS

1½	tablespoons **grill seasoning**, such as McCormick's Montreal Steak Seasoning, 1½ palmfuls
1	tablespoon **dark Mexican chili powder**, a palmful
	Zest of 1 lime
2	to 2¼ pounds **flank steak**
2	tablespoons **butter**
1½	cups **long-grain white rice**
1	small **onion**, chopped
½	**red bell pepper**, chopped
1	**jalapeño pepper**, seeded and chopped
2	**garlic cloves**, chopped
3	cups **chicken stock**
2	tablespoons **tomato paste**
2	teaspoons **hot sauce** (eyeball it)
1	pound small to medium **shrimp**, peeled and deveined

2 tablespoons finely chopped **fresh cilantro** or flat-leaf parsley
  Salt
  Cooking spray or oil, to coat the grill or grill pan
2 ripe **beefsteak tomatoes**, sliced
2 **Hass avocados**, halved, scooped from skin, and sliced
  Juice of ¹/₂ lemon
1 small **red onion**, thinly sliced
¹/₂ cup **crumbled queso asadero** (Mexican white mild cheese),
  goat cheese, queso fresco, or queso blanco

Preheat an outdoor grill or indoor grill pan over high heat. Combine the grill seasoning, chili powder, and lime zest and rub into both sides of the meat. Let the meat stand for 10 minutes while you get the rice going.

Heat a medium sauce pot over medium heat. Add the butter and when it melts add the rice and toast it for a couple of minutes. Add the onions, bell peppers, jalapeños, and garlic and cook for a few minutes to begin to soften the veggies. Add the stock and raise the heat to bring it up to a bubble. Stir in the tomato paste and the hot sauce. Reduce the heat to a simmer, cover the pot, and cook for 13 minutes. Add the shrimp to the pot so they can steam on top of the rice and cook until they are pink and firm, 5 minutes longer. Stir the shrimp and cilantro into the rice and season it with salt.

Oil the grill surface or grill pan and cook the meat for 7 to 8 minutes on the first side and 5 to 6 minutes on the flip side for medium doneness. Let the meat rest, covered loosely with aluminum foil.

Season the sliced tomatoes with salt and dress the avocados with the lemon juice. Make 4 stacks, alternating the tomatoes with avocado and onion slices.

Slice the steak and serve the slices on a bed of shrimp rice, with the guacamole stacks alongside. Garnish the guacamole stacks with cheese crumbles.

4 SERVINGS

HOT SPANISH NIGHTS

- "Hot Olives"
- **Charred Serrano and Manchego Melts**
- **Grilled Shrimp and Chorizo Skewers**
- **Piquillo Pepper Gazpacho**

I love Spain! At least I think I do; technically I've never been to the country. But I love Gaudí's architecture (at least in pictures), Almodóvar's films, flamenco guitar music and dancing, chorizo sausage, macho gazpacho, and rioja. I should have dual citizenship for all that. Have a hot night in Barcelona, baby!

GRILLED SHRIMP AND CHORIZO SKEWERS WITH PIQUILLO PEPPER GAZPACHO

4 **wooden skewers**

1 **lemon**

16 extra-large **shrimp,** peeled and deveined

Coarse salt

EVOO (extra-virgin olive oil), for liberal drizzling

1 ³/₄-pound package fully cooked **chorizo,** such as Gaspar's brand, cut into 16 thick slices on an angle

A generous handful of fresh **flat-leaf parsley** leaves

A generous handful of fresh **cilantro** leaves

2 **garlic cloves,** cracked from their skins

1 jar **roasted Spanish piquillo peppers,** available in most markets (roasted red peppers may be substituted, about 1 cup packed, drained peppers)

1 28-ounce can **fire-roasted tomatoes,** diced or crushed

1 small **yellow onion,** coarsely chopped

¹/₂ **seedless cucumber,** peeled, chopped

2 **celery ribs** from the heart, chopped

2 thick slices **crusty bread**, crusts trimmed, chopped
1 tablespoon **hot sauce**, such as Tabasco, for medium to spicy heat level, to taste

Preheat a grill or grill pan over medium-high heat. Soak the skewers in cold water for 10 minutes to prevent them from burning.

Zest the lemon and reserve the zest on a cutting board.

Place the shrimp in a shallow dish and season it with salt, the juice of half the zested lemon, and a liberal drizzle of EVOO—just enough to coat the shrimp. Thread 4 shrimp alternately with 4 slices of chorizo onto each skewer.

Place the parsley leaves on the cutting board with the lemon zest. Add $1/2$ palmful of cilantro leaves to the pile as well as 1 clove of garlic. Finely chop this mixture and reserve.

Place the remaining herbs and garlic in the food processor or in a large blender with the peppers, tomatoes, chopped vegetables, bread, and hot sauce. Process the gazpacho until smooth.

Grill the shrimp and chorizo for 3 to 4 minutes on each side until the shrimp are firm and opaque. Sprinkle small bowls of gazpacho with the reserved zest and herb mixture. Rest a shrimp skewer across the top of each bowl for dipping and dunking.

4 SERVINGS

TIDBIT

A word about ingredients here: Serrano ham is similar to prosciutto and is available at deli counters or in pre-sliced packages near the deli. If you can't find it, go for the prosciutto. Spanish manchego cheese is found in many markets today; look for it with the imported cheeses. Roasted piquillo peppers are available in most markets; if you can't get them, a packed cup of drained jarred roasted red peppers can stand in.

MEALS FOR 4

CHARRED SERRANO AND MANCHEGO MELTS AND "HOT" OLIVES WITH HERB AND SPICES

8 ¹/₂-inch-thick slices **crusty bread** from a good-size loaf
5 inches across and 3 inches wide

¹/₃ pound thinly sliced **Serrano ham**

¹/₃ to ¹/₂ pound **manchego cheese**, thinly sliced with a sharp knife or cheese plane

1 cup **giardiniera**, drained

¹/₂ cup **sweet pickled red pepper relish** or sweet pickle relish

2 cups good-quality mixed **olives**

2 tablespoons fresh **thyme** leaves, finely chopped

1 tablespoon **lemon zest**

1 teaspoon **cumin seeds**

1 teaspoon **red pepper flakes**

EVOO (extra-virgin olive oil), for drizzling

Preheat a grill pan or outdoor grill to medium high.

On 4 of the bread slices, layer Serrano and cheese in equal amounts. Combine the spicy giardiniera and the sweet pickled relish in a food processor and pulse or chop them to make a relish. Spread the relish evenly on the sandwich tops and set them into place.

Tear off a sheet of aluminum foil and place the olives in the center. Season with the thyme, lemon zest, cumin seeds, and red pepper flakes and drizzle them with EVOO. Fold in the sides to form a sealed packet. Place the packet on the grill and cook it for a few minutes on each side to heat the olives, herb, and spices. (The packet also can be roasted in a 350-degree oven until heated through, 10 to 15 minutes.)

Place the sandwiches on the grill and weight them down with a heavy skillet or a brick covered in foil. Char and heat the sandwiches for 2 to 3 minutes on each side.

Cut the sammies in half and serve with "hot" olives alongside.

4 SERVINGS

■ ■ ■

MOTHER'S DAY MEAL FOR ELSA

- **BLT and P (Bacon, Leek, Tomato, and Potato) Soup**
- **BLCC (Berries, Lemon Curd, and Cake) Dessert**

This soup is surprisingly light, colorful, and full of vegetables. It warms you up, soul and stomach, just like Mom's cooking. My mom, Elsa, and I first made this soup a few months ago when we returned from a drive up to our favorite smokehouse, Oscar's in Warrensburgh, New York. We love their bacon so much we made a soup with it so we could have a whole potful of that great flavor. Invite over your mom, or someone who gives you great advice. Make this for them and turn any day into your own Mother's Day.

BLT AND P (BACON, LEEK, TOMATO, AND POTATO) SOUP

    EVOO (extra-virgin olive oil), for drizzling
6 slices lean, smoky **bacon**, chopped into $1/2$-inch pieces
3 small **celery ribs** from the heart, finely chopped
2 small or medium **carrots**
3 **leeks**, trimmed of rough tops and root ends
1 **bay leaf**
    Salt and **black pepper**
3 medium-size starchy **potatoes**, such as Idaho, peeled
2 quarts **chicken stock**
1 15-ounce can **petite diced tomatoes**, drained
    A handful of fresh **flat-leaf parsley** leaves, finely chopped
    Crusty bread, for dunking and mopping

Heat a medium soup pot or deep-sided skillet over medium-high heat. Add a drizzle of EVOO and the bacon to the hot pan. Cook the bacon until it's brown and crisp. Remove the bacon to a paper-towel-lined plate and reserve. Drain off all but 2 tablespoons of the remaining fat

continued

and return to the heat. Add the chopped celery and cook over medium heat. As the celery cooks, use the vegetable peeler to make long, thin strips of the carrots. Chop the thin strips into small bits or carrot chips, $1/2$ inch wide. Add the chips to the celery and stir. Halve the leeks lengthwise and then cut into $1/2$-inch half moons. Place the slices into a colander and run them under cold water, separating all the layers to wash away all the trapped grit. When the leeks are clean, shake off the water and add them to the celery and carrots. Stir the veggies together, add the bay leaf, and season them with salt and pepper. While the leeks cook to wilt, 3 to 4 minutes, slice the potatoes.

Cut each potato crosswise into thirds. Stand each potato third upright and thinly slice it. The pieces will look like raw potato chips.

Add the stock to the vegetables and bring to a boil. Reduce the heat and add the potatoes and tomatoes. Cook them for 8 to 10 minutes, until the potatoes are tender and starting to break up a bit. Add the bacon and parsley and stir. Discard the bay leaf and adjust the seasonings. Serve immediately with crusty bread.

4 SERVINGS

BLCC DESSERT (BERRIES, LEMON CURD, AND CAKE)

4 small **individual sponge cakes**, sold in packages of 6 on the baking aisle
1 jar **prepared lemon curd**
$1/2$ pint **raspberries**
1 canister **whipped cream**, from the dairy case
2 teaspoons **lemon zest**

Arrange the sponge cakes on a serving dish. Remove the lid from the lemon curd jar and heat the lemon curd in the microwave for 30 seconds on high to warm and loosen it. Fill the cakes with the curd. Top the curd with berries, whipped cream, and lemon zest.

4 SERVINGS

SNOW DAY MENU

- **Hungarian-ish Mini Dumpling and Egg Noodle Soup**
- **Cucumber and Celery Salad**

The soup in this menu is both light and hearty at the same time. It is great in any season for any reason, but it is especially delish on cold, snowy days. Plus, it's made from many items you can keep on hand. I always have a package each of ground turkey and ground chicken in the freezer—they are both so lean and easy to work with.

CUCUMBER AND CELERY SALAD

3 tablespoons **pickle relish**

2 tablespoons **cider vinegar** or red wine vinegar

3 tablespoons **EVOO** (extra-virgin olive oil; eyeball it)

1 **seedless cucumber**, quartered lengthwise and sliced $1/2$ inch thick (you can use a regular cuke, but seed it and, if the skin is waxy, peel it)

5 to 6 **celery ribs** from the heart, sliced $1/2$ inch thick

$1/4$ cup chopped **hot or roasted red peppers** or $1/2$ small fresh bell pepper

1 small jar **marinated mushrooms** or artichoke hearts or 1 cup **giardiniera** (pickled vegetable salad), chopped

Salt and **black pepper**

Place the relish in the bottom of a bowl. Whisk in the vinegar then the EVOO. Add the cucumbers, celery, peppers, and marinated vegetable of choice to the bowl. Toss the salad and adjust the flavor with salt and pepper.

4 SERVINGS

HUNGARIAN-ISH MINI DUMPLING AND EGG NOODLE SOUP

8 cups **chicken stock**, such as Kitchen Basics (2 1-quart boxes)

1 pound **ground chicken** or ground turkey breast

1 **egg**

1 cup plain **bread crumbs**

1/4 teaspoon freshly grated or ground **nutmeg** (eyeball it)

1 teaspoon **smoked sweet paprika**

Handful of fresh **flat-leaf parsley** leaves, finely chopped

Salt and **black pepper**

1 1/2 to 2 cups **thin egg noodles**

1/2 cup **Spanish piquillo peppers** or roasted red peppers, cut into quarters lengthwise then very thinly sliced

6 **scallions**, cut into 2-inch pieces then shredded into thin sticks

3 tablespoons **fresh dill**, finely chopped, a handful

In a large soup pot, bring the stock to a boil and reduce the heat to a simmer.

Mix the chicken with the egg, bread crumbs, nutmeg, paprika, parsley, salt, and pepper. Roll the mixture into 1-inch dumplings and add them to the simmering stock. Let the dumplings cook for 3 to 4 minutes, then add the egg noodles, piquillo peppers, and scallions and stir. Cook for another 4 to 5 minutes, until the noodles are just tender. Stir in the dill. Season the soup with salt and pepper to taste and serve it immediately.

4 SERVINGS

■ ■ ■

SUMMER SALAD SUPPER

- **Sliced Grilled Portobello Mushroom Sorta-Caesar Salad**
- **Tipsy Triple-Chocolate Shakes and Strawberries**

This dinner is meat free and guilt free so of course, you can have dessert! I love give-and-take thinking. It's like when I go shopping. If I buy some two-hundred-dollar shoes on sale for seventy-five dollars, then I can go buy a one-hundred-twenty-five-dollar dress to go along with them.

SLICED GRILLED PORTOBELLO MUSHROOM SORTA-CAESAR SALAD

$^1/_3$ cup **EVOO** (extra-virgin olive oil), plus some for brushing (eyeball it)

8 **portobello mushroom** caps (discard the stems)

1 tablespoon **grill seasoning**, such as McCormick's Montreal Steak Seasoning, a palmful

1 tablespoon finely chopped fresh **rosemary**, from a few sprigs

2 crusty **semolina rolls**, split, or $^1/_2$ small loaf semolina bread, sliced

2 **garlic cloves**, cracked away from their skins and split

Black pepper

Juice of 1 lemon

2 teaspoons **Dijon mustard**

2 teaspoons **Worcestershire sauce** (eyeball it)

1 teaspoon **hot sauce**, such as Tabasco (eyeball it)

2 teaspoons **anchovy paste**—a must for me, optional for you

3 **hearts of romaine**, chopped

1 cup grated **Parmigiano-Reggiano or Romano cheese**, 4 generous handfuls

Heat a grill pan or an outdoor grill to medium-high heat. Brush EVOO evenly over the mushroom caps, then rub them with the grill season-

continued

MEALS FOR 4

ing and rosemary. Grill for 3 to 4 minutes on each side, or until they are dark and tender. Remove the caps and reserve.

While the mushrooms cook, toast the split rolls or bread under the broiler or on the grill until they are deeply golden, then rub them with 1 clove of cracked, split garlic. Drizzle EVOO over the bread and season it with a little pepper, then chop the bread into cubes.

Rub the inside of a salad bowl with the remaining clove of garlic. Combine the lemon juice, Dijon, Worcestershire, hot sauce, and anchovy paste, if using, in the salad bowl. Whisk in the $1/3$ cup of EVOO. Add the greens and bread to the bowl and toss with the dressing to coat. Add the cheese to the salad and toss it again, then season it with black pepper to taste. Slice the mushrooms about $1/2$ inch thick and arrange over each serving of salad.

4 SERVINGS

TIPSY TRIPLE-CHOCOLATE SHAKES AND STRAWBERRIES

  8 shots **chocolate cream liqueur**, such as Bailey's
 12 scoops **chocolate ice cream**
  4 cups **chocolate milk**
     Whipped cream, from a canister (in the dairy case)
  1 **dark chocolate bar**, for garnish
 16 **large-stem strawberries**, rinsed and dried

Working in 2 batches, combine the chocolate liqueur, ice cream, and chocolate milk in a blender and whir until it is thick but smooth. Pour the shakes into tall glasses and garnish them with whipped cream. Use a vegetable peeler to shave the dark chocolate over each. Serve them with straws and long spoons on plates to catch the drips, with 4 large-stem berries alongside for dunking.

4 SERVINGS

WINGS AWAY

• **Wingless Buffalo Chicken Pizza**
• **Celery Succotash Salad**

I am always trying to make the foods that are bad for my figure less of a guilty pleasure. Case in point: Buffalo chicken wings. The chicken here is all white meat; it's not fried; and as an added attraction, it's sitting on top of a pizza. The celery sticks you would munch alongside are here, too, chopped up in a healthful salad. Put a game on or pop a movie in and enjoy. Wings away!

WINGLESS BUFFALO CHICKEN PIZZA

3/4 pound **chicken breast cutlets**
EVOO (extra-virgin olive oil), for drizzling
2 teaspoons **grill seasoning**, such as McCormick's Montreal Steak Seasoning (eyeball it)
1 **pizza dough**, store-bought or from your favorite pizzeria
Cornmeal or flour, for dusting
2 tablespoons **butter**
1 tablespoon **Worcestershire sauce** (eyeball it)
2 to 3 tablespoons **hot sauce**, to taste
1/2 cup **tomato sauce**
1 cup shredded **Monterey Jack cheese**, 4 generous handfuls
1/2 cup **crumbled blue cheese**
3 **scallions**, thinly sliced

Preheat the oven to 425° F. Preheat a grill pan over high heat.

Place the chicken on a plate and drizzle with EVOO. Season it with the grill seasoning. When the grill pan is hot, cook the chicken for about 3 minutes on each side, until it is cooked through.

continued

MEALS FOR 4

Stretch the dough to form a pizza, using cornmeal or flour to help you handle it. If you let it rest and warm up for a few minutes, it will handle more easily. Set the pizza on a pizza pan to the side.

In a medium skillet over medium heat, melt the butter and stir in the Worcestershire, hot sauce, and tomato sauce.

Remove the chicken from the grill pan and slice it thin. Add the chicken to the sauce and stir to coat. Cover the pizza dough with the saucy Buffalo chicken, cheeses, and scallions. Bake for 18 minutes, or until crisp.

4 SERVINGS

CELERY SUCCOTASH SALAD

2 tablespoons **Dijon mustard**
2 tablespoons **honey**, a healthy drizzle
Juice of 1 lemon
2 tablespoons **red wine vinegar** (eyeball it)
1/3 cup **EVOO** (extra-virgin olive oil; eyeball it)
Salt and **black pepper**
1 **celery heart**, thinly sliced
1/2 cup **shredded carrots**
1 10-ounce box **frozen corn kernels**, thawed
1 15-ounce can **chickpeas**, drained
1/2 **red bell pepper**, chopped
1/2 small or medium **red onion**, chopped
2 tablespoons **fresh thyme** leaves, chopped

In a medium bowl, combine the mustard, honey, lemon juice, and vinegar. Whisk in the EVOO and season the dressing with salt and pepper. Add the celery, carrots, corn, chickpeas, bell peppers, onions, and thyme. Toss to combine the salad and adjust the salt and pepper to taste.

4 SERVINGS

■ ■ ■

MAKE YOUR OWN TAKE-OUT, SUB-STYLE

- Chicken Parm Meatball Subs
- Shredded Veggie Salad
- Campari Citrus Soda

Chicken Parm Subs are truly tasty but that's for some fattening reasons: the cutlets are deep-fried and the subs are buried in cheese. Here, the cheesy meatballs are made with lean ground chicken and they are baked, not fried. Open wide! The salad was inspired by cold sub sandwiches: the veggies are all shredded up like sandwich toppings.

SHREDDED VEGGIE SALAD

2 **hearts of romaine** or 1 small head of iceberg lettuce, shredded
1 medium **beefsteak tomato**, halved then very thinly sliced
1 small **green bell pepper**, seeded, cored, and very thinly sliced
1/2 medium **onion**, very thinly sliced
1/4 cup **hot pepper rings** or pepperoncini, drained and chopped
2 tablespoons **red wine vinegar** (eyeball it)
1/4 cup **EVOO** (extra-virgin olive oil; eyeball it)
Salt and **black pepper**

In a large bowl, combine the lettuce, tomatoes, bell peppers, onions, and hot pepper rings. Dress with the vinegar, oil, salt, and pepper.

4 SERVINGS

CHICKEN PARM MEATBALL SUBS

1¹/₂ pounds **ground chicken**

1 tablespoon **grill seasoning**, such as McCormick's Montreal Steak Seasoning

1 **egg**, beaten

1 cup grated **Parmigiano-Reggiano cheese**

¹/₂ cup **Italian-style bread crumbs**

Handful of chopped fresh **flat-leaf parsley** leaves

3 tablespoons **EVOO** (extra-virgin olive oil), plus some for liberal drizzling

2 large **garlic cloves**, cracked from their skins and split

¹/₄ teaspoon **red pepper flakes**, a couple of healthy pinches

1 28-ounce can **crushed tomatoes**, San Marzanos if available

1 cup **chicken stock**

Salt and **black pepper**

8 to 10 **fresh basil** leaves, torn or shredded

4 6- to 8-inch **crusty sub rolls**

1¹/₂ cups **shredded Provolone**

Preheat the oven to 425° F.

Place the chicken in a bowl and season it with the grill seasoning. Add the egg, half of the grated cheese, the bread crumbs, parsley, and a serious drizzle of EVOO. Combine the mixture and form 12 large meatballs, placing them on a baking sheet. Squish the balls to flatten them a bit—like mini oval meat loaves. Be careful not to form the balls wider than your bread. The flattened balls will stay put on your sub—no roll-aways! Bake the meatballs for 15 minutes, or until golden and firm. Switch the broiler on.

While the chicken balls bake, heat a medium skillet over medium heat. Add the 3 tablespoons of EVOO and the garlic and cook them for 5 minutes. Discard the garlic, add the red pepper flakes and the tomatoes, then stir in the chicken stock. Season the sauce with salt and pepper and simmer for 10 minutes. Adjust the seasonings and stir in the basil.

Use a thin spatula to loosen the chicken balls from the baking sheet and add them to the sauce, turning the meatballs to coat.

Cut the sub rolls, making the bottom a little deeper than the top. Hollow out a little of the bread and lightly toast the sub rolls under the broiler. Fill the bottoms of the breads with the sauced meatballs. Combine the Provolone and the remaining Parmigiano cheese. Cover the meatballs with cheese and return to the broiler to melt the cheese until it's golden. Set the roll tops in place. Pour any leftover sauce into a bowl and serve at the table for dipping.

4 SERVINGS

CAMPARI CITRUS SODA

1 shot of **Campari**
3 to 4 ounces **grapefruit juice**
   Ginger ale

Fill a tall glass with ice. Add the Campari to the ice and nearly fill the glass with grapefruit juice. Top it off with ginger ale and enjoy!

1 SERVING

TIDBIT

When you make your own take-out, you control the quality of the ingredients and the cooking method, making you feel better about eating more!

HOLD THE MAYO

• Grilled Chicken Posole Salad
• Chipotle Potato Salad
• Tortilla Chips and Salsas (store-bought)

Picnics are a birthright for us all. Eating outside, on a big blanket, amidst the grass and trees, the birds—hold the bees! Dress it up. Pack real plates and silver, along with some chilled rosé and pretty glassware. This is a picnic-perfect spicy salad menu, made mayo-free so you don't have to worry about the food temp. (You have better things to do, like going to fly a kite!)

GRILLED CHICKEN POSOLE SALAD

4   6-ounce boneless, skinless **chicken breasts**
3   tablespoons **EVOO** (extra-virgin olive oil), plus some for drizzling
1   tablespoon **grill seasoning**, such as McCormick's Montreal Steak Seasoning
2   teaspoons ground **cumin**, $2/3$ palmful
1   teaspoon ground **thyme** or poultry seasoning, $1/3$ palmful
3   **garlic cloves**, chopped
1   medium **onion**, chopped
12   **tomatillos**, husks removed, rinsed and dried, then coarsely chopped
4   Spanish **piquillo peppers** or 2 roasted red peppers, drained and chopped
3   **celery ribs**, with green tops, chopped
$1/2$ cup **green olives** with pimientos, drained and chopped
1   15-ounce can **hominy**, drained
1   tablespoon **hot sauce** (eyeball it)
     Juice of 2 limes
     Salt and **black pepper**
2   cups lightly crushed **tortilla chips**, any color or variety

Preheat a grill pan or outdoor grill to high. Coat the chicken with a generous drizzle of EVOO. Combine the grill seasoning with the cumin and ground thyme and sprinkle it evenly over the chicken. Grill the meat for 5 to 6 minutes on each side. Remove it from the heat and set aside until cool enough to handle.

While the chicken works, heat a skillet over medium-high heat. Add 1 tablespoon of the EVOO (once around the pan), the garlic, and the onions and cook them together for a few minutes. Add the tomatillos and cook for 3 to 4 minutes just to take the bitter edge off the tomatillos. Remove the skillet from the heat.

In a large bowl, combine the chopped peppers, celery, olives, and hominy. Dice and add the chicken. Add the hot sauce and lime juice to the salad and dress it with the remaining 2 tablespoons of EVOO (eyeball it). Toss the salad, then add the tomatillo mixture and combine. Season the salad with salt and pepper and serve with crushed tortilla chips as a garnish.

4 SERVINGS

TIDBIT

Hominy, the key ingredient in posole, is hulled corn kernels. You can find canned, ready-to-eat hominy in the Latin food section.

CHIPOTLE POTATO SALAD

4 large **Russet potatoes**, about 2^1/$_2$ pounds, peeled and thinly sliced
Salt

2 **chipotles in adobo**, chopped, plus 2 tablespoons of the adobo sauce

3 tablespoons **orange marmalade**

3 tablespoons **orange juice**

3 tablespoons **red wine vinegar**

3 tablespoons **EVOO** (extra-virgin olive oil; eyeball it)

1 small **red onion** or ^{1}/$_2$ large red onion, chopped

2 tablespoons chopped **fresh cilantro**, a handful
A couple **fresh oregano** sprigs, finely chopped, or a couple pinches
of dried
Salt and **black pepper**

Place the potatoes in a pot and cover them with water. Bring the water to a boil and season liberally with salt, then cook the potatoes until they are just fork tender, 8 to 9 minutes.

Combine the chipotles and adobo sauce, marmalade, orange juice, and vinegar in a bowl, then whisk in the EVOO.

Drain the potatoes well, return them to the hot pot to let the water evaporate, then add them immediately to the dressing. (The dressing will be better absorbed by warm taters.) Toss them with the onions and herbs and season the salad with salt and pepper. Serve it warm or chilled. Drizzle with a little more EVOO if the salad gets dry.

4 SERVINGS

■ ■ ■

- Get the potatoes for the crab cakes going.

- Grill the mushrooms.

- Mix and form the crab cakes.

- While the crab cakes fry, stuff the mushrooms and make the salad.

HORS D'OEUVRE DINNER

- **Killer Crab and Potato Cakes**
- **Bitter Salad with Sweet Dressing**
- **Giant Stuffed Mushrooms**

I think that crab cakes and stuffed mushrooms should be more than just party snacks. Here, they take center plate. I make many versions of crab cakes and this one, made with a bit of potato, is more substantial than most.

GIANT STUFFED MUSHROOMS

1/4 cup **EVOO** (extra-virgin olive oil), plus more for liberal brushing
5 large **portobello mushroom** caps
   Salt and **black pepper**
1 cup diced, stale **chewy bread**
2 **plum tomatoes**, chopped
2 **celery ribs** from the heart, with green tops, very thinly sliced
1/2 small **onion**, chopped
   A couple handfuls of fresh **flat-leaf parsley** leaves, chopped
   Leaves from 3 to 4 fresh **thyme** sprigs, chopped
   Juice of 1 lemon
   Small chunk of **Parmigiano-Reggiano cheese**, for shaving

Preheat a grill pan over medium-high heat.

Brush EVOO over 4 of the mushrooms and grill them for 5 minutes on each side. Season with salt and pepper, then remove them from the grill.

While the portobellos cook, cut the remaining portobello into 4 thick slices, then thinly slice each piece across. Mix the fresh mushroom

continued

bits with the bread, tomatoes, celery, onions, parsley, and thyme, then dress the stuffing with the lemon juice and the ¹/₄ cup of EVOO. Toss and season the stuffing with salt and pepper.

Top the grilled mushrooms with mounds of the stuffing and shavings of Parmigiano-Reggiano.

4 SERVINGS

KILLER CRAB AND POTATO CAKES AND BITTER SALAD WITH SWEET DRESSING

1 large **Idaho potato**, peeled and cubed

2 **garlic cloves**, chopped

Coarse salt

A handful of fresh **flat-leaf parsley** leaves, chopped

Leaves from 2 fresh **thyme** sprigs, finely chopped

1 lemon, zested, then cut into wedges

¹/₂ teaspoon **red pepper flakes**

2 6-ounce tubs **fresh lump crab meat**, available at the seafood counter

1 tablespoon **seafood seasoning**, such as Old Bay

1 cup **Italian-style bread crumbs**, 3 overflowing handfuls

7 tablespoons **EVOO** (extra-virgin olive oil)

1 **roasted red pepper**, chopped

1 small **shallot**, chopped

2 teaspoons **sugar**

2 tablespoons **apricot preserves** or orange marmalade

2 tablespoons **red wine vinegar**

Black pepper

1 small **head of escarole**, chopped

1 small **head of radicchio**, chopped

1 Belgian **endive**, chopped

Cook the potatoes in boiling water for 6 to 7 minutes, until tender. Drain, the potatoes and scatter the pieces across a large flat surface to cool and dry for 5 minutes, then scoop into a mixing bowl. Make a paste with the garlic and salt and add it to the potatoes along with the parsley, thyme, lemon zest, and red pepper flakes. Feel through the crab meat as you add it to the potatoes to check for shells and bits of cartilage. Add the seafood seasoning and combine the mixture gently. Form four super-size 4- to 5-inch killer crab cakes. Place the bread crumbs on a plate and coat the crab cakes on both sides with crumbs to set them.

Heat 3 tablespoons of the EVOO in a nonstick skillet over medium to medium-high heat. Add the cakes and cook for 3 to 4 minutes on each side, or until they are deeply golden.

Combine the roasted red peppers, shallots, sugar, preserves, and red wine vinegar in a food processor. Stream in the remaining 4 tablespoons of EVOO. Stop the processor and season the dressing with salt and pepper. Combine the greens in a salad bowl and toss with the dressing; adjust the salt and pepper to your taste. Serve the crab cakes on a bed of the salad, with lemon wedges to squeeze over the cakes.

4 SERVINGS

■ ■ ■

SIDEWALK CAFÉ SUMMER SUPPER

- **Beef Tenderloin Bites on a Bed of Arugula**
- **Amaretti Ice Cream Dessert**

From Montreal to Rome, sidewalk cafés often have the most surprising, simple, satisfying dishes. This supper reminds me of many al fresco café meals I've shared with my husband or family members while traveling. The tenderloin bites are based on a dish I never actually ordered but read about on a menu in a tiny tavern while traveling through a small neighborhood in a midwestern American city.

BEEF TENDERLOIN BITES ON A BED OF ARUGULA

$1^1/_2$ cups **Italian-style bread crumbs** (eyeball it)

Handful of fresh **flat-leaf parsley** leaves, chopped

$^1/_2$ cup grated **Parmigiano-Reggiano** cheese, a couple handfuls

$^1/_4$ cup **EVOO** (extra-virgin olive oil), plus some for drizzling for the salad

3 to 4 **garlic cloves**, finely chopped

4 **tenderloin steaks**, 1 inch thick, cut into bite-size pieces

Salt and **black pepper**

5 to 6 cups **arugula**, chopped

Juice of 1 lemon

Preheat the broiler.

Mix the bread crumbs with the parsley and cheese. Warm the $^1/_4$ cup of EVOO and garlic over low heat for 5 minutes to infuse the oil with flavor. Pour the oil and garlic into the bread-crumb mixture and combine to distribute equally and moisten the bread crumbs.

Season the meat with salt and pepper, then toss the meat in the bread-crumb mixture to coat evenly. Spread the meat on a baking sheet and place under the broiler until the coating is crisp and the meat is tender, 6 to 7 minutes. Dress the arugula with a drizzle of EVOO, the lemon juice, and salt and pepper to taste, tossing to coat well. Serve the meat on a bed of the arugula.

AMARETTI ICE CREAM DESSERT

16 **Amaretti cookies**
 4 shots of **Amaretto** or other almond liqueur
 8 scoops of **French vanilla ice cream**
   Whipped cream, from a canister (in the dairy case)
¼ cup **slivered almonds**

Crumble 4 Amaretti cookies into each of 4 dessert cups and douse them with the liqueur. Top with ice cream, whipped cream, and almonds.

■ ■ ■

IRISH BREAKFAST OF CHAMPIONS

- Cream Eggs with Irish Cheese and Chives
- Spiked Beans and Toast
- Sausage O'Patties
- Harvey's Tea

- Get the bacon for the beans going.

- Mix and form the sausage patties.

- While the beans finish cooking, cook the sausage, eggs, and toast.

- Make the tea just before serving.

I call this a breakfast but it's a hearty enough meal to eat for brunch or lunch as well. Try not to break out in a brogue while making it. It will annoy most of your friends, especially the Irish. Harvey, who's from Ireland, wrote the tea-making method and he's very specific about it. Don't stray from the form, please; you'll have him to answer to. He'll know. He's serious about the tea.

SAUSAGE O'PATTIES

- 1 small **Idaho potato**, peeled
  Salt
- 1 small **onion**, coarsely chopped, about ¹/₃ cup
- ³/₄ pound **ground pork**
  A few sprigs of fresh **flat-leaf parsley**
- 1 teaspoon **ground thyme**, ¹/₃ palmful
  Black pepper
- 2 tablespoons **EVOO** (extra-virgin olive oil)

Grate the potato onto a cutting board, salt it, then transfer it to a paper-towel-lined bowl or plate to drain.

Place the potato, onions, pork, parsley, thyme, and salt and pepper in a food processor and pulse to form a sausage mixture. Heat a large nonstick skillet over medium heat with the EVOO. When the oil is hot, form 8 potato-sausage patties 3 inches wide, $^1/_2$ inch thick. Cook the patties for 6 to 7 minutes on each side, until they are deeply golden brown in color.

4 SERVINGS

SPIKED BEANS AND TOAST

2 **bacon** slices, chopped
1 small **onion**, chopped
1 28-ounce can **baked beans**
2 shots **Irish whisky**
 Black pepper
2 tablespoons **butter**, softened
1 tablespoon **honey**
4 slices **white bread**, toasted

Heat a medium skillet over medium-high heat. Add the bacon and cook until crisp, 5 minutes. Add the onions to the skillet and reduce the heat to medium. Cook the onions with the bacon until they are soft, 5 to 6 minutes more. Stir in the baked beans. Heat the beans through, then reduce the heat to low. Remove the pan from the heat, add the whisky, and stir it in, then return it to the heat. If the whisky flames, the flame will die out in less than 10 seconds—just be prepared. For a full whisky-spike flavor, the trick is to avoid the flame and just warm the alcohol: think hot toddy. Season the spiked beans with black pepper.

Combine the softened butter with the honey, then spread the mixture evenly on the toasted bread. Serve the beans with honey-buttered toast.

4 SERVINGS

CREAM EGGS WITH IRISH CHEESE AND CHIVES

2 tablespoons **Irish butter**, such as Kerrygold brand, or regular butter, cut into small bits

8 large **eggs**

1/3 cup **heavy cream** (eyeball it)

Salt and **black pepper**

1/2 pound **Blarney cheese** or Irish farmhouse cheddar, shredded or diced

12 **fresh chives,** chopped

Melt the butter in a medium nonstick pan over medium-low heat.

Whisk the eggs with the cream and salt and pepper. Add the egg mixture to the pan and stir just until softly scrambled. Stir in the cheese and chives and continue to cook for a minute more, then serve.

4 SERVINGS

HARVEY'S TEA

First, the tea must be Barry's Tea Gold Blend. Next, boil the water in a kettle. Pour a little boiling water into the teapot and swish it around to warm it, then pour it out. (I have no idea why. Harvey says so, that's why.) Place 2 tea bags in the teapot for every 3 cups of water. Place the teapot over the lowest flame for 30 seconds to 1 minute. Remove the pot and cover it with a cozy or a kitchen towel. Pour the tea into cups and add a splash of whole milk after the tea is poured.

■ ■ ■

JAZZ FEST

- **Muffaletta Salad**
- **Shrimp Po'boys**

I live near Saratoga Springs, New York, home of SPAC, a huge performing-arts center. Every summer a huge jazz fest is held here. The center's sprawling lawn is dotted with hundreds of blankets with fans settling in for hours of music. All that's missing is great food, since they limit what you can bring in (no drinks allowed!). I like to have my own jazz fest at home, with plenty of New Orleans--style food and drink to enjoy with the music. Load up the stereo with your favorite music and whip up this gut-bustin' feast.

MUFFALETTA SALAD

1 cup mixed **pitted olives**, coarsely chopped

2 cups **giardiniera** (pickled cauliflower, hot peppers, and carrots), drained

5 to 6 **celery ribs** from the heart, chopped

1/4 cup soft (not oil packed) **sun-dried tomatoes**, chopped

1 **green bell pepper**, seeded and chopped

1/2 **red onion**, chopped

1/2 pound **stick salami**, diced

1/2 pound thick-cut **ham**, chopped

1/2 pound **Provolone**, chopped

3 tablespoons **red wine vinegar**

1/4 cup **EVOO** (extra-virgin olive oil; eyeball it)

Salt and **black pepper**

In a large salad bowl, combine the veggies, meats, and cheese. Dress with the vinegar and EVOO, season with salt and pepper, and let the salad stand for a few minutes before serving.

4 SERVINGS

MEALS FOR 4

SHRIMP PO'BOYS

Vegetable or peanut oil, for frying

1 large **egg**

1 cup **milk** (eyeball it)

Salt

1 1/2 pounds **large shrimp**, peeled and deveined, tails removed

1/2 cup all-purpose **flour**

1 cup **cornmeal** or **plain bread crumbs**

2 tablespoons **Old Bay** or other seafood seasoning, a couple palmfuls

8 leaves **Bibb or butter lettuce**

1 **beefsteak tomato**, thinly sliced

4 **soft club rolls** or sub rolls, split

1 **lemon**, cut into wedges

1/4 cup **sweet pickle relish**

1/2 cup **spicy, grainy mustard**

Preheat an inch of oil in a deep skillet over medium to medium-high heat.

Beat the egg and milk together in a large bowl. Salt the shrimp, then set them in the milk batter. Before you begin breading the shrimp, cover a plate with plastic wrap for easy cleanup, then mix together the flour, cornmeal or bread crumbs, and seafood seasoning on the plate. Using tongs, remove a few shrimp at a time from the batter and coat in the breading. Add the breaded shrimp to the hot oil and fry them for 5 to 6 minutes, or until they are firm and deeply golden all over. Repeat until all the shrimp are fried, draining them on paper towels.

Pile lettuce and tomatoes on the roll bottoms, top with the shrimp, and douse the shrimp with a little lemon juice. Mix the relish and mustard and dot the roll tops with spoonfuls of the sauce before setting them into place.

4 SERVINGS

■ ■ ■

CONTINENTAL CUISINE

• **Where's Waldorf? Salad with Izzy's Epic Dressing**
• **Almond-Crusted Chicken Cutlets and Asparagus with Scallion Beurre Blanc**

Continental and classic French cuisines were big back in the late 1960s and early '70s. Couples would actually dress for dinner and take turns dining at each other's homes. This is a meal I might have served, back in the day, to newly wed neighbors. Today, I'd make it for me, my hubby, our neighbor Judy, and our pit bulls.

WHERE'S WALDORF? SALAD WITH IZZY'S EPIC DRESSING

My friend Izzy is a crazy Swede who taught me how to snowboard and lowered my geek quotient by teaching me expressions like "Mad Steeze!" (You'll have to ask Iz if you don't know.) This is her dad's dressing.

1 cup **whole walnut halves**
1 **celery heart** with greens, wiped clean and chopped
$1/2$ **red onion**, thinly sliced
1 cup **red seedless grapes**, split
2 **Gala apples**, cored and chopped
1 **Belgian endive**, shredded
Juice of $1/2$ lemon
3 tablespoons **honey** (eyeball it)
2 tablespoons **apple cider vinegar**
1 teaspoon **ground cardamom** (eyeball it)
3 tablespoons finely chopped fresh **dill**
$1/3$ cup **EVOO** (extra-virgin olive oil; eyeball it)
3 tablespoons **heavy cream** (eyeball it)
Salt and **black pepper**
1 head of **Bibb or butter lettuce**

continued

MEALS FOR 4

119

Toast the nuts in a small skillet over medium heat in a small pan until an aroma develops and the nuts crisp a bit, 5 to 6 minutes. Cool the walnuts, then combine in a bowl with the celery, onions, grapes, apples, and endive. Whisk the lemon juice, honey, vinegar, cardamom, and dill together, then whisk in the EVOO in a slow, steady stream. When the oil is incorporated, slowly whisk in the cream, then season the dressing with salt and pepper. Dress the salad and adjust the salt and pepper. Use 2 leaves of lettuce to form a bed for each serving of the salad.

4 SERVINGS

ALMOND-CRUSTED CHICKEN CUTLETS AND ASPARAGUS WITH SCALLION BEURRE BLANC

1/4 cup plus 2 tablespoons **heavy cream**

1/4 cup **dry white wine** (eyeball it)

2 **scallions**, very finely chopped, whites and greens separated

1 large **egg**

8 thin **chicken breast cutlets**, 1 1/4 to 1 1/2 pounds total

1/2 cup **sliced almonds**

1/2 cup **plain bread crumbs**

1/4 teaspoon grated or ground **nutmeg** (eyeball it)

Salt and **black pepper**

3 tablespoons **EVOO** (extra-virgin olive oil) or vegetable oil

1 pound **asparagus**, tough ends trimmed

1/2 cup (1 stick) cold **butter**, cut into pieces

Place a baking sheet in the oven and turn the oven on low, 250° F.

Combine 1/4 cup of the cream, the white wine, and the whites of the scallions in a sauce pot and bring to a boil over medium heat. Cook until reduced to 1/4 cup liquid, 5 to 6 minutes.

While the sauce is working, beat the egg with the remaining 2 tablespoons of cream and add the chicken pieces. Combine the almonds, bread crumbs, nutmeg, salt, and pepper in a food processor and process until finely ground. Cover a plate with plastic wrap (this makes for easy cleanup after breading) and pour the almond and bread-crumb mixture onto it.

Heat the EVOO, three times around the pan, in a large nonstick skillet over medium to medium-high heat. One at a time, remove cutlets from the egg mixture and coat in the almond crumbs, covering entirely. Add the cutlets to the skillet and cook for 3 minutes on each side; transfer them to the oven to keep them warm. You may need to do this in 2 batches; don't overcrowd the pan.

While the chicken cooks, bring an inch of water to a boil in a skillet. Reduce to a simmer, add a pinch of salt, and add the asparagus. Cook for 3 minutes. Remove the asparagus to a plate.

Take the sauce off the heat, add the scallion greens, then whisk in the cold butter a few bits at a time. Hit the pan with just a touch of heat if necessary. The sauce will be white and thick and the volume will triple. Season the sauce with salt and pepper.

Place a cutlet on each dinner plate, top with a few asparagus spears, then place a second cutlet on top. Spoon the beurre blanc sauce over the cutlets and asparagus.

4 SERVINGS

■ ■ ■

SMOTHERED IN FLAVOR

- 30-Minute Garlic-Almond Chicken Under a Brick
- Smothered Mushrooms and Kale

When you are pressed for time, pressing your food can help get you better and bigger flavors in a fewer ticks of the clock. The chicken breasts get extra crispy under a brick and the smothered mushrooms and kale will make you want to eat not only your own veggies but also those of the guy sitting next to you!

30-MINUTE GARLIC-ALMOND CHICKEN UNDER A BRICK

4 large **garlic cloves**, cracked away from their skins

1 cup fresh **flat-leaf parsley** leaves, a few generous handfuls

1/2 cup **Marcona almonds** (Spanish skinned, toasted nuts available in the bulk section of many markets) or toasted slivered almonds

1 **lemon**, grated for 1 tablespoon zest, then cut into wedges

4 bone-in, skin-on **chicken breasts** or thighs

EVOO (extra-virgin olive oil), for liberal drizzling

2 tablespoons **grill seasoning**, such as McCormick's Montreal Steak Seasoning

Preheat a heavy-bottomed skillet over medium heat and preheat the oven to 400° F.

Combine the garlic, parsley, almonds, and lemon zest in a food processor and pulse to chop them into a dry paste. Loosen the skin on the chicken and spread one fourth of the mixture under the skin of each piece. Wash your hands, grease the breasts with a liberal drizzle of EVOO, and season them with grill seasoning. Place the breasts in the skillet skin side down and top them with another, smaller skillet. Weight the pan with a brick. Cook them to crisp the skin, 6 to 8 minutes. Transfer the pan to the hot oven and roast them for another 15 minutes.

SMOTHERED MUSHROOMS AND KALE

  2 tablespoons **EVOO** (extra-virgin olive oil)
  2 tablespoons **butter**, cut into small pieces
  4 **garlic cloves**, chopped
 24 small **cremini mushrooms**, wiped clean, halved
1¼ pounds **kale** (1 large bunch)
¼ cup **Marsala** or other sherry
   Salt and **black pepper**

Heat a medium skillet with the EVOO and butter over medium to medium-high heat. When the butter melts, add the mushrooms and place a lid which is too small for the skillet down into the pan, pressing and smothering the mushrooms. Cook them for 5 or 6 minutes, stirring once, then add the garlic. Cook another minute or two. While the mushrooms cook, strip the kale from its stems and coarsely chop. Add to the pan with the mushrooms, turning the kale with tongs to combine it with the mushrooms. Smother the greens for a minute or two, then deglaze the pan with the Marsala and season the mixture with salt and pepper.

■ ■ ■

RENOVATION MENU

- **Renaissance of Tuna Casserole**
- **Iceberg Salad with Shrimp**

I love tuna casserole and iceberg lettuce. I like gourmet fare, too, but I'm no aristocrat—food snobs lose out on comfort foods and home-cooking gems like tuna casserole and icy iceberg salad. Here, I dress up these two old favorites. I hope to convert at least a few upper-crusters, and get them religion when it comes to respecting comforting American classics like tuna casserole.

ICEBERG SALAD WITH SHRIMP

1 head of **iceberg lettuce**

1/2 cup prepared **cocktail sauce**

A few drops of **hot sauce**

2 teaspoons **lemon zest plus juice of 1 lemon**

1/4 cup **mayonnaise** (eyeball it)

1 cup small cooked **shrimp**, 100 count

Salt and **black pepper**

2 to 3 tablespoons snipped fresh **chives**

Slam the core of the head of lettuce on the counter, then twist and remove it. Quarter the head of lettuce lengthwise.

In a medium bowl, combine the cocktail sauce, hot sauce, lemon zest and juice, and mayo. Stir the shrimp into the dressing and spoon it evenly over the lettuce quarters. Season the salads with a little salt and pepper, sprinkle with the chives, and serve.

4 SERVINGS

RENAISSANCE OF TUNA CASSEROLE

Salt

1 pound **fettuccine**

3 tablespoons **EVOO** (extra-virgin olive oil)

4 **garlic cloves**, finely chopped

1 small **onion**, chopped

2 6-ounce cans **Italian tuna in water or oil**, drained

$^1/_2$ cup tender **sun-dried tomatoes** (available in small pouches in the produce department), thinly sliced

$^1/_2$ cup **dry white wine**

$^1/_2$ cup **heavy cream**

1 cup **frozen peas**, a couple handfuls

$^1/_2$ cup grated **Parmigiano-Reggiano**, a few generous handfuls

Black pepper

1 cup shredded **fresh basil,** 20 leaves

Bring a large covered pot of water to a boil for the pasta. Salt the water, then add the pasta and cook to al dente.

While the pasta cooks, heat a deep skillet over medium heat with the EVOO. Sauté the garlic and onions until tender, 4 to 5 minutes. Add the tuna and sun-dried tomatoes and stir to heat them through, another minute or two. Add the wine and cook it down for a minute, then add the cream. When it comes to a bubble, stir in the cheese and season the sauce with salt and pepper. Stir in the pens and heat through. Toss the drained hot pasta with the sauce. Serve topped with shredded basil.

4 SERVINGS

■ ■ ■

GAME PLAN

- Get the potatoes into the oven to roast; rehydrate the cranberries.

- Mix and form the burgers.

- Finish the salad while the burgers cook.

BURGER NIGHT

- **Onion and Mushroom Smothered Super Swiss Turkey Burgers**
- **Warm Potato-Cranberry Dressed Salad**

When it is said in relation to food, the word *smothered* always means something good. These burgers are not only smothered but also are studded with cheese, and that spells yum-o! With the potato-cranberry salad addition, this burger night is like a casual Thanksgiving any night of the year.

ONION AND MUSHROOM SMOTHERED SUPER SWISS TURKEY BURGERS

2 tablespoons **EVOO** (extra-virgin olive oil), plus some for drizzling

1 large **onion**, sliced

Salt and **black pepper**

$1/2$ pound **button mushrooms**, trimmed and thinly sliced

2 teaspoons all-purpose **flour**

$1/4$ cup **dry white wine** (eyeball it)

$3/4$ cup **chicken stock** (eyeball it)

$1 1/4$ pounds **ground turkey breast**, the average weight of 1 package

$1/3$-pound block of **Swiss cheese**, such as Emmentaler, or Jarlsberg, cut into $1/4$-inch dice

2 teaspoons **poultry seasoning**, $2/3$ palmful

$1/4$ teaspoon **cayenne pepper** (eyeball it)

4 sandwich-size **English muffins**, toasted

Preheat a large skillet over medium-high heat with the 2 tablespoons of EVOO, 2 times around the pan. Add the onions and season them with a little salt and pepper. Cover them with foil and set a lid or a plate on the onions to smother them, for 5 minutes. Add the mushrooms to the onions and smother them for another 5 minutes, stirring occasionally. Uncover the pan and let the juices cook off a little, then sprinkle the mixture with the flour. Cook for 1 minute, add the wine then the chicken stock, and cook until nice and thick, 2 minutes.

Combine the ground turkey, Swiss cheese, salt and pepper, poultry seasoning, and cayenne pepper in a medium bowl. Score the meat with the side of your hand to separate it into 4 equal amounts. Form the mixture into 4 large patties no more than 1 inch thick. Drizzle the patties liberally with EVOO. Preheat a large nonstick skillet over medium-high heat. Once the skillet is hot, add the patties and cook them for 5 to 6 minutes on each side, or until the turkey is cooked through.

Serve the turkey burgers on the toasted English muffins, smothered with the onions and mushrooms.

4 SERVINGS

WARM POTATO-CRANBERRY DRESSED SALAD

2 to 2^1/$_2$ pounds **red potatoes**
^{1}/$_4$ cup **EVOO** (extra-virgin olive oil), plus some for drizzling
5 fresh **sage leaves**, chopped
1 tablespoon, a palmful, **grill seasoning**, such as McCormick's Montreal Steak Seasoning
^{1}/$_4$ cup **dried cranberries**, a generous handful
Salt
^{1}/$_2$ pound **green beans**, stem ends trimmed
^{1}/$_2$ pound **wax beans**, stem ends trimmed
2 tablespoons **Dijon mustard**
3 tablespoons **white wine vinegar** (eyeball it)
2 large **shallots**, chopped
Freshly ground black pepper
^{1}/$_2$ cup fresh **flat-leaf parsley** leaves, 2 generous handfuls, chopped

continued

Preheat the oven to 450° F.

Cut the potatoes into wedges and drop them onto a rimmed baking sheet. Liberally drizzle EVOO over the potatoes, sprinkle them with the sage and grill seasoning, and toss to coat. Roast the potatoes, turning them once, for 25 minutes.

Fill a medium skillet or pot with a few inches of water, cover it with a tight-fitting lid, and bring it up to a boil over high heat. Place the cranberries in a small mixing bowl. Once the water comes up to a boil, remove a small ladle of the hot water from the pot and pour it over the cranberries to hydrate and soften them.

Add some salt to the remaining water in the skillet, and add both types of beans, and cook them for 2 minutes. Drain and reserve the beans.

When the cranberries have softened, drain off the water; your fingers make the best strainer for this. To the bowl of drained cranberries, add the mustard, white wine vinegar, shallots, and a little salt and pepper. Stir to combine, then whisk in the $1/4$ cup of EVOO in a slow, steady stream.

Transfer the roasted potatoes to a serving bowl. Add the cranberry dressing and the beans and mix, then add the parsley and toss to combine. Taste and adjust the seasoning.

4 SERVINGS

■ ■ ■

TUSCAN COMFORTS OF HOME

- **Veal and Sage Meat Loaf with Gorgonzola Gravy**
- **Smashed Potatoes with Prosciutto and Parmigiano**
- **Wine-Steeped Greens**

I love Tuscany, veal meatballs, and wine. All those loves converge in this classy comfort-food menu.

WINE-STEEPED GREENS

    2 tablespoons **EVOO** (extra-virgin olive oil)
    1 **garlic clove**, crushed from its skin
1¼ pounds cleaned **kale**, 1 large bunch
    2 cups **dry red wine**
      Salt and **black pepper**
    2 teaspoons **lemon zest** (eyeball it)

Heat a deep skillet over medium heat. Add the EVOO, 2 times around the pan, and the garlic. Cook the garlic for a couple of minutes while you strip the kale from its stems and chop it, then remove the garlic. Crank the heat up a notch, then add the greens and wilt them down; 2 to 3 minutes of turning and stirring is involved here. Add the wine, salt, and pepper and reduce the heat to a simmer. Steep the greens in the wine for 10 minutes, stir in the zest, then serve.

4 SERVINGS

VEAL AND SAGE MEAT LOAF WITH GORGONZOLA GRAVY AND SMASHED POTATOES WITH PROSCIUTTO AND PARMIGIANO

3 large **Idaho potatoes**, peeled and chopped, $2^1/4$ to $2^1/2$ pounds
Salt
$1^1/2$ pounds **ground veal**
1 large **egg**, beaten
$^1/2$ cup Italian-style **bread crumbs**, a couple handfuls
1 cup grated **Parmigiano-Reggiano** cheese
Leaves from 4 to 6 fresh **sage** sprigs, thinly sliced
Black pepper
3 tablespoons **EVOO** (extra-virgin olive oil)
10 to 12 **cremini (baby portobello) mushrooms**, thinly sliced
1 cup **chicken stock**
3 tablespoons **butter**
1 **garlic clove**, crushed from its skin
2 tablespoons all-purpose **flour**
3 cups **milk**
$^1/4$ teaspoon freshly grated or ground **nutmeg** (eyeball it)
$^1/4$ pound **prosciutto di Parma**, finely chopped (have the deli slice it as thick as bacon, rather than shaving it)
$^3/4$ cup crumbled Gorgonzola cheese

Preheat the oven to 400° F.

Place the potatoes in a pot, cover them with water, then bring the water to a boil. Salt it and cook the potatoes until fork tender, 10 to 12 minutes or so.

While the potatoes are working, combine the veal with the egg, bread crumbs, $^1/2$ cup of the Parmigiano, the sage, salt, and pepper. Form four 1-inch-thick oval meat loaves. Heat a large nonstick skillet over medium-high heat with 2 tablespoons of the EVOO, 2 times around the pan. Brown the meat loaves for 2 to 3 minutes on each side, then transfer them to a nonstick baking sheet and finish them in the oven for 6 to 8 minutes. Return the skillet to the heat, add the remaining tablespoon of EVOO, and add the mushrooms. Cook the mushrooms until they are dark and tender, 5 to 6 minutes, then add salt and pepper and deglaze the pan with the chicken stock.

While the mushrooms cook, melt the butter over medium heat in a medium sauce pot. Add the garlic and cook until golden, a minute or so; discard the garlic. Add the flour and cook for a minute or two. Whisk in the milk and season with the nutmeg, salt, and pepper. Cook the sauce for a few minutes to thicken it a bit.

Drain the potatoes and return them to the warm pot. Add half of the milk sauce to the potatoes with the prosciutto and the remaining $1/2$ cup of Parmigiano. Smash the potatoes to the desired consistency and season them with salt and pepper.

Stir the Gorgonzola into the remaining milk sauce to melt it, then stir the mushrooms and stock into the sauce. Serve the meat loaves with gorgonzola-mushroom gravy over the top and prosciutto potatoes alongside.

4 SERVINGS

■ ■ ■

WARM UP

- **Stuffed Cabbage Stoup**
- **Grilled Cheese and Watercress Sandwiches**

I love making thick soups, or *stoups* as I call them; they're thicker than soup and thinner than stew. A fan of *30-Minute Meals* wrote in and asked me to come up with one based on stuffed cabbage, so I did. It's quite a warm-up for any chilly night.

STUFFED CABBAGE STOUP

2 tablespoons **EVOO** (extra-virgin olive oil)

$1^1/_2$ pounds **ground meat loaf mix** (a combination of beef, pork, and veal)

$^1/_2$ teaspoon **allspice** (eyeball it)

$^1/_2$ tablespoon ground **coriander**, half a palmful

2 teaspoons **smoked sweet paprika** (eyeball it in your palm)

Salt and **black pepper**

1 **bay leaf**

1 **onion**, chopped

2 **garlic cloves**, minced

1 **carrot**, thinly sliced with a vegetable peeler into strips, then finely chopped

1 pound **Savoy cabbage**, thinly sliced (1 small or $^1/_2$ to $^3/_4$ larger head)

1 28-ounce can **diced tomatoes**

1 cup **tomato sauce**

1 quart **chicken stock**

1 cup **white rice**

Handful of fresh **flat-leaf parsley** leaves, chopped

3 tablespoons fresh **dill**, finely chopped

Heat a deep pot over medium-high heat. Add the EVOO, twice around the pan, then add the meat and brown it for 2 to 3 minutes. Season the meat with the allspice, coriander, smoked paprika, salt, and pepper, then add the bay leaf, the onions, garlic, and carrots. Cook the veggies for 2 to 3 minutes to begin to soften them, then add the cabbage and wilt it down a bit. Add the tomatoes, tomato sauce, and stock and cover the pot. Raise the heat to bring the stoup to a boil, then add the rice and reduce the heat to a simmer. Cook for 16 to 18 minutes, until the rice is just tender. Stir in the parsley and dill, discard the bay leaf, adjust the salt and pepper, and serve.

4 SERVINGS

GRILLED CHEESE AND WATERCRESS SANDWICHES

- 8 slices **pumpernickel** or marble rye bread
- $1/2$ pound your choice of **Muenster, Havarti with dill, or Leyden cheese** (Gouda with cumin seeds), thinly sliced
- 1 cup **watercress leaves**, shredded or chopped
- 2 tablespoons **dill pickle relish** or sweet red pepper relish
- 4 tablespoons ($1/2$ stick) **butter**, softened

Preheat a griddle or large skillet over medium-low heat. Make 4 sandwiches of sliced cheese, chopped greens, and relish, distributing the ingredients evenly among them. Butter the outsides of the sammies with softened butter and cook them in the preheated pan until they are golden and the cheese has melted.

4 SERVINGS

GAME PLAN

• Make the soup (and serve it if you want) while the pasta water heats.

EAT GREEK

- Lemon and Egg Soup
- Greek-Style Shrimp Scampi and Linguine

I love tavernas because in many of these Greek eateries you sit community style and make new friends. The ouzo flows, the scent of garlic and oil fills the air, a wood-burning stove crackles in the background. At the last taverna I visited, I ended up belly dancing on the tabletops. Go Greek!

LEMON AND EGG SOUP

6 cups **chicken stock**
Pinch of **saffron** or saffron powder
1 **bay leaf**
Peel of 1 **lemon**, removed in long strips with a vegetable peeler, plus 4 to 5 tablespoons lemon juice (from 2 or 3 lemons)
2 large **eggs**
2 large **egg yolks**
A couple drops of **hot sauce**
Handful of fresh **flat-leaf parsley** leaves, chopped
Salt and **black pepper**
Pita chips, any brand or flavor you like

Bring the stock to a boil with the saffron, bay leaf, and lemon peel. Cover, turn off the heat, and steep for 5 minutes, then remove the bay leaf and lemon peel.

In a medium bowl, whisk the eggs and yolks with the lemon juice and hot sauce. Whisk in $1/2$ cup of the hot stock to temper the eggs. Whisk the egg mixture into the stock, then turn the heat on low and whisk them together until the soup thickens slightly, 4 to 5 minutes. Stir in the parsley and season with salt and pepper. Ladle the soup into bowls, and top it with a few pita chips.

4 FIRST-COURSE SERVINGS

GREEK-STYLE SHRIMP SCAMPI AND LINGUINE

Salt
1 pound **linguine**
1 pound medium to large **shrimp**, peeled and deveined, tails removed
Black pepper
1/3 cup **EVOO** (extra-virgin olive oil; eyeball it)
4 **garlic cloves**, thinly sliced
1/2 teaspoon **red pepper flakes**
2 fresh **oregano** sprigs, finely chopped
Handful of pitted **kalamata olives**, chopped
1/2 cup **white wine** (eyeball it)
Zest and juice of 1 lemon
Handful of fresh **flat-leaf parsley** leaves, chopped
1 cup **feta cheese crumbles**

Place a large covered pot of water on the stove to boil. Salt the water and cook the pasta to al dente. Heads up: you'll need some of the pasta cooking water before you drain the pasta.

Season the shrimp with salt and pepper.

While the pasta cooks, heat the EVOO in a deep skillet and brown the garlic slices. Remove the garlic and reserve. Add the shrimp and cook for 3 to 4 minutes. Add the red pepper flakes, oregano, olives, wine, and lemon zest and cook together for a couple more minutes. Remove from the heat. Add a ladle of the starchy pasta cooking water to the sauce, then add the lemon juice. Add the drained pasta to the skillet. Let the pasta absorb the juices for a minute, then toss with the parsley, feta, and reserved garlc slices. Use tongs to pull the pasta from the skillet, giving it a turn to twist in as many ingredients as possible. Then, use the tongs to remove and arrange the shrimp and ingredients that may remain in the pan, distributing them evenly among the portions.

4 SERVINGS

■ ■ ■

SPORTS AND SAMMY NIGHT

- Grilled Kielbasa Reubens with Warm Mustard-Caraway Sauerkraut
- Smoked Paprika O-Rings
- Root Beer Floats (store-bought)

This meal is a touchdown whether you eat it while watching the NFL or after playing a little light-tackle with your buddies.

GRILLED KIELBASA REUBENS WITH WARM MUSTARD-CARAWAY SAUERKRAUT

1 teaspoon **caraway seeds**

1 (1-pound sack) of **sauerkraut**, drained

1 cup **beer or apple cider**

1/4 cup **spicy brown, grainy mustard**

2 sticks or 1 long folded **link kielbasa** or turkey kielbasa, 1 1/4 pounds

2 tablespoons **butter**, softened

8 slices **marble rye bread**

8 deli slices **Emmentaler** or other Swiss cheese

1/2 cup **sweet red pepper relish**

Preheat a griddle pan to medium high.

Heat a medium skillet over medium heat. Toast the seeds for a couple of minutes, then stir in the sauerkraut, beer or cider, and mustard and simmer for 10 minutes.

Cut the kielbasa into 4 portions and split the sausage pieces lengthwise, opening them like a book. Grill the sausages on the hot griddle until they are crispy on both sides, 7 to 8 minutes total. Wipe some of the grease off the griddle and turn the heat down to low.

Lightly butter 1 side of each slice of bread. With the buttered sides out, build sandwiches of grilled kielbasa, sauerkraut, and 2 slices of cheese; spread the top slice of bread with red pepper relish before setting in place. Cook the sandwiches on the griddle until they are crispy, lightly pressing wih a spatula to set the layers. Cut and serve.

4 SERVINGS

SMOKED PAPRIKA O-RINGS

About 6 cups **vegetable oil**, for frying
1 large **Vidalia onion**, sliced into rings about $1/4$ inch thick
3 cups **buttermilk**
$1^1/2$ cups all-purpose **flour**
$1^1/2$ cups **cornmeal**
2 tablespoons **smoked sweet paprika**, a couple palmfuls
1 tablespoon **chili powder**, a palmful
1 tablespoon **ground cumin**, a palmful
1 tablespoon **salt**
$1^1/2$ cups **sour cream**
2 **pimiento peppers** or 1 roasted red pepper, patted dry and chopped
3 tablespoons chopped fresh **dill**

Heat a couple inches of oil in a deep pot over medium to medium-high heat. When it's hot enough, 10 minutes or so, a piece of bread dropped into the oil should brown in a count of 20

Separate the onion rings and toss them in the buttermilk. Cover a large, deep plate with plastic wrap for easy cleanup. Combine the flour, cornmeal, spices, and salt on the plate. Toss one third of the rings in the breading at a time, coating them evenly, then fry them in the hot oil for 3 to 4 minutes, or until they are deep golden. Drain them on a paper-towel-lined plate. Repeat with the remaining onion rings.

Combine the sour cream with the peppers and dill in a food processor and process them to make a smooth sauce. Transfer the sauce to a dish for dipping, surround it with o-rings, and serve.

4 SERVINGS

COOK WITH A KID

• Chicken Parm Pizza
• Salad on a Stick
• Cake and Berries with Melted Ice Cream Sauce

This menu is a real kid-pleaser. Whether you have kids of your own or not, cooking with a kid rocks! Kids are more honest, funny, and self-effacing than almost any of my grown friends, and kids today are really getting into good food. They love to cook and to watch food-related TV. If you don't have one of your own, borrow a kid tonight; enjoy a laugh and a tasty meal, together.

CHICKEN PARM PIZZA

Cornmeal or flour, to handle dough

1 **pizza dough**, store-bought or from your favorite pizzeria

2 tablespoons **EVOO** (extra-virgin olive oil), plus a drizzle

1 pound **ground chicken**

3 **garlic cloves**, chopped

1 small **onion**, chopped

Salt and **black pepper**

Handful of fresh **flat-leaf parsley** leaves, chopped

A couple pinches of **red pepper flakes**

A couple pinches of **dried oregano**

1 8-ounce can **tomato sauce**

1 cup grated **Parmigiano-Reggiano** cheese

1½ cups shredded **Provolone cheese**

5 or 6 fresh **basil leaves**, shredded or torn

Preheat the oven to 425° F.

Coat your hands and the work surface with a little cornmeal or flour and, using your hand or a rolling pin, form a 14-inch round pizza. Place the pizza on a pizza baking tray and prick the dough with the tines of a fork in several places. Drizzle a little bit of EVOO over the dough and place it in the oven. Bake it for 10 minutes.

Meanwhile, heat a deep skillet over medium-high heat with the 2 tablespoons of EVOO, 2 times around the pan. Add the meat and brown it, breaking it up with a wooden spoon. To the browned meat, add the garlic and onions and season them with salt and pepper. Cook them together for 5 to 6 minutes, then add the parsley, red pepper flakes, oregano, and tomato sauce. Heat the sauce through.

Remove the pizza from the oven after 10 minutes and top it with the meat sauce, then scatter the cheeses over all. Return it to the oven and bake it until it's golden and bubbly, another 10 to 12 minutes. Top the pizza with shredded basil, cut, and serve.

4 SERVINGS

SALAD ON A STICK

- $^1/_2$ cup **heavy cream** or whole milk
- 1 5.4-ounce container **garlic-and-herb flavored soft cheese**, such as Boursin
  Salt and **black pepper**
- 1 **green or red bell pepper**, seeded and cut into 1-inch dice
- $^1/_3$ **seedless cucumber**, diced
- $^1/_2$ pint **grape tomatoes**
- 4 **celery ribs**, cut into 1-inch pieces
- 2 1-inch-thick pieces **Genoa salami** from the deli, cubed
- 4 **wooden skewers**

Blend together the cream or milk and cheese. Pour into a dipping dish and season the dressing with salt and pepper. Place the dip on a platter. Arrange the veggies and salami on the platter with 4 bamboo skewers, 1 per person. Use the skewers to spear the salami and veggies, stacking them up a mouthful at a time. Dip each bite in the dressing as you eat, but don't double dip, please! Yum-o! Salad on a stick!

4 SERVINGS

CAKE AND BERRIES WITH MELTED ICE CREAM SAUCE

$^1/_2$ pint **strawberries**, sliced

$^1/_2$ pint **blueberries** or blackberries

2 teaspoons **sugar**

$^1/_2$ loaf of **pound cake**, cut into cubes

2 cups **strawberry or vanilla ice cream**

Mix the berries together with the sugar in a bowl. Pile the cake cubes into goblets or sundae cups. Top the cake with berries. Melt the ice cream in a microwave for 15 to 20 seconds. Stir out any lumps in the melted ice cream, then pour it evenly over the cake and berries.

4 SERVINGS

GAME PLAN

- Get the pasta water going.

- While the chicken sautés, cook the pasta and the saté sauce.

- Make the orange sauce for the chicken.

- Toss the noodles with the saté sauce.

MAKE-YOUR-OWN-TAKE-OUT NIGHT, CHINESE STYLE

- **Chicken in Orange-Scallion-Sesame Sauce**
- **Big Fat Spicy Saté Noodles**

I know I say this all the time but making your own take-out is really the way to go. YOU are in control of all the stuff that's important to you: the oil, the flavor, the spice, and the quality of the ingredients. Plus, you don't use any MSG, right? Since life can seem so out of control sometimes, why not take it back where you can?

CHICKEN IN ORANGE-SCALLION-SESAME SAUCE

- 1 tablespoon **ground coriander**, a palmful
- 1/2 teaspoon **cayenne pepper** (eyeball it)
  Salt and **black pepper**
- 4 boneless, skinless **chicken breasts**, 6 ounces each
- 2 tablespoons **vegetable oil** (eyeball it)
- 2 **navel oranges**
  2-inch piece of **fresh ginger**, peeled and grated
- 3 large **garlic cloves**, chopped
- 1/4 to 1/2 teaspoon **red pepper flakes**
- 1 1/2 cups **chicken stock** (eyeball it)
- 3 tablespoons **tamari** (dark soy sauce; eyeball it)
- 3 **scallions**, thinly sliced
- 1 teaspoon **toasted sesame oil**
- 2 tablespoons **toasted sesame seeds**, 2 palmfuls

continued

MEALS FOR 4

In a bowl, combine the coriander, cayenne, and some salt and pepper. Season the chicken breasts with the spicy mixture. Preheat a large skillet over medium-high heat with the vegetable oil, 2 times around the pan. Add the chicken and cook it on each side for 5 to 6 minutes, or until cooked through.

While the chicken is cooking, zest both oranges and reserve the zest. With a paring knife, slice off the peel and all of the pith from each orange. Slice each orange into $1/4$-inch-thick disks and reserve.

Remove the chicken from the skillet to a plate and cover it loosely with a piece of aluminum foil. Return the skillet to the stovetop over medium-high heat and add the ginger, garlic, salt, pepper, and red pepper flakes—a little or a lot, you're in charge! Cook, stirring constantly, for 1 to 2 minutes, then add the chicken stock and tamari and turn the heat up to high. Cook until you've reduced the liquids by half. Add the reserved orange zest, orange disks, and the scallions. Continue to cook for 1 minute to heat the oranges and scallions. Add the sesame oil and toasted sesame seeds.

Slice the chicken breasts and arrange them on a mound of the Big Fat Spicy Saté Noodles. Top them with the orange-scallion-sesame sauce. Things are so tasty when YOU are in control!

4 SERVINGS

BIG FAT SPICY SATÉ NOODLES

Salt

1 pound **bucatini** pasta

2 tablespoons **vegetable oil** (eyeball it)

3-inch piece of **fresh ginger**, peeled and grated

3 large **garlic cloves**, chopped

1 teaspoon **red pepper flakes**, 1/3 palmful

1 cup **chicken stock** (eyeball it)

1/3 cup **tamari** (dark soy sauce; eyeball it)

1/2 cup **smooth peanut butter**

Juice of 2 limes

1 cup **unsalted roasted peanuts**

A generous handful of fresh **cilantro** or fresh flat-leaf parsley leaves, chopped

Bring a large covered pot of water to a boil for the pasta. Add some salt and the pasta and cook the pasta to al dente. Right before you drain it, remove and reserve 1 cup of the pasta cooking liquid. Drain the noodles and reserve.

Return the pot to the stovetop over medium-high heat; add the vegetable oil, 2 times around the pan. Add the ginger, garlic, and red pepper flakes and cook for 2 minutes. Add 1/2 cup of the reserved pasta cooking liquid, the chicken stock, and tamari and bring it up to a bubble over high heat. Cook for 2 to 3 minutes. Turn the heat off, add the peanut butter, and whisk to combine. If the sauce gets too thick, add a couple more splashes of the reserved pasta cooking liquid. Add the lime juice and the drained noodles, toss to coat the noodles, then add the chopped peanuts and cilantro and toss again.

4 SERVINGS

> **TIDBIT**
>
> Here's a little confession for you: when I make this, I've been known to reserve a little serving of it in a bowl and hide it way in the back of the refrigerator, concealed behind the milk, mustard, and jellies. They are mighty good cold the next day and I'm not afraid to eat them for breakfast.

04

HALLOWEEN HOOPLA

• Pumpkin-Peanut Curry Noodles
• Five-Spice Seared Scallops and Shrimp
• Looking for Mr. Goodbar Sundaes

Cabbage Night, or prank night—traditionally the night before Halloween—is the perfect time to invite over a few grown ghouls to help ring in the kids' favorite haunted holiday. Here's a spooky-good menu for just such an occasion. The sundaes taste like Mr. Goodbar candy bars. The mini Mr. Goodbars were the first things I looked for in my trick-or-treat bag.

PUMPKIN-PEANUT CURRY NOODLES WITH FIVE-SPICE SEARED SCALLOPS AND SHRIMP

Salt

1 pound **spaghetti**

8 tablespoons **vegetable oil** or peanut oil (Don't worry! You're not gonna wind up eating all that oil!)

3 **garlic cloves**, finely chopped

2-inch piece of fresh **ginger**, peeled and minced or grated

1 **red bell pepper**, thinly sliced

$1/2$ teaspoon **red pepper flakes**

$1/4$ cup **creamy peanut butter**

$1/4$ to $1/3$ cup **tamari** (dark soy sauce; eyeball it)

1 15-ounce can **cooked pumpkin**

2 rounded tablespoons **mild or hot curry paste**, such as Patak's, found on the international foods aisle

3 tablespoons **five-spice powder**

12 large **sea scallops**, trimmed and patted dry

12 **jumbo shrimp**, 6 to 8 count, peeled and deveined

4 **scallions**, cut into 2-inch pieces, then thinly sliced lengthwise into matchsticks

Heat a large covered pot of water for the pasta. When the water boils, salt it, drop in the pasta, and cook to al dente. Heads up: you'll need to reserve a cup or so of the cooking water before you drain the pasta.

While the pasta cooks, heat a large, deep skillet over medium heat with 2 tablespoons of the vegetable or peanut oil. Add the garlic, ginger, red bell peppers, and red pepper flakes to the pan and cook them together for a couple of minutes, then add the peanut butter and stir until it melts. Whisk the tamari into the peanut butter, then stir in the pumpkin and curry paste—the sauce should now be very thick. Turn the heat down to low. Add a ladle or two of the boiling pasta cooking water to thin the sauce a bit, and simmer the sauce over low heat. Adjust the salt to taste.

Heat a large skillet over high heat. Pour the five-spice powder onto a plate with some salt. Press both sides of the scallops and shrimp into the spices. Add 3 tablespoons of the remaining oil to the hot skillet. Add the shrimp and sear on both sides, until opaque. Remove to a plate and reserve. Wipe the skillet out and add the last 3 tablespoons of oil to the skillet. Make sure the pan gets super hot again before you add the scallops, and sear on both sides until opaque. Remove to the same plate as the shrimp.

TIDBIT

Diver scallops are sea scallops that have been harvested by hand by divers, not by boats dragging the ocean floor with nets. They tend to be the choicest—and priciest.

Drain the pasta, and return it to the pot. Add the pumpkin-peanut sauce to the pasta pot and toss until the pasta is thoroughly coated. Top the noodles with the scallions and seafood, then serve.

4 SERVINGS

LOOKING FOR MR. GOODBAR SUNDAES

2 pints **vanilla ice cream**

1 jar **chocolate fudge sauce**

1 cup **red-skinned salted peanuts**, available on the snack aisle of the market

1/4 cup **honey**

Whipped cream, from a canister (in the dairy case)

8 **mini Mr. Goodbars**, for garnish (optional)

Get 4 sundae cups or goblets out and place a huge scoop of ice cream in each. Heat the fudge sauce for 30 seconds in a microwave, with the lid off the jar. Sprinkle a handful of nuts into each dish, then top each with a layer of fudge, another scoop of ice cream, and a spoonful more of fudge. Heat the honey in a microwave for 10 to 15 seconds. Top the sundaes with whipped cream and a drizzle of warm honey, then garnish them with a few more red peanuts and a couple of mini candy bars. Serve them on plates, to catch any overflow, and pass out the long sundae spoons.

4 SERVINGS

■ ■ ■

ITALIAN THANKSGIVING

- **Drunken Risotto with Porcini and Barolo**
- **Milanese-Style Turkey Cutlets with Peppers and Basil**

Red wine, turkey, and starch: this meal is as tasty as it is tiring, though not because it's a lot of work to put together. It's full of starch and turkey, both of which can make you sleepy. This easy, richly flavored turkey feast is a meal you'll be thankful for, but be careful not to operate any heavy machinery after dinner, please! You *will* need a nap.

DRUNKEN RISOTTO WITH PORCINI AND BAROLO

1	ounce **dried porcini mushrooms**
4	cups **chicken stock**
2	tablespoons **EVOO** (extra-virgin olive oil)
1	medium **onion**, finely chopped
	Salt and **black pepper**
1^1/$_2$	cups **Arborio rice**
1^3/$_4$	to 2 cups **dry Italian red wine**, such as Barolo, about ^{1}/$_3$ bottle to ^{1}/$_2$ bottle
	Leaves from 4 to 5 fresh **rosemary** sprigs, finely chopped, about 2 tablespoons
2	tablespoons cold **butter**, cut into pieces
^{2}/$_3$	to 1 cup grated **Parmigiano-Reggiano** or Romano cheese, 3 or 4 generous handfuls

Place the mushrooms and stock in a small sauce pot and bring to a simmer over medium-low heat. Keep at a loud simmer until needed for the risotto.

Heat the EVOO in a medium to large skillet over medium to medium-high heat. Add the onions, season them with salt and pepper, and cook them for a couple of minutes to soften. Add the Arborio rice, coat the grains in the oil, and cook for a minute more. Add half of the wine and stir until it is absorbed into the rice. Stir in the rest of the wine along with the rosemary. When the second addition of wine is fully absorbed, ladle off some of the stock simmering with the mushrooms and add it to the rice. Keep adding stock every few minutes until it is fully absorbed. Chop the softened porcinis and add to the risotto. The total cooking time for the risotto should be 20 to 22 minutes. The rice should be creamy from the frequent stirring and cooked to al dente, with just a bit of a bite left to it. Remove it from the heat and stir in the butter, then the cheese. Serve immediately.

4 SERVINGS

MILANESE-STYLE TURKEY CUTLETS WITH PEPPERS AND BASIL

  4 **turkey breast cutlets**, 6 ounces each
      Coarse salt and **black pepper**
  1 tablespoon **poultry seasoning**, a palmful
  1 cup all-purpose **flour**
$3/4$ cup Italian-style **bread crumbs**
$1/4$ cup grated **Parmigiano-Reggiano** cheese, a handful
$1/8$ teaspoon freshly grated or ground **nutmeg** (eyeball it)
  2 **eggs**, beaten
  3 tablespoons **EVOO** (extra-virgin olive oil)
  2 tablespoons **butter**
  2 **light green cubanelle peppers**, seeded and thinly sliced
  1 **red bell pepper**, seeded and very thinly sliced
  4 **lemon wedges**
$1/2$ cup thinly sliced fresh **basil**, about 10 leaves

Preheat the oven to 250° F and set a baking sheet in the center of the oven.

Place the turkey cutlets between wax paper or plastic and pound thin with a small skillet. Each cutlet should measure 8 inches across and be between $1/8$ and $1/4$ inch thick. Season the cutlets with salt and pepper. Mix together the poultry seasoning and flour. Combine the bread crumbs with the cheese and nutmeg. Dredge the cutlets in the flour, then dip them in the egg and coat them in the bread-crumb mixture.

Heat a large nonstick skillet over medium heat with 1 tablespoon each of EVOO and butter. When the butter melts, cook 2 of the cutlets for 3 to 4 minutes on each side. Transfer them to the baking sheet in the oven and repeat with the remaining cutlets.

While the cutlets cook, heat 1 tablespoon of the EVOO in a medium skillet over medium to medium-high heat. Add the peppers, season them with salt and black pepper, and cook them until they are just tender, 5 minutes.

Top the crispy cutlets with an extra pinch of coarse salt and serve them with lemon wedges to squeeze over the top. Divide the peppers evenly among the cutlets and garnish them with a generous amount of basil.

4 SERVINGS

04

■ ■ ■

INTERNATIONAL DIPLOMACY

- Pierogi and Spicy Beet Salsa
- Roasted Carrots with Fresh Dill and Lemon

Delicious Polish pierogi may have started out as pirozhki back in Russia but when they take a trip south of the border, they meet up with this Spicy Beet Salsa. They kick back, hang out on the beach, sipping tequila, and ask each other why they've never hung out before. (Air fares, even for root vegetables, are really high these days.)

PIEROGI AND SPICY BEET SALSA

3 tablespoons **butter**, softened

1 (16- to 19-ounce) package **frozen potato-filled pierogi**, any brand or variety

1 15-ounce can **sliced beets**, drained, finely chopped

1 small **red onion**, finely chopped

Juice of 1 lime

Hot sauce to taste or 1 small jalapeño, seeded and finely chopped

$1/4$ cup fresh **flat-leaf parsley** leaves, a generous handful, chopped

$1/4$ cup fresh **cilantro leaves**, a generous handful, chopped

$1/4$ cup **sour cream** (eyeball it)

Salt and **black pepper**

Spread the softened butter on the bottom of a skillet. Arrange the pierogi in the pan in a single layer. Add 1 cup of water to the pan, cover the pan, and place it over medium-high heat. Cook it for 8 minutes, then remove the lid from the skillet and cook off any liquid in the pan. When all the water evaporates the pierogi will start to "stick" and brown in the butter. Once the dumplings are nice and brown and crispy, remove them from the skillet to serving plates or a platter.

While the pierogi cook, throw together the spicy beet salsa. In a bowl, combine the chopped beets, red onions, lime juice, hot sauce or chopped jalapeños, parsley, cilantro, sour cream, and a little salt and pepper.

Serve the pierogi topped with some of the spicy beet salsa.

4 SERVINGS

ROASTED CARROTS WITH FRESH DILL AND LEMON

2 8-ounce bags **baby carrots**, halved lengthwise
   EVOO (extra-virgin olive oil), for liberal drizzling
   Salt and **black pepper**
3 tablespoons cold **butter**, cut into pieces
   Zest and juice of 1 lemon
$^{1}/_{4}$ cup chopped fresh **dill**, a generous handful

Preheat the oven to 400° F.

Arrange the carrots on a rimmed baking sheet, drizzle them with EVOO, and season them with salt and pepper. Toss the carrots around to make sure they are well coated. Shake the baking sheet to spread the carrots in an even layer and roast them for 15 minutes, or until they are tender and the sides that are touching the baking sheet are lightly browned. Shake up the carrots twice while they roast. (This will prevent the ones on the edges of the baking sheet from burning before the ones in the center are cooked.)

While the carrots are roasting, combine the cold butter, lemon zest and juice, and dill in a serving bowl. Transfer the roasted carrots to the bowl while they are piping hot. Toss them until the butter has completely melted, then serve.

4 SERVINGS

■ ■ ■

WHOLE-GRAIN TRAIN

- **Whole-Wheat Penne with Cauliflower Sauce**
- **Kale and Portobello Mushrooms**

Whole grains have a rich, chewy texture that is nicely complemented by a creamy, hearty cauliflower sauce. Deep, rich greens and earthy portobellos stand up to the texture and flavors of the pasta for a strong showing as a hearty side dish.

WHOLE-WHEAT PENNE WITH CAULIFLOWER SAUCE

	Salt
1	pound **whole-wheat penne rigate**
1/4	cup **EVOO** (extra-virgin olive oil)
3	**garlic cloves**, sliced
1	**red onion**, finely chopped
1	head of **cauliflower**, stemmed and chopped
1	cup **chicken stock**
	Leaves from 4 fresh **rosemary** sprigs, finely chopped
3/4	cup grated **Romano cheese**, 3 handfuls
	Black pepper

Bring a large covered pot of water to a boil for the pasta. Add the salt and pasta and cook to al dente. Heads up: you'll need some of the pasta cooking water before you drain the pasta.

While the water is coming up to a boil and the pasta cooks, make the sauce. Heat the EVOO in a deep skillet over medium heat. Add the garlic and cook for 3 minutes, then discard the garlic. Add the onions and cook for 5 minutes, then add the cauliflower, chicken stock, and rosemary. Cover the pan and cook for 15 minutes. Uncover the sauce, add a ladle or two of the hot pasta water, and mash the cauliflower with the back of a wooden spoon or potato masher. Drain the pasta and add it to the cauliflower. Add the cheese and toss to combine with the pasta and the sauce. Season the dish with salt and pepper and serve.

4 SERVINGS

KALE AND PORTOBELLO MUSHROOMS

3 tablespoons **EVOO** (extra-virgin olive oil)
4 **portobello mushroom caps**, sliced
$1^{1}/_{4}$ pounds **kale**, 1 large bunch, stemmed and chopped
   Salt and **black pepper**
$^{1}/_{4}$ teaspoon freshly grated or ground **nutmeg**, or to taste
$^{1}/_{2}$ cup **dry Italian red wine**

Heat the EVOO in a large skillet over medium-high heat. When the oil is hot, add the mushrooms and cook them until they are dark and tender, then add the kale, turning it with tongs until it wilts. Season the mushrooms and greens with salt, pepper, and nutmeg. Add the wine and stir to deglaze the pan. Reduce the heat to low and cook the greens for 5 minutes longer, then serve.

4 SERVINGS

■ ■ ■

- Get the steaks going.

- Cook the veggies and make the brown butter while the steaks cook.

- Make the garlicky bread chunks while the steaks rest.

- Toss the veggies with the brown butter.

WOULD YOU LIKE SOME STEAK WITH YOUR BREAD? MENU

- **Garlicky, Cheesy Bread Chunks Topped with Steaks**
- **Green Onions and String Beans with Balsamic Brown Butter**

No need for a basket of bread on the table tonight: we're putting the bread to work soaking up the steak juices and making for a mighty nice bite of steak-y, garlicky, cheesy goodness. Can I hear a YUM-O, a DELISH—and throw in a loud YOWZA while you're at it? It's a week-night or company's-coming hit. The green onions (or perhaps you call them scallions) and string beans (or perhaps you call them green beans or snap beans, it all works), are a great way to shake up a humdrum veggie side, so what are you waiting for? Go get cooking.

GARLICKY, CHEESY BREAD CHUNKS TOPPED WITH STEAKS

4 **beef tenderloin steaks**, 1¹/₂ inches thick

Leaves from 4 fresh **thyme** sprigs, chopped

Salt and **black pepper**

1 tablespoon **EVOO** (extra-virgin olive oil; eyeball it)

5 tablespoons really soft **butter**

1 large **garlic clove**, finely chopped

A generous handful of fresh **flat-leaf parsley** leaves, chopped

6 fresh **basil leaves**, chopped

A generous handful of grated **Parmigiano-Reggiano** cheese

4 2-inch-thick slices **Italian sesame-semolina bread**, cut on an angle

Season the steaks with the thyme, salt, and pepper. Place a large skil-let over high heat with the EVOO, once around the pan. When the oil is hot, using a pair of tongs and a folded paper towel, spread the oil lightly over the surface of the pan. Place the steaks in the hot pan and sear the meat, cooking it for 2 minutes on each side. Reduce the heat to medium and cook the steaks for 3 to 4 minutes longer on each side. Remove the steaks to a plate, cover them loosely with aluminum foil, and let rest for about 5 minutes.

While the steaks cook, combine the soft butter, garlic, parsley, basil, Parmigiano, and some pepper in a bowl. Spread the butter mixture evenly on all the cut sides of the bread slices. Once the steaks are out of the skillet and resting, return the skillet to the stovetop over medium heat. Add the slices of bread and cook until the first side is golden, 2 to 3 minutes. Flip and toast the second buttered side.

Serve the steaks on top of the cheesy, garlicky bread chunks.

4 SERVINGS

GREEN ONIONS AND STRING BEANS WITH BALSAMIC BROWN BUTTER

Salt
1¼ pounds **string beans**, trimmed
3 tablespoons **butter**
1 tablespoon **balsamic vinegar** (eyeball it)
1 bunch of **green onions**, cut into 1-inch pieces
Freshly ground black pepper

Fill a skillet with about an inch of water, place it over high heat, and bring it up to a boil. Add some salt and the string beans and cook them until just barely tender, 2 to 3 minutes. Drain and reserve the beans.

Return the skillet to the stovetop and turn the heat down to medium. Add the butter and cook until it is lightly browned and has a nutty fragrance. It will go from melted to bubbling and then quickly to browning. Once the butter is brown, add the vinegar, a small splash of water, the reserved green beans, the green onions, and some salt and pepper. Toss around to combine and coat the beans in the balsamic brown butter and continue to cook for about 1 minute.

4 SERVINGS

FAMILY SUPPER

• Marinate the turkey cutlets.

• Get the potatoes going, then start on the cutlets.

• Make the beans and finish the potatoes while the cutlets cook.

- **Sage, Thyme, and Lemon Turkey Cutlets with a Quick Pan Sauce**
- **Balsamic-Glazed Pearl Onions and Green Beans**
- **Garlic Chip and Parsley Smashed Potatoes**

This one is great for weeknights with the family. You can also prepare the entrée with chicken cutlets or thin pork chops; the recipe will be just as delicious and easy.

SAGE, THYME, AND LEMON TURKEY CUTLETS WITH A QUICK PAN SAUCE

6 fresh **sage leaves**, chopped

Leaves from 6 fresh **thyme sprigs**, coarsely chopped

Juice of 2 lemons

Salt and **black pepper**

1^1/$_3$ pounds **turkey breast cutlets**

2 tablespoons **EVOO** (extra-virgin olive oil)

^{1}/$_2$ cup **dry white wine** or dry vermouth (eyeball it)

1 cup **chicken stock** (eyeball it)

^{1}/$_4$ cup **heavy cream** or half-and-half (eyeball it)

^{1}/$_4$ cup fresh **flat-leaf parsley** leaves, a generous handful, chopped

In a shallow bowl, combine the sage, thyme, lemon juice, salt, and pepper. Add the turkey cutlets and let them marinate for 10 minutes.

Preheat a large skillet over medium-high heat with the EVOO, 2 times around the pan. Remove the turkey cutlets from the marinade, letting any excess drip back into the bowl, and add the cutlets to the hot skillet in a single layer, working in 2 batches if necessary. Sauté the cutlets for 4 to 5 minutes on each side, transfer them to a warm plate, and cover them loosely with aluminum foil to keep warm.

Return the skillet to the heat, add the wine, and stir, scraping up any brown bits with a wooden spoon. Add the chicken stock and cream, turn the heat up to high, and simmer until the sauce is slightly thickened. Stir in the parsley and pour the sauce over the turkey cutlets.

4 SERVINGS

BALSAMIC-GLAZED PEARL ONIONS AND GREEN BEANS

Salt

1 to 1$^{1}/_{4}$ pounds trimmed **green beans** (many markets sell 1-pound packages of trimmed raw beans in the fresh produce department)

3 tablespoons **EVOO** (extra-virgin olive oil; eyeball it)

$^{1}/_{2}$ pound **frozen pearl onions**, defrosted and dried in a dish towel

3 tablespoons **balsamic vinegar** (eyeball it)

$^{1}/_{2}$ cup **chicken stock** (eyeball it)

Black pepper

2 tablespoons **butter**

Heat 2 inches of water in a skillet with the lid on. Once it comes to a boil, add some salt and the beans and cook them for 3 to 4 minutes with the lid off. Drain the beans and reserve. Put the skillet back on the stove over medium-high heat and add the EVOO. Once hot, add the pearl onions and cook them for about 5 minutes, or until they start to take on a little color. Stir in the balsamic vinegar, chicken stock, and a little salt and pepper; turn the heat up to high and cook until the liquids have reduced by half. Return the beans to the pan, toss them around a bit, then add the butter and turn off the heat. Stir until the butter melts. Serve.

4 SERVINGS

GARLIC CHIP AND PARSLEY SMASHED POTATOES

2¹/₂ pounds **small potatoes**, such as baby Yukon Golds, halved
      Salt
      EVOO (extra-virgin olive oil)
  4 large **garlic cloves**, thinly sliced
¹/₃ cup **half-and-half** or heavy cream (eyeball it)
  3 tablespoons **butter**
  2 handfuls of fresh **flat-leaf parsley** leaves, chopped
      Black pepper

Place the potatoes in a sauce pot and cover them with water by about an inch. Place a lid on the pot and put it over high heat to bring it to a boil. Once the water is boiling, remove the lid, add some salt, and cook for 12 minutes, or until the potatoes are tender. Drain and reserve the potatoes in a colander while you cook the garlic chips.

Return the pot to the stovetop over medium-low heat and add enough EVOO to cover the bottom of the pot in a thin layer, about 3 tablespoons. Add the thinly sliced garlic, spreading the slices out evenly, and cook until the garlic is golden, giving the pot a shake every now and then. Once the garlic is golden, add the half-and-half, butter, and parsley; bring it up to a bubble; and add the reserved potatoes. Smash the potatoes with a fork or potato masher to the desired consistency. Taste and adjust the seasoning with a little more salt and some pepper.

4 SERVINGS

■ ■ ■

ONE OF THE ORIGINAL THREE SQUARE MEALS

- **Sliced Steak Sensation**
- **Sweet Tomato and Blue Cheese Salad with Basil Vinaigrette**
- **Lemony Parsley Boiled Potatoes**
- **Chocolate Cake and Milk (store-bought)**

Meat and potatoes are always crowd pleasers and this menu also pleases the cook with its ease; nobody's gonna break a sweat putting this one together! For dessert, I recommend a little slice of store-bought chocolate cake. Okay, who are we kidding? Make that a BIG slice of chocolate cake with a huge glass of ice-cold milk. (Wear your "loose" pants tonight!)

LEMONY PARSLEY BOILED POTATOES

$2^{1}/_{2}$ to 3 pounds **small white or red Bliss potatoes**, halved
Salt
A generous handful of fresh **flat-leaf parsley** leaves, chopped
3 tablespoons cold **butter**
Zest of 2 lemons
Black pepper

Place the potatoes in a sauce pot with cold water to cover by about 1 inch. Cover the pot with a lid to bring it up to a boil quickly. Remove the lid, add salt, and cook the potatoes until they are tender, about 12 minutes. Drain the potatoes; return them to the pot and place them over medium-low heat for about a minute to dry out a bit. Add the parsley, butter, lemon zest, salt, and pepper, and toss until the butter has melted, then serve hot.

4 SERVINGS

SLICED STEAK SENSATION

The trick to serving London broil is to let it rest, then slice it super thin and against the grain. Use a very sharp knife.

3 tablespoons **Worcestershire sauce** (eyeball it)
2 teaspoons **hot sauce** (eyeball it)
1 tablespoon **white wine vinegar** (eyeball it)
2 tablespoons **EVOO** (extra-virgin olive oil; eyeball it)
Salt and **freshly ground black pepper**
1 **top round steak** (also labeled London broil), 1 to 1^1/$_2$ inches thick, about 2 pounds

Preheat the broiler on high.

Combine the Worcestershire, hot sauce, vinegar, EVOO, and some salt and pepper and coat the steak with the mixture. Put the steak on a broiler pan and situate the pan on the rack closest to the flame; broil for 6 minutes per side. Remove the steak from the broiler and allow it to rest for 5 minutes, tented with a piece of aluminum foil. Then slice it very thin against the grain to serve.

4 SERVINGS

SWEET TOMATO AND BLUE CHEESE SALAD WITH BASIL VINAIGRETTE

- 1 pint red **cherry tomatoes**
- ¹/₂ pint **yellow grape tomatoes**
- ¹/₂ cup **crumbled blue cheese**
- 1 small **red onion**, thinly sliced
- 1 head of **Bibb or butter lettuce**, torn into bite-size pieces
- 1 **shallot**, peeled and cut into quarters
- 20 fresh **basil** leaves, about 1 cup
- A generous handful of fresh **flat-leaf parsley** leaves, chopped
- 1 tablespoon **Dijon mustard** (eyeball it)
- 3 tablespoons **white wine vinegar** (eyeball it)
- **Salt** and **freshly ground black pepper**
- ¹/₄ cup **EVOO** (extra-virgin olive oil; eyeball it)

Cut the tomatoes in half and place them in a salad bowl. Add the crumbled blue cheese, red onions, and lettuce. In a blender, combine the shallots, basil, parsley, mustard, white wine vinegar, and a little salt and pepper. Turn the blender on and, in a slow, steady stream, pour in the EVOO.

> **TIDBIT**
>
> This dressing is fabulous on pasta salad. Cook and cool your favorite shape of pasta, toss into the salad mix, and there ya go: yum-o!

When you're ready to serve, give the vinaigrette a quick stir and then pour the dressing over the tomatoes and lettuce, and toss well.

4 SERVINGS

GAME PLAN

• Mix up the dip-ins
  while the chicken
  and veggies fry.

DIP ON DOWN SOUTH OF THE BORDER

- **Tex-Mex Mixed Crunchy Fry**
- **Chipotle Mayo Dip-in**
- **Sweet, Spicy, and Sour Dip-in**

I double-coat the chicken and veggies in this mixed fry, making good use of the thick and tangy buttermilk. The results are a super-crunchy and satisfying crust that's full of flavor.

TEX-MEX MIXED CRUNCHY FRY

Vegetable oil, for frying

3 cups all-purpose **flour**

1 tablespoon **ground cumin**, a palmful

1 tablespoon **chili powder**, a palmful

2 cups **buttermilk** (eyeball it)

2 **limes**, zested, then cut into wedges

2 pounds **chicken tenders**

Salt and **black pepper**

A very generous handful of fresh **cilantro** or flat-leaf parsley leaves, chopped

1 large **red onion**, cut into $1/4$-inch-thick slices, rings separated

1 large **red bell pepper**, seeded and cut into $1/4$-inch-thick rings

Chipotle Mayo Dip-in and Sweet, Spicy, and Sour Dip-in, for dipping (page 160)

Preheat the oven to 250° F.

Preheat $1^1/2$ inches of vegetable oil in a high-sided, large skillet over medium to medium-high heat. To test the oil, submerge a wooden spoon handle in the oil and see if bubbles rise out and away from it—that says you're good to go.

While the oil is heating, set up a breading station right near the stove. Combine the flour, cumin, and chili powder in a large, wide bowl. In a second large, wide bowl, mix the buttermilk and lime zest. Season the chicken tenders with a little salt and pepper and toss them with all of the chopped cilantro or parsley.

Working in small batches, run the chicken tenders through the flour, shake off the excess, and then coat them in the buttermilk. Transfer them back to the flour and coat them thoroughly, then back into the buttermilk. Dip them back into the flour for a third and final coating. Carefully place the first batch of coated tenders in the hot oil. Fry the tenders for 6 to 7 minutes, turning when the first side is golden brown. Remove them from the oil to a paper-towel-lined plate and immediately sprinkle them with a little salt. Repeat with the remaining chicken pieces. Transfer them to a cookie sheet and keep them warm in the oven while you fry the veggies.

Sprinkle the red onion rings and red bell pepper rings with a little bit of water, and toss them around a bit; the water will help the first coating of flour stick to the veggies. Repeat the same flour-buttermilk, flour-buttermilk-flour process with the veggie rings. Cook the veggies for 4 to 5 minutes then drain on paper towels. As you are frying and draining the veggie rings, transfer the fried items to a second cookie sheet and keep them warm in the oven while you continue to fry.

Serve the chicken, onions, and peppers with the lime wedges and dips.

4 SERVINGS

CHIPOTLE MAYO DIP-IN

1 1/2 cups **mayonnaise**
1 to 2 **chipotle peppers in adobo sauce**, finely chopped, plus
1 to 2 tablespoons of the adobo sauce
Juice of 1 lime

In a bowl, combine the mayonnaise, chopped chipotle, adobo sauce, and lime juice.

4 SERVINGS

SWEET, SPICY, AND SOUR DIP-IN

3/4 cup **red wine vinegar**
1/2 cup **sugar**
1 small **jalapeño pepper**, cut in half lengthwise
Pinch of salt
2 **scallions**, thinly sliced
1/4 cup fresh **cilantro leaves**, a generous handful, chopped

In a small sauce pot combine the red wine vinegar, sugar, and 1/4 cup water, and bring them up to a simmer to dissolve the sugar. Once the sugar has dissolved, turn off the heat and add the jalapeño and the salt. The residual heat will release the jalapeño's flavor into the vinegar. Cool to room temperature, remove the jalapeño halves, and add the scallions and cilantro. Now go get dipping.

4 SERVINGS

MAKE YOUR OWN TAKE-OUT, THAI-STYLE

- **Thai-Style Chicken and Veggies**
- **Ginger-Lemon Rice**

In hot peppers the heat lives in the ribs and the seeds. If you like extra-spicy Thai when you order out, add some seeds and ribs to the pepper chop. If you like some heat in your dishes but you want to remain in control of your sweat glands, seed the pepper completely. For a lighter version, decrease the amount of coconut milk by as much as one cup and replace it with chicken stock.

THAI-STYLE CHICKEN AND VEGGIES

4 tablespoons **vegetable oil** (eyeball it)

4 6-ounce boneless, skinless **chicken breasts**, cut into bite-size pieces
   Salt and **black pepper**

1 cup **shredded carrots** (available in the produce department; or shred your own)

1 large **onion**, thinly sliced

3 large **garlic cloves**, chopped
   3-inch piece of **fresh ginger**, peeled and grated

1 **serrano or jalapeño pepper**, seeded (or not) and finely chopped

1 **red bell pepper**, seeded and thinly sliced

3/4 cup **chicken stock** (eyeball it)

1 13.5-ounce can **light coconut milk**

1 10-ounce box **frozen peas**, thawed

20 fresh **basil leaves**, about 1 cup

1/4 cup fresh **cilantro leaves**, a generous handful, coarsely chopped
   Zest and juice of 1 lime

continued

Heat a large skillet over medium-high heat with 2 tablespoons of the vegetable oil, 2 times around the pan. Add the chicken to the skillet, season with salt and pepper, and brown it for about 5 minutes. Remove the chicken to a plate. Add the remaining 2 tablespoons of oil to the skillet, then add the carrots, onions, garlic, ginger, hot peppers, and bell peppers and cook, stirring frequently, for 2 to 3 minutes. Add the chicken stock and the coconut milk, turn the heat up to high, and simmer for 5 minutes. Return the chicken to the skillet and cook it for another 3 to 4 minutes, or until cooked through. Add the peas, basil, cilantro, and lime zest and juice, and cook for 1 more minute. Serve on a bed of the ginger-lemon rice.

4 SERVINGS

GINGER-LEMON RICE

$2^3/_4$ cups **chicken stock**
     Zest and juice of 1 lemon
     3-inch piece of **fresh ginger**, peeled
$1^1/_2$ cups **white rice**
   4 **scallions**, chopped

In a sauce pot that has a tight-fitting lid, combine the chicken stock, lemon zest, and ginger. Cover and bring it up to a boil over high heat. Add the rice, stir, bring it back up to a simmer, then cover and cook over low heat for 18 minutes, or until tender. Discard the ginger. Add the scallions and lemon juice, and fluff the rice with a fork until the scallions are well distributed.

4 SERVINGS

■ ■ ■

HAM IT UP

GAME PLAN

- Start the pasta water then get the zucchini in the oven.
- Make the pasta and sauce while the zucchini roasts.

- **Walnuts, Ham, and Cheese . . . Oh, My!**
- **Roast Zucchini**

This is one of those dinners that came to me after a long, hard stare into what looked like an empty fridge. You know the stance: fridge door open, one hand hanging on the door handle and the other hand on your hip. You stare, close the door, reopen it, and resume the stance. You continue to stare, trying not to blink, hoping that the fridge will reveal something to your inner self. Well, this time it did—and boy did my Zen fridge come through for us!

WALNUTS, HAM, AND CHEESE . . . OH, MY!

Salt

1 pound **bowtie pasta** (farfalle)

$1/2$ cup **walnuts**, finely chopped

3 tablespoons **EVOO** (extra-virgin olive oil; eyeball it)

10 slices **Canadian bacon** or breakfast ham, cut into thin strips

2 large **garlic cloves**, chopped

$1/2$ teaspoon **red pepper flakes**

Juice of 1 lemon

$3/4$ cup fresh **flat-leaf parsley** leaves, 3 generous handfuls, chopped

2 tablespoons **butter**

1 cup grated **Parmigiano-Reggiano**, plus some to pass at the table

Place a large covered pot of water over high heat and bring it up to a boil for the pasta. Once the water boils, salt it and cook the pasta to al dente. Note: right before draining the pasta, you'll want to remove and reserve 1 cup of the pasta cooking water.

Place a large skillet over medium-high heat, add the chopped walnuts, and toast them, stirring every now and then, until they are golden and smell toasty—a couple of minutes. Remove the nuts

continued

MEALS FOR 4

from the skillet and reserve. When the pasta is nearly done, return the skillet you cooked the walnuts in to the stovetop over medium-high heat with the EVOO, 3 times around the pan. Once the EVOO is hot, add the Canadian bacon and cook it for 2 to 3 minutes, or until it starts to lightly brown. Add the garlic and red pepper flakes and cook for another minute. Add the reserved pasta cooking liquid and cook it until the liquid has reduced by half. Add the drained pasta, toasted walnuts, lemon juice, and parsley to the skillet, toss it to coat the noodles, and continue to cook until the pasta has soaked up almost all of the liquid. Turn the heat off, add the butter and grated cheese, and toss until the butter has melted. Serve with extra Parmigiano to pass at the table.

4 SERVINGS

ROAST ZUCCHINI

3 **zucchini** (about 2 pounds), sliced into 1-inch disks
3 tablespoons **EVOO** (extra-virgin olive oil; eyeball it)
 Salt and **black pepper**
2 large **garlic cloves**, chopped
20 fresh **basil leaves**, coarsely chopped (about 1 cup)

Preheat the oven to 450° F.

Arrange the zucchini on a baking sheet and drizzle them generously with the EVOO. Season them with salt and pepper, toss to coat evenly, and roast the zucchini for 10 minutes. Remove from the oven, add the garlic, toss to distribute, and then continue to roast them for another 5 minutes, or until tender. Once they are roasted, transfer the zucchini to a serving bowl and toss them with the chopped basil.

4 SERVINGS

■ ■ ■

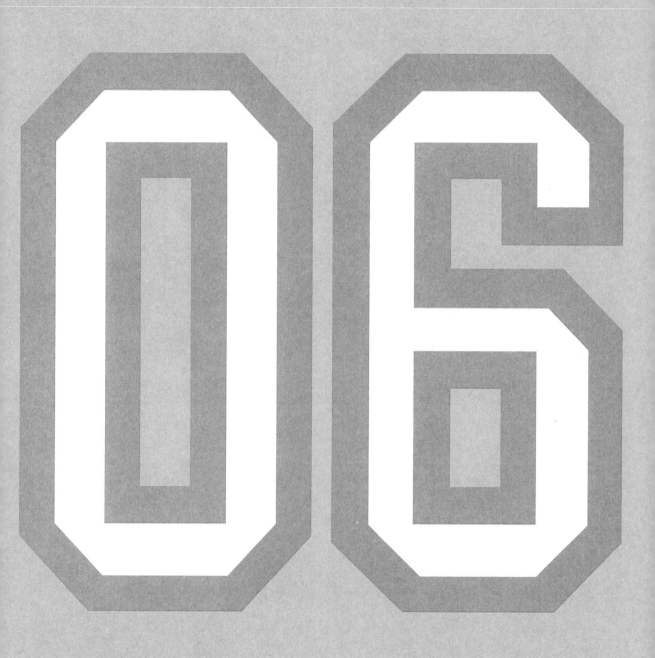

SIX IS A NICE, ROUND, FRIENDLY-LOOKING NUMBER AND IT'S SPECIAL TO ME BECAUSE IT'S THE MINIMUM NUMBER THAT CLASSIFIES AS A "GROUP" IN MY MIND. FOUR MAKES ME PICTURE A FAMILY OR A DOUBLE DATE BUT SIX, WELL, THERE'S SOME HANGING OUT GOING ON AND SOME LAUGHTER IN THE AIR WITH THAT GROUP! EVEN FAMILIES OF SIX SEEM TO GET ALONG BETTER. WHEN I SEE BIG FAMILIES IN THE SUPERMARKET THEY LOOK AND SOUND LIKE THEY KNOW HOW TO SHARE AND TALK MORE EASILY BECAUSE THEY ARE A GROUP: ONE UNIT. GATHER UP YOUR GROUP TONIGHT OR SOME NIGHT SOON. YOU'LL BE READY FOR THEM!

06

08

MY DADDY'S BIRTHDAY SUPPER

• **Jimmy's Jazzed-Up Jambasta (Jambalaya Pasta, Deluxe)**
• **Mini Pecan Ice Cream Pies**

My dad, Jim, is from Louisiana and he loves spicy food and smooth jazz. That's how this entrée got half its title. Now, the mix up of a *jambalaya* with *pasta*, well, that jumble came about because my mama is Sicilian and we put everything on spaghetti, at least once. I've been making and perfecting my jambasta for years. This is the current edition of the recipe. It can turn any Wednesday, Monday, or Sunday into Fat Tuesday!

JIMMY'S JAZZED-UP JAMBASTA

Salt
1 pound **penne rigate**
2 tablespoons **EVOO** (extra-virgin olive oil)
3/4 pound **andouille sausage**, casing removed and diced, any brand
2 tablespoons **butter**
4 **garlic cloves**, chopped
2 **jalapeño peppers**, seeded and thinly sliced
1 **red bell pepper**, seeded and chopped
2 **celery ribs** from the heart, with greens, chopped
1 **onion**, chopped
Black pepper
2 tablespoons all-purpose **flour**
1 cup **beer**
1 cup **chicken stock**
1 14-ounce can **crushed fire-roasted tomatoes**
2 tablespoons **hot sauce**, such as Frank's Red Hot or Tabasco (eyeball it)

2 tablespoons fresh **thyme** leaves, chopped

$^3/_4$ pound **chicken breast tenders**, sliced $^1/_2$ inch thick

$^1/_2$ pound medium to large **shrimp**, peeled, deveined, and tails removed

$^1/_3$ cup **heavy cream** (eyeball it)

3 **scallions**, thinly sliced

Bring a large covered pot of water to a boil for the pasta and add the salt to it, then the pasta. Cook the pasta to al dente and drain.

While the pasta works, heat a deep skillet over medium-high heat. Add the EVOO and the andouille. Brown the sausage for 2 to 3 minutes to render the fat, then remove it with a slotted spoon to a bowl. Add the butter, and when it melts add the garlic, peppers, celery, and onions to the skillet and sauté for 5 to 6 minutes. Season the mixture with salt and pepper and add the flour to the pan. Cook the flour with the veggies for 2 minutes more, then whisk in the beer and cook until it is almost all evaporated, about 2 minutes. Add the chicken stock, tomatoes, hot sauce, and thyme. Bring the liquid to a bubble and add the chicken and shrimp. Cook for 6 to 7 minutes, until the chicken is firm and the shrimp are opaque. Stir to mix in the cooking juices, then add the cream. Add the drained pasta to the sauce. Ladle up the jambasta and top it with the scallions and the reserved crispy andouille.

6 SERVINGS

MINI PECAN ICE CREAM PIES

1¹/₂ cups **pecan halves**
6 individual **mini graham-cracker-crumb pie shells**
2 pints **butter pecan ice cream**
1 jar **caramel sauce**
Whipped cream, from a canister (in the dairy case)

Place the pecans in a dry skillet and toast them over moderate heat until fragrant; remove them from the skillet. Place the pie shells on a small tray. Soften the ice cream in the microwave for 20 seconds on high. Fill the pie shells with ice cream, mounding it into each shell. Smooth the edges of the ice cream pies and freeze them for 20 minutes to set. Remove the lid of the caramel sauce and warm the sauce in the microwave for 1 minute on high. Top the pies with caramel sauce and lots of toasted pecans and whipped cream.

6 SERVINGS

■ ■ ■

A NIGHT IN AMALFI

- Lemon Spaghetti
- Flounder Francese with Toasted Almonds, Lemon, and Capers
- Limoncello liqueur (in the liquor department)
- Lemon sorbet (store-bought)

On the Amalfi coast of Italy, lemons the size of melons grow from the edge of the sea to the top of the sky on the rocky cliffs that disappear up into the clouds. This is a menu that takes me back there, to my lemon heaven.

LEMON SPAGHETTI

Salt
1 pound **spaghetti**
3 tablespoons **EVOO** (extra-virgin olive oil)
4 **garlic cloves**, finely chopped
1/2 teaspoon **red pepper flakes**
Zest and juice of 2 lemons
3/4 cup **heavy cream**
1 cup grated **Parmigiano-Reggiano cheese**
Handful of fresh **flat-leaf parsley** leaves, finely chopped
1/2 cup fresh **basil** leaves, 10 or 12 leaves, shredded

Bring a large covered pot of water to a boil. Salt the water and drop the spaghetti into the pot.

Heat a large, deep skillet over low heat. Add the EVOO, garlic, red pepper flakes, and lemon zest.

continued

When the pasta has been cooking for about 5 minutes, to the garlic mixture add the lemon juice, a ladle of the cooking water from the pasta, and the cream. Raise the heat a bit to bring the sauce to a bubble.

Drain the pasta when it still has a good bite to it. Add the pasta to the skillet and turn off the heat. Add half the cheese to the pasta and toss the pasta with the sauce for a minute or two, allowing it time to soak up the sauce. Add the parsley and toss. Use tongs or a meat fork to gather one sixth of the pasta and twist it to form a bundle, or pasta nest. Top each serving with a sprinkle of the remaining cheese and lots of shredded basil.

6 SERVINGS

FLOUNDER FRANCESE WITH TOASTED ALMONDS, LEMON, AND CAPERS

6 **flounder fillets**, 6 to 8 ounces each
  Salt and **black pepper**
  All-purpose **flour**, for dredging
2 large **eggs** plus 2 egg yolks
5 tablespoons **EVOO** (extra-virgin olive oil)
4 tablespoons ($^1/_2$ stick) cold **butter**, each tablespoon cut into small pieces
$^2/_3$ to $^3/_4$ cup **dry white wine** (eyeball it)
  Handful of fresh **flat-leaf parsley** leaves, finely chopped
  Zest and juice of 1 lemon
3 tablespoons **capers**, drained
$^1/_2$ cup **sliced almonds**, toasted
4 **garlic cloves**, finely chopped
2 pounds **triple-washed spinach**, tough stems removed, coarsely chopped
$^1/_4$ teaspoon freshly grated or ground **nutmeg** (eyeball it)

Preheat a large nonstick skillet over medium to medium-high heat. Season the fish with salt and pepper and dredge in flour. Beat the eggs with the egg yolks in a shallow dish. Add 1 tablespoon of the EVOO to the skillet, 1 time around the pan, then add 1 tablespoon of the butter. Dip 3 pieces of fish into the eggs and coat them evenly, then fry them until they're golden, 5 to 6 minutes total. Transfer the fish to a plate and cover it with a loose foil tent to retain the heat. Repeat the process with the remaining fish fillets, using another tablespoon of the oil and of the butter.

Add the wine to the skillet and cook until it has reduced by half, 1 minute. Add the parsley, lemon zest and juice, and capers. Stir the remaining 2 tablespoons of cold butter into the sauce. Pour the sauce over the fish and sprinkle with the sliced almonds.

Return the skillet to the heat. Heat the remaining 3 tablespoons of EVOO. Add the chopped garlic and let it "speak" by coming to a sizzle. Add the spinach and wilt it, turning it to coat it in EVOO. Season the spinach with salt, pepper, and nutmeg, and serve it alongside the flounder.

6 SERVINGS

TIDBIT

To toast almonds, heat them in a dry skillet over medium-high heat until they are just starting to color. Shake often as they toast and trasnfer to a bowl to cool to avoid burning them. You can also toast almonds in a 350°F oven for about 10 minutes, stirring once or twice.

SLOW-YOU-DOWN FOOD

- **Cabbage and Straw Pasta**
- **Almond and Chocolate Cream Trifle**

Slow food is a big movement now, and there's no doubt long cooking times benefit the development of full flavor. But don't discount what you can achieve in just 30 minutes. This meal is fast to prepare but eating it will slow you way down. Wide noodles prepared with cabbage, potatoes, and sage make up the classic Genoa comfort food called *pizzoccheri*. Have a pillow handy. This is another supper that'll leave you needing a nap.

CABBAGE AND STRAW PASTA

Salt
2 **Idaho potatoes**, peeled and cut into $1/2$-inch dice
1 pound **fettucine** or pappardelle pasta
1 small head of **Savoy cabbage**, quartered, cored, and finely shredded
$1/2$ cup (1 stick) **butter**, cut into pieces
3 to 4 **garlic cloves**, crushed from their skins and halved
16 fresh **sage leaves**, 10 thinly sliced, 6 left whole
1 teaspoon **coarse black pepper**
$1^1/2$ to 2 cups grated **Romano cheese**

Bring a large covered pot of water to a boil and salt it. Add the potatoes and cook them for 7 minutes. Add the pasta and cook it for 2 minutes, then stir in the cabbage and cook it for 5 minutes longer.

While the potatoes and pasta cook, in a large, deep skillet, melt the butter over medium heat and add the garlic and 6 whole sage leaves. Cook for 3 to 4 minutes, remove the garlic and whole leaves (reserve the leaves), then add the sliced sage leaves and the black pepper. Just before draining the pasta and cabbage, add 2 ladles of starchy cooking water to the skillet.

Drain the potatoes, pasta, and cabbage and add them to the butter and sage. Toss the pasta to combine it with the sage butter, adding lots of cheese as you work. Toss it for 1 or 2 minutes to form a cheesy, buttery coating on the pasta and cabbage, then adjust the salt and serve. Use the reserved whole sage leaves to garnish the pasta.

6 SERVINGS

ALMOND AND CHOCOLATE CREAM TRIFLE

2 packages **ladyfingers**
$^1/_2$ to $^2/_3$ cup **almond liqueur**, such as Amaretto
2 cups **heavy cream**
$^1/_4$ cup **sugar**
$^1/_4$ cup **slivered almonds**
3$^1/_2$ ounces **bittersweet chocolate**, finely chopped
Cocoa powder, for dusting
1 pint **raspberries**, for garnish

Line an 8- or 9-inch square or round glass dish or bowl with ladyfingers. Douse the cake with half of the liqueur. Whip the cream with the sugar until it's stiff, then fold in the almonds and the chopped chocolate. Layer half the whipped cream over the ladyfingers and top it with another layer of ladyfingers. Sprinkle the remaining liqueur over the cake and top with the remaining whipped cream. Dust with cocoa powder, garnish with raspberries, and serve; or chill until ready to serve.

6 SERVINGS

■ ■ ■

- Get the fries in the oven.

- While the fries bake, make the chili.

- Make the cheese sauce for the fries while the polenta cooks.

SUPER BOWLS

- Smoky Cheese Fries
- Polenta with Chunky Chicken and Chorizo Chili

This one is for all you armchair lady linebackers as well as you big, burly male quarterbacks. These Super Bowls are fare good enough for the owner's box. Have a double or triple date night and take in a great game!

SMOKY CHEESE FRIES

1 large package **frozen waffle-cut fries**

2 tablespoons **tomato paste**

2 tablespoons **butter**

2 tablespoons all-purpose **flour**

2 cups **milk**

2 cups grated **cheddar cheese**

2 **chipotles in adobo**, chopped, plus 1 to 2 tablespoons adobo sauce
  Salt

Preheat the oven and bake the waffle fries according to the package directions.

Heat the tomato paste in a small pot over medium heat and cook it for a minute or two. Heat the butter in another small pot over medium heat and whisk in the flour. Cook the flour for a minute, then add the tomato paste. Cook for a minute longer, then whisk in the milk. When the sauce bubbles, stir in the cheese, chipotles, and adobo sauce. Season the sauce with salt. Remove the fries from the oven when they are crisp and golden brown. Spoon the thick cheese sauce over the waffle fries and serve.

6 SERVINGS

POLENTA WITH CHUNKY CHICKEN AND CHORIZO CHILI

- 1 tablespoon **EVOO** (extra-virgin olive oil)
- ¾ pound packaged **chorizo** (not smoked), chopped
- 2 pounds **ground chicken**
- 3 tablespoons **chili powder**, 3 palmfuls
- 1 tablespoon ground **cumin**, a palmful
- 1 **onion**, chopped
- 3 **garlic cloves**, finely chopped
- 1 **red bell pepper**, chopped
- 1 15-ounce can **red kidney beans**, drained
- 1 12-ounce bottle of **beer**
- 1 28-ounce can diced **fire-roasted tomatoes**
  Salt
- 6 cups **chicken stock**
- 2 cups **quick-cooking polenta**
- 2 tablespoons **butter**
- 2 **scallions**, finely chopped
- 2 tablespoons fresh chopped **thyme**

Heat a big, deep skillet over medium-high heat with the EVOO, once around the pan. Add the chorizo and cook to render its fat, 2 minutes. Push the chorizo off to the side of the pot and add the chicken meat. Brown and crumble the chicken, 5 to 6 minutes, seasoning the chicken with the chili powder and cumin while it cooks. Add the onions, garlic, peppers, and beans to the skillet and cook for another 5 to 6 minutes. Stir the beer into the chili, cook for a minute to reduce the liquid, then add the tomatoes and heat through. Season the chili with salt and reduce the heat to low.

Bring the stock to a boil in a medium pot, then stir in the polenta. Keep stirring until the polenta masses and thickens enough to mold to the sides of a bowl, 2 to 3 minutes. Stir in the butter, scallions, and thyme and season it with salt.

Fill 6 bowls halfway with polenta and make a well in the center, pushing the polenta up the sides. Top the polenta with chili and serve.

6 SERVINGS

ZITI ALWAYS PLEASES

- **Double Eggplant Parm Fake-Baked Ziti**
- **Chopped Salad with Olives and Roasted Red Pepper Dressing**

Nothing pleases like baked ziti, the universal carried dish that is welcome at any occasion. It's always the empty chafing dish on any buffet and the first request when Mom asks you what you want for dinner. This is one of my best: in 30 minutes, you can turn out eggplant baked ziti with both breaded eggplant and eggplant sauce. It is a hands-down winner by a knockout—no need to tally the scorecards.

DOUBLE EGGPLANT PARM FAKE-BAKED ZITI

2 medium **eggplants**, 1 peeled and chopped, 1 thinly sliced

$1/2$ cup plus 2 tablespoons **EVOO** (extra-virgin olive oil)

Salt and **black pepper**

2 **eggs**

$1/4$ to $1/3$ cup **milk** or cream (eyeball it)

1 pound **ziti rigate** or rigatoni

$1 1/2$ cups grated **Parmigiano-Reggiano cheese**

1 cup **Italian-style bread crumbs**, 4 generous handfuls

3 tablespoons fresh chopped **rosemary** leaves, from 4 to 5 sprigs

2 **garlic cloves**, crushed from their skins

1 teaspoon **red pepper flakes**

1 28-ounce can **crushed tomatoes or crushed fire-roasted tomatoes**

Handful of fresh **flat-leaf parsley** leaves, chopped

2 cups shredded **Provolone cheese**

Heat the oven to 500° F.

Place a large covered pot of water on to boil.

Spread the chopped eggplant on a nonstick rimmed baking sheet. Pour about $^1/_4$ cup of the EVOO in a small dish, then, using a pastry brush, coat the eggplant with oil and season liberally with salt and pepper. Roast the eggplant for 20 minutes, or until the eggplant pieces are dark and tender.

Preheat about $^1/_4$ cup of the EVOO in a large nonstick skillet over medium heat.

Beat the eggs with the milk or cream in a wide, shallow dish and season the mixture with salt and pepper.

When the water comes to a boil, salt it liberally and add the pasta. Cook the pasta to al dente (with a bite to it). Drain the pasta and reserve.

In a wide, shallow dish combine about $^1/_2$ cup of the grated cheese with the bread crumbs and rosemary. Coat the eggplant slices in the egg mixture then the bread crumbs and cook in the hot EVOO for 3 to 4 minutes on each side. Work in two batches if necessary. Drain the eggplant on paper towels.

Preheat another large skillet over medium heat. Add the remaining 2 tablespoons of EVOO and the garlic. Cook for a couple of minutes, then remove the garlic and add the red pepper flakes, tomatoes, parsley, and salt.

When the roasted eggplant is done, switch the oven to broil. Scrape the roasted eggplant pieces into a food processor and process them until they're smooth. Add the pureed eggplant to the tomato sauce and stir to combine.

Toss the drained hot pasta with half of the sauce and the remaining 1 cup of grated Parmigiano cheese. Spread the pasta in a baking dish and top it with the eggplant slices, the remaining sauce, and all of the Provolone. Place the fake-baked ziti under the broiler for 2 to 3 minutes to brown the cheese.

6 SERVINGS

CHOPPED SALAD WITH OLIVES AND ROASTED RED PEPPER DRESSING

8 cups store-bought **chopped mixed salad greens**—take your pick

3/4 cup **pitted mixed olives**, chopped

2 **roasted red peppers**, drained and patted dry, chopped

3 tablespoons **red wine vinegar**

1/3 cup **EVOO** (extra-virgin olive oil)

Salt and **black pepper**

Handful of **sliced toasted almonds**

Place the salad greens in a bowl and top with the olives. Combine the peppers and red wine vinegar in a food processor, turn the machine on, then stream in the EVOO. Pour the dressing over the salad, toss, and season it with salt and black pepper. Garnish the salad with the nuts.

6 SERVINGS

■ ■ ■

SPRING FLING

- **Fried Vermicelli and Green Onions**
- **Sautéed Pork Chops with Sherry-Berry Pan Gravy**
- **Rhubarb Chutney**
- **Strawberry Ice Cream and Wafer Cookies (store-bought)**

I'm not much for sweets and I cannot bake, so you won't spy me making rhubarb pies, but I do love the flavor of rhubarb. Rhubarb chutney is the key to making *every* flavor in this menu shine. Fried Vermicelli is a great side dish to keep in mind for any spring brunch or lunch menu as well.

FRIED VERMICELLI AND GREEN ONIONS

    Salt

1 pound **vermicelli** or thin spaghetti

3 tablespoons **EVOO** (extra-virgin olive oil)

3 tablespoons **butter**, cut into small pieces

3 **garlic cloves**, crushed from their skins

6 **scallions**, cut into 3-inch pieces then shredded lengthwise

    Black pepper

1 cup fresh **basil**, about 20 leaves, very finely sliced

Bring a large covered pot of water to a boil and salt it. Add the pasta and cook to al dente, then drain it.

Heat the EVOO and butter in a large skillet with the garlic over medium heat and cook the garlic until it begins to soften, 4 to 5 minutes. Remove the garlic and raise the heat. Fry the scallions in the seasoned oil for 3 to 4 minutes. Add the well-drained pasta to the pan and season it with salt and pepper. Toss the pasta with the scallions and seasoned oil. Press the pasta by placing a plate smaller than

continued

the pan directly onto the pasta and weighing it with a few cans or a heavy skillet. Let the pasta brown and crisp up a bit. Remove the weights and the plate and invert the pasta onto a serving platter. Garnish with the basil.

6 SERVINGS

SAUTÉED PORK CHOPS WITH SHERRY-BERRY PAN GRAVY AND RHUBARB CHUTNEY

- 5 tablespoons **butter**
- 3 tablespoons **sugar**
- 2 tablespoons **fresh lemon juice**
- 1/4 cup **balsamic vinegar**
- 3/4 pound **rhubarb**, trimmed and chopped
  Handful of **golden raisins** (a snack-size box)
- 2 tablespoons **EVOO** (extra-virgin olive oil)
- 6 boneless **center-cut pork loin chops**, 8 ounces each
  Salt and **black pepper**
- 1 tablespoon all-purpose **flour**
- 1/2 cup **dry sherry**
- 1/2 cup **chicken or beef stock**
- 3 tablespoons **strawberry, blackberry, or raspberry all-fruit preserves**, such as Polaner

In a medium skillet, melt 2 tablespoons of the butter over medium heat. Add the sugar, lemon juice, and vinegar and bring to a bubble. Add the rhubarb and raisins and cook for 10 to 12 minutes, or until the rhubarb is tender. Turn off the heat and set the chutney aside until the pork chops are done.

Heat the EVOO, 2 times around the pan, in a nonstick skillet over medium-high heat. When the oil smokes or ripples, add the chops, season them with salt and pepper, and cook them for 6 minutes on each side. Remove the chops to a plate and keep them warm under a foil tent while the meat rests. Add the remaining 3 tablespoons of butter to the pan and when it melts add the flour. Cook the flour for a minute, then whisk in the sherry and cook until it has reduced by half. Whisk in the stock, then the preserves. Season the gravy with a little black pepper. Serve the chops with gravy ladled over the top and rhubarb chutney alongside.

6 SERVINGS

■ ■ ■

GAME PLAN

• Roast the tomatoes along with the mushrooms.

• Make the dressing and assemble the salad while they roast.

• Finish the pasta and sauce.

• Toss the salad and dressing together.

IL FORNO

- Roasted Mushroom Pasta with Prosciutto
- Roasted Tomato and Spinach Salad
- Pistachio Ice Cream and Amaretti Cookies (store-bought)

When I'm having a crowd over, my oven often gets a workout, which means less work for me. Roast up the extra mushrooms and tomatoes. Enjoy them cold, as an appetizer or in a salad. They are truly delicious.

ROASTED MUSHROOM PASTA WITH PROSCIUTTO

Salt

1½ pounds **bowtie pasta** (farfalle)

6 large **portobello mushroom** caps

¼ cup **EVOO** (extra-virgin olive oil), plus some for drizzling

Black pepper

5 large **garlic cloves**, thinly sliced

½ cup **white wine** (eyeball it)

3 tablespoons cold **butter**

1 cup fresh **flat-leaf parsley** leaves, 4 generous handfuls, chopped

12 slices **prosciutto di Parma**, cut into strips

1 cup grated **Parmigiano-Reggiano**, 3 overflowing handfuls, plus more to pass at the table

Preheat the oven to 450° F.

Bring a large covered pot of water to a boil over high heat for the pasta. Once it's boiling, salt the water, add the pasta, and cook the pasta to al dente. Reserve 1 cup of the pasta cooking water, then drain the pasta.

While the water is heating, place the portobello mushrooms on a cookie sheet and drizzle both sides with a little EVOO. Roast the mushrooms for 10 minutes, or until they are tender. Remove them from the oven, season them with salt and pepper, slice, and reserve.

Drain the pasta and return the pasta pot to the stove over medium-high heat. Add the $^1/_4$ cup of EVOO and the garlic and cook until the garlic is golden. Add the wine and the reserved pasta cooking liquid, a little salt, and a lot of freshly ground black pepper. Return the pasta to the pot along with the sliced roasted mushrooms and stir to combine them. Turn the heat off, add the butter, parsley, prosciutto, and grated cheese, and stir it until the butter has melted and the parsley and prosciutto are distributed through the pasta. Serve immediately, with more cheese to pass at the table.

6 SERVINGS

ROASTED TOMATO AND SPINACH SALAD

  2 pints **red or yellow cherry tomatoes**
$^1/_3$ cup **EVOO** (extra-virgin olive oil), plus some for drizzling
     Salt and **freshly ground black pepper**
     Leaves from 6 fresh **thyme** sprigs, coarsely chopped
  1 **shallot**, finely chopped
  2 tablespoons **Dijon mustard** (eyeball it)
     Juice of 2 lemons
  2 pounds **prewashed spinach leaves**, thick stems removed, leaves torn into bite-size pieces
  2 **Belgian endives**, leaves separated from the core, then thickly sliced
$^3/_4$ pound **Gorgonzola cheese**

Preheat the oven to 450° F.

Spread the cherry tomatoes on a rimmed baking sheet. Drizzle them with a little EVOO, season them with salt and freshly ground black pepper, and sprinkle them with the thyme, then toss them around a

continued

bit on the baking sheet to make sure they are thoroughly coated. Roast the tomatoes for 15 minutes, or until they start to flirt with bursting. Remove them from the oven and let them cool for a bit.

While the tomatoes are roasting, combine the shallots, mustard, and lemon juice in a bowl and add a little salt and pepper. Whisk in the $1/3$ cup of EVOO in a slow, steady stream.

Combine the spinach and endive in a salad bowl with the roasted tomatoes. Crumble and break up the Gorgonzola cheese over the salad and then add the mustard-lemon dressing. Toss the salad gently, adjust the seasoning, and serve.

6 SERVINGS

■ ■ ■

- Get the tender-
  loins in the oven.

- Start the gravy
  and mix and fry
  the pancakes
  while the onions
  cook and the
  sauce simmers.

VERY ENTERTAINING TENDERLOIN

- Roasted Pork Tenderloins with Sweet Apple Gravy
- Pea and Potato Pancakes with Scallion-Lemon Sour Cream
- Warm Apple Pie (store-bought)

Entertaining, whether for family or friends, has it good when pork tenderloins are on the menu—and you have it pretty easy, as well. Serving low-maintenance pork tenderloins means you get more time to hang out and have a laugh with everyone at the table—and that translates into more minutes of living what I call the good life!

ROASTED PORK TENDERLOINS WITH SWEET APPLE GRAVY

06

$2^1/2$ to $2^3/4$ pounds **pork tenderloins**, trimmed of fat and connective tissue

3 tablespoons **EVOO** (extra-virgin olive oil; eyeball it), plus some for the pan

Leaves from 8 fresh **thyme sprigs**, coarsely chopped, and 4 whole thyme sprigs

Salt and **black pepper**

3 tablespoons **butter**

$1/2$ large **onion**, chopped

3 large **garlic cloves**, chopped

Pinch of **red pepper flakes**

1 heaping tablespoon all-purpose **flour**

$1/2$ cup **white wine** (eyeball it)

1 cup **apple juice** or cider (eyeball it)

$1^1/2$ cups **chicken stock** (eyeball it)

1 bunch of fresh **chives**, chopped

continued

MEALS FOR 6

Preheat the oven to 475° F.

Rub the tenderloins with the 3 tablespoons of EVOO, the chopped thyme, and a liberal amount of salt and pepper. Brush a rimmed baking sheet or broiler pan with oil and arrange the tenderloins on the pan. Roast the pork for 25 minutes. They will still be slightly pink inside; if you prefer the pork well done, cook an additional 5 minutes.

For the sweet apple gravy, preheat a skillet over medium high with the butter. When the butter melts, add the onions, garlic, red pepper flakes, whole thyme sprigs, and a little salt and pepper and cook, stirring every now and then, until the onions start to take on some color, 5 to 8 minutes. Sprinkle with the flour and continue to cook the onions for 1 minute, then whisk in the wine and apple juice or cider. Bring the mixture up to a bubble and add the stock. Bring that up to a simmer and continue to cook the gravy over medium heat until it's thick. Discard the thyme stems, then stir in the chopped chives.

To assemble, slice the tenderloins thin and pile the meat on a platter. Drizzle the slices with the sweet apple gravy.

6 SERVINGS

PEA AND POTATO PANCAKES WITH SCALLION-LEMON SOUR CREAM

1 **egg**
1 18-ounce package **shredded potatoes,** such as Simply Potatoes, available on the dairy aisle
1/2 large **onion**, grated
1/2 of a 10-ounce box **frozen peas**, defrosted
Zest and juice of 1 lemon
1/2 cup fresh **flat-leaf parsley** leaves, 2 generous handfuls, chopped
3 tablespoons all-purpose **flour**
Salt and **black pepper**
Vegetable oil, for frying

1¹/₂ cups **sour cream** (eyeball it)

  5 **scallions**, thinly sliced

Crack the egg into a bowl and beat it with a fork. Squeeze the excess liquid from the potatoes and then add them to the bowl along with the grated onions, peas, lemon zest, parsley, and flour. Season the potatoes with some salt and pepper and combine them thoroughly.

Preheat a large skillet with about $^1/_4$ inch of vegetable oil over medium-high heat. Working in batches and using a large spoonful of the potato mixture for each potato cake, make three or four 3-inch cakes in the skillet. Cook the cakes for 3 or 4 minutes on each side, until they are golden brown and cooked through. Transfer the cooked pancakes to a paper-towel-lined plate to drain and sprinkle them with a little salt while they are still piping hot. Repeat the process until the potato mixture is gone, making 12 pancakes. Some of the peas can get a little frisky and escape from the pancakes, but don't sweat it, they're just asserting their individuality.

While the potato cakes are cooking, throw together the scallion-lemon sour cream. In a bowl, combine the sour cream, lemon juice, sliced scallions, and a little salt and pepper.

Serve each pancake with a small dollop of the scallion-lemon sour cream.

6 SERVINGS

■ ■ ■

GAME PLAN

• Get the rice going.

• While the fish marinates, make the cucumber relish.

• Cook the salmon fillets.

SWIM UPSTREAM FOR IT

- **Sweet and Sour Cucumber and Red Onion Relish**
- **Spicy Cilantro-Scallion Rice**
- **Seared Salmon with Soy and Garlic**
- **Citrus Sorbets (store-bought)**

They say we should all be eating more fish, but *they* aren't coming over and making it for us, now are *they*? This is a fast, easy way to feed your crowd without tons of ingredients and lots of work. And yes. *They* are right about eating more fish. It *is* good for us.

SWEET AND SOUR CUCUMBER AND RED ONION RELISH

$1/2$ cup **rice wine or cider vinegar** (eyeball it)

2 rounded tablespoons **sugar**

$1/2$ teaspoon **red pepper flakes**

Salt

1 **European seedless cucumber**, cut in half lengthwise then thinly sliced into half moons

1 **red onion**, thinly sliced

In a small sauce pot, combine the vinegar, sugar, red pepper flakes, and a little salt. Bring it up to a simmer over medium-high heat and cook until the sugar has completely dissolved. While the sugar is dissolving, combine the cucumbers and red onions in a bowl. Pour the hot vinegar mixture over the cucumbers and onions, stir to coat, and let them cool to room temperature.

6 SERVINGS

SPICY CILANTRO-SCALLION RICE

    2 tablespoons **vegetable oil** (eyeball it)
    1 **serrano or jalapeño pepper**, halved lengthwise and seeded
    2 **garlic cloves**, crushed
    2 cups **long-grain white rice**
      Salt and **freshly ground black pepper**
    4 cups **chicken stock**
  $^{1}/_{2}$ cup fresh **cilantro** leaves, 2 generous handfuls, chopped
    6 **scallions**, thinly sliced

Heat a medium sauce pot over medium-high heat with the vegetable oil, 2 times around the pan. Add the pepper halves and the garlic cloves, cook for about 1 minute, then add the rice and stir to coat it with the oil. Season with salt and pepper. Add the chicken stock and bring the liquid to a boil. Cover the rice, reduce the heat to very low, and cook the rice for 18 to 20 minutes, until it's tender. Add the cilantro and scallions and fluff the rice with a fork.

Remove what's left of the pepper halves; some small pieces may have broken away but they will be tender and flavorful.

6 SERVINGS

SEARED SALMON WITH SOY AND GARLIC

  $^{1}/_{4}$ cup **tamari** (dark soy sauce; eyeball it)
    1 **garlic clove**, finely chopped
  $^{1}/_{2}$ tablespoon **ground coriander**, $^{1}/_{2}$ palmful
    6 skinless **salmon fillets**, 6 ounces each
    3 tablespoons **vegetable oil** (eyeball it)
      Freshly ground black pepper

In a shallow dish, combine the tamari, garlic, and coriander. Add the salmon fillets, turn to coat them, and let them marinate for about 5 minutes.

continued

Preheat a large nonstick skillet over medium-high heat with the vegetable oil, 3 times around the pan. Remove the salmon fillets from the marinade; season them with a little pepper and add them to the hot skillet skin side down. Cook the salmon until it's just cooked through, 3 to 4 minutes on each side.

Serve the salmon on the rice, topped with some of the relish.

6 SERVINGS

■ ■ ■

SANDWICH NIGHT

- **Uptown Sweet and Spicy Sausage Hoagies**
- **Bitter Greens and Dijon Dressing**
- **Brownies à la mode**

Not that I ever really tire of the typical downtown or ballpark sausage, pepper, and onion hoagies with melted Provolone, but stake them to a ride uptown and you can entertain with them! Entertaining with casual foods always makes for a good time. The beets (yes, I said beets) in this hoagie make a yum-o balance with the spicy sausage and peppers.

UPTOWN SWEET AND SPICY SAUSAGE HOAGIES

1	pound **sweet Italian sausages**
1	pound **hot Italian sausages**
3	tablespoons **EVOO** (extra-virgin olive oil), plus a little more for drizzling
3	large **garlic cloves**, crushed
2	large **red onions**, thinly sliced
2	**cubanelle peppers** (light green, mild Italian peppers), seeded and thinly sliced
2	**red bell peppers**, seeded and thinly sliced
	Leaves from 6 fresh **thyme sprigs**, coarsely chopped
$^1/_2$	teaspoon **red pepper flakes**
	Salt and **black pepper**
6	crusty **semolina submarine sandwich rolls**, sesame seeded or plain
3	tablespoons **balsamic vinegar** (eyeball it)
$^1/_2$	cup **chicken stock** (eyeball it)
1	15-ounce can **sliced beets**, drained and cut into sticks
8	ounces **ricotta salata cheese**, crumbled
4	cups **arugula**, washed, stemmed, and coarsely chopped

continued

Preheat the broiler.

Place the sausages in a large nonstick skillet and pierce the casings with a fork. Add 1 inch of water to the pan and a drizzle of oil. Cover the skillet and bring the liquid to a boil. Remove the cover, reduce the heat, and simmer for 10 minutes. Let the water cook off and the casings crisp in the rendered fat.

Heat a second large skillet over medium-high heat. Add the EVOO, garlic, red onions, peppers, thyme, red pepper flakes, salt, and black pepper. Cook the veggies, stirring frequently, for 8 to 10 minutes, or until they start to take on color.

Drain the sausages and slice them on an angle into 2-inch pieces. Return the skillet to the stove, turning the heat to medium high. Add a drizzle of oil to the skillet, then add the sliced sausage pieces and brown up the cut sides.

Split the sub rolls and toast them under the broiler until golden.

Add the vinegar, chicken stock, and beets to the peppers and onions and cook until the beets are heated through and the liquid has almost completely cooked away. Add the veggies to the browned sausage slices and toss them to combine and pick up the drippings from the meat. Pile the sausages and veggies into the sub rolls. Top each with crumbled cheese and arugula.

6 SERVINGS

BITTER GREENS AND DIJON DRESSING

- 2 tablespoons **grainy Dijon mustard**
- 3 tablespoons **white wine vinegar** (eyeball it)
  Salt and **black pepper**
- $^1/_3$ cup **EVOO** (extra-virgin olive oil; eyeball it)
- 1 pint **red cherry tomatoes**, halved
- 1 pint **yellow cherry tomatoes**, halved
- 2 heads of **escarole**, washed and torn into bite-size pieces

In a salad bowl, combine the mustard, white wine vinegar, salt, and pepper. In a slow, steady stream, whisk in the EVOO. Add the tomatoes and escarole. Toss to combine. Serve.

6 SERVINGS

BROWNIES À LA MODE

- 6 large **store-bought brownies**
- 1 pint **cherry vanilla ice cream**
- 1 pint **chocolate ice cream**
- 8 ounces **store-bought chocolate sauce**, such as Hershey's chocolate syrup

Arrange the brownies on a microwave-safe plate and heat them in the microwave, checking them at 40-second intervals, until they are nice and warm. Arrange each warm brownie on a dessert plate, top each with a small scoop of the cherry vanilla and a small scoop of chocolate ice cream, then drizzle them with some of the chocolate sauce.

6 SERVINGS

RICH FLAVOR, SMALL PRICES

- **Hearty Sausage and Mushroom Stew over Polenta**
- **Caramelized Cayenne Pear and Blue Cheese Salad**
- **Flourless Chocolate Cake with Whipped Cream and Raspberries (store-bought)**

Polenta is as cheap as pasta, and quick-cooking polenta is five times faster to make. Need I explain further? It is simply a great go-to when you have people coming over.

HEARTY SAUSAGE AND MUSHROOM STEW OVER POLENTA

4 cups **chicken stock**

2 cups **milk**

5 **garlic cloves**, 2 crushed from their skins, 3 chopped

Salt and **black pepper**

1 cup **beef stock**

1 2-ounce package **dried porcini mushrooms**

4 tablespoons **EVOO** (extra-virgin olive oil; eyeball it)

1 pound **bulk hot Italian sausage**

2 pounds small **button mushrooms**, wiped clean with a damp towel, left whole if small, halved if larger

4 large **portobello mushroom caps**, thickly sliced (don't be precious about it, just run your knife through them)

1 pound fresh **shiitake mushrooms**, stemmed, caps halved

6 to 8 fresh **sage** leaves, chopped

1 large **onion**, finely chopped

3/4 cup **dry red wine**

2 cups **quick-cooking polenta**, found in the Italian or specialty foods aisles

1 cup grated **Parmigiano-Reggiano** cheese

3 tablespoons **butter**

1¹/₂ cups fresh **basil**, about 25 leaves, coarsely chopped or torn

Combine the chicken stock, milk, crushed garlic cloves, and a little salt and pepper in a large sauce pot. Bring it up to a simmer and then lower the heat until you are ready to add the polenta.

In a small sauce pot, bring the beef stock to a boil over high heat. Add the dried mushrooms, turn the heat off, and let them steep to rehydrate while you get the fresh mushrooms going.

Preheat a large skillet over medium-high heat with 2 tablespoons of the EVOO, 2 times around the pan. Add the sausage and break it up into little bits, using a wooden spoon. Brown it, stirring every now and then, for 5 minutes. Once it is brown, remove the sausage from the skillet and drain it on a paper-towel-lined plate. Drain all but about 2 tablespoons of the fat from the skillet, return the skillet to the stove over high heat, and add the remaining 2 tablespoons of EVOO. Add the fresh mushrooms, sage, and some pepper. Cook the mushrooms without stirring for 3 to 4 minutes, then give them a stir and cook for another 10 minutes, stirring every now and then. Add the chopped garlic, onions, and a little salt and continue to cook for 3 or 4 minutes. Add the wine and let it cook down for about a minute. Use a slotted spoon to remove the rehydrated porcini mushrooms from the beef stock and add them to the sautéed mushrooms. Line a small strainer or the corner of a colander with a paper coffee filter and pour all of the fortified beef stock through it and into the skillet. (Sometimes the dried mushrooms contain a little grit; you're removing it without giving up a drop of that fortified stock.) Return the sausage to the skillet, bring the mixture up to a bubble, and cook it until the liquids have reduced by half.

continued

Back to the polenta: remove the crushed garlic cloves from the chicken stock and milk, whisk in the polenta in a slow and steady stream, and cook, stirring frequently, for about 5 minutes. Turn the heat off and add the cheese, stirring it to combine. If the polenta gets a little too thick for your liking, add a little more stock or milk and that will loosen it up. Polenta is very understanding and forgiving.

Once the liquids in the stew have reduced by half, turn the heat off, add the butter and basil, and stir the stew until the butter has melted.

Serve each helping of the sausage and mushroom stew over a portion of the polenta.

6 SERVINGS

CARAMELIZED CAYENNE PEAR AND BLUE CHEESE SALAD

    3 tablespoons **sugar**
 1/4 teaspoon **cayenne pepper**
    2 **firm pears**, halved, cored, and cut into 10 to 12 long wedges
       Juice of 2 lemons
       Salt and **freshly ground black pepper**
 1/4 cup **EVOO** (extra-virgin olive oil; eyeball it)
    1 cup **crumbled blue cheese**
    2 pounds **triple-washed spinach** or mixed greens
    1 cup **toasted walnut pieces**

Thoroughly combine the sugar, cayenne, and 2 tablespoons water in a medium-size nonstick skillet and place the skillet over high heat. Once it starts getting hot, you will notice that the bubbles will start out slow, speed up, and then slow down again. Once they slow down again, it's time to really keep your eye on the skillet. The sugar will start to brown and get dark soon after the bubbles slow down that second time, but don't let it burn. Once the sugar browns up a bit, add the pear wedges, toss to coat in the sugar mixture, and cook them for 1 or 2 minutes. Transfer the pear wedges to a cookie sheet and spread them out in a single layer to cool.

While the pears are cooling, combine the lemon juice with a little salt and pepper in a salad bowl. In a slow, steady stream, whisk in the EVOO.

Once you are ready to serve and the pears are completely cool, add the blue cheese crumbles and the greens to the lemon and olive oil dressing. Add the pears and walnuts, then toss to coat.

6 SERVINGS

■ ■ ■

• Get the water for the noodles going and toast the nuts for the salad.

• Make the salad and dressing while the chicken simmers.

• Cook the noodles and toss the salad.

FRENCH AND FABULOUS

- **White Burgundy Chicken over Buttered Egg Noodles**
- **Honey-Dijon Dressed Greens with Toasted Pecans**
- **Mixed Fruit Tart (store-bought)**

The key to achieving great flavor in this style of French country cooking is getting the ingredients nice and brown and caramelized. Since you're making such a large amount of food, I've split up the browning between two pots. True, it means another pot to wash, but you cooked, so you shouldn't have to do the dishes, too. Even if you do get stuck scrubbing, the full flavor will be worth it.

WHITE BURGUNDY CHICKEN OVER BUTTERED EGG NOODLES

Salt

1¹/₂ pounds **wide egg noodles**

6 tablespoons (³/₄ stick) **butter**

¹/₂ cup fresh **flat-leaf parsley** leaves, 2 generous handfuls, coarsely chopped

Black pepper

4 tablespoons **EVOO** (extra-virgin olive oil), plus a little more as necessary

6 boneless, skinless **chicken breasts**, 6 ounces each, cut into bite-size pieces

2 cups **white burgundy wine**

1 16-ounce bag **frozen pearl onions**, defrosted and patted dry on kitchen towels

4 **garlic cloves**, smashed

¹/₂ pound **baby carrots**

5 **celery ribs**

6 **fresh thyme** sprigs

2 **bay leaves**, fresh or dried

3 tablespoons all-purpose **flour**

3 cups **chicken stock**

1 10-ounce box **frozen peas**, defrosted

Fill a large covered pot with water and bring to a boil over high heat. Once it's at a boil, add some salt and the egg noodles and cook them according to the package directions. Drain the noodles really well, then transfer them to a large bowl. Add 3 tablespoons of the butter, the parsley, and a little salt and pepper. Keep warm.

While the water is coming up to a boil, preheat a large nonstick skillet with 2 tablespoons of the EVOO, 2 times around the pan, over medium-high to high heat. Preheat a second pan, a large Dutch oven or heavy-bottomed soup pot, over medium heat. Season the chicken liberally with salt and pepper, add half of the chicken to the skillet, and brown it for about 2 minutes on each side. Remove the browned chicken to a plate and return the skillet to the heat. Add a little more oil and the remaining chicken, and brown it on both sides. Combine all the browned meat and deglaze the pan with 1 cup of the wine, using a wooden spoon to scrape up all the brown bits. Remove from the heat.

While the first batch of chicken is cooking, add the remaining 2 tablespoons of EVOO and 3 tablespoons of butter to the Dutch oven or soup pot. Once the butter starts to bubble, add the pearl onions and garlic cloves and brown them for 4 to 5 minutes, until they are nice and brown all over. Cut the baby carrots in half lengthwise and cut the celery into $1^{1}/_{2}$- to 2-inch pieces, about the same length as the carrots. Strip the leaves off the thyme sprigs and chop, then add the baby carrots, celery, thyme, and bay leaves to the pearl onions and season them with salt and pepper. Cook the vegetables, stirring them frequently, for 2 minutes more. Sprinkle them with the flour and cook them for 1 minute, then add the remaining cup of wine and the liquid from the chicken skillet. Add the chicken stock and bring everything up to a bubble, then add the reserved chicken and simmer everything together for 10 minutes. Add the peas and cook them until they're heated through, about 1 minute. Discard the bay leaves.

Serve over the buttered egg noodles.

6 SERVINGS

HONEY-DIJON DRESSED GREENS WITH TOASTED PECANS

1¹/₂ cups **pecan halves**

2 tablespoons **Dijon mustard**

2 tablespoons **honey**

3 tablespoons **white wine vinegar**

Salt and **black pepper**

¹/₄ cup **EVOO** (extra-virgin olive oil)

6 really big handfuls of **mixed greens**

Preheat the oven to 350° F.

Place the pecans on a rimmed baking sheet and toast them in the oven for 10 to 12 minutes, or until they smell and look nice and toasted. Remove them from the oven, cool them a bit, then run your knife through them once, just to break them up a little.

For the dressing, combine the mustard, honey, vinegar, and a little salt and pepper in a bowl. Whisk in the EVOO in a slow, steady stream. Arrange the greens in a large salad bowl, top them with the nuts and dressing, and toss them to coat thoroughly.

6 SERVINGS

■ ■ ■

FIREHOUSE SPECIAL

- Get the pasta water going.

- While the pasta cooks, brown the beef and start the bacon.

- Toast the chick-peas while the chili simmers.

- Finish the salads while the chili mac browns.

- Smoky Bacon and Bean Salad
- Three-Alarm Italian-Style Chili Mac
- Pistachio Ice Cream (store-bought)

Firemen are HOT! There's something about *any* man in a uniform, it's true, but firemen—wow! They carry big, heavy axes, not guns. They have that smoky, battle-worn gear—and look so strong and sexy. They know how to tame a wild hose and, best of all, they know how to cook! They're all locked up together around the clock when they're on duty, so they know their way around a flaming stovetop better than most. Keep those pots hot, gentlemen. This one's for you! If you'll excuse me, I think I need a tall drink of cold water now.

THREE-ALARM ITALIAN-STYLE CHILI MAC

Salt

1 pound **penne rigate** or cavatappi (hollow corkscrew pasta)

2 tablespoons **EVOO** (extra-virgin olive oil)

1½ pounds **ground sirloin**

2 tablespoons **chili powder**, 2 palmfuls

Black pepper

1 **onion**, chopped

1 **cubanelle pepper**, seeded and chopped

1 **red bell pepper**, seeded and chopped

3 to 4 **garlic cloves**, chopped

1 cup **beef stock**

1 28-ounce can **crushed fire-roasted tomatoes**

Handful of fresh **basil leaves**, torn

2 cups **shredded smoked cheddar** or scamorza (smoked aged mozzarella)

Bring a large covered pot of water to a boil for the pasta. When it boils, salt the water, add the pasta, and cook to al dente. Preheat the broiler.

continued

While the water for the pasta comes up to a boil and the pasta cooks, heat the EVOO in a deep skillet over medium-high heat. When the oil ripples or smokes, add the beef and break it up with a wooden spoon, stirring and crumbling it for 5 to 6 minutes. Season the meat with the chili powder and salt and pepper. When the meat has browned, add the onions, peppers, and garlic. Cook until the vegetables are soft, 6 to 7 minutes. Add the stock and scrape up the pan drippings. Stir in the crushed tomatoes and simmer the sauce for 10 minutes. Fold in the basil, drain the pasta, toss the pasta in the pan to combine, and transfer the mixture to a casserole dish. Sprinkle the chili mac with the cheese and brown it under the broiler for 3 to 4 minutes.

6 SERVINGS

SMOKY BACON AND BEAN SALAD

1/3 cup **EVOO** (extra-virgin olive oil), plus some for drizzling

4 slices **bacon**, chopped

2 15-ounce cans **chickpeas**, rinsed and patted dry with paper towels
   Salt
   A few healthy pinches of **red pepper flakes**

3 **hearts of romaine**, chopped

1 rounded teaspoon **Dijon mustard**

3 tablespoons **balsamic vinegar** (eyeball it)

Heat a small skillet over medium-high heat. Add a drizzle of EVOO and the bacon. Crisp the bacon, then transfer it to a paper-towel-lined plate. Add the chickpeas and reduce the heat to medium. Cook them until they're toasted and lightly browned, 10 to 12 minutes. Season the chickpeas with salt and red pepper flakes and let them cool.

Place the greens in a salad bowl with the chickpeas. Whisk together the mustard, vinegar, and the 1/3 cup of EVOO. Add the bacon and dressing to the salad and toss to coat it evenly.

6 SERVINGS

EAT YOUR VEGETABLES AND ENJOY

- **Creamy Polenta with Veggie Ragù**
- **Angel Food Cake with Strawberries and Apricots and Sweetened Whipped Cream (store-bought)**

Rarely has going veggie tasted so satisfying as with the help of creamy polenta. You can make this one hundred percent vegetarian by using vegetable stock rather than chicken stock, but if a little meat is what you and yours like, then add some bulk sweet Italian sausage to the skillet before you start to cook up the fennel and other veggies. Or, you can simply finish off the ragù with some strips of prosciutto or Serrano ham.

CREAMY POLENTA WITH VEGGIE RAGÙ

1 large head of **cauliflower**, about 2 pounds, cut into bite-size florets

3 tablespoons **EVOO** (extra-virgin olive oil; eyeball it), plus some for drizzling
  Salt and **black pepper**

6 cups **chicken or vegetable stock**

2 cups **milk** (eyeball it)

1 large **fennel bulb**, cored and thinly sliced

1 large **onion**, thinly sliced

4 large **garlic cloves**, chopped

2 **red bell peppers**, seeded and sliced

$^1/_2$ teaspoon **red pepper flakes**

$^1/_2$ cup **golden raisins**, 1 overflowing handful

2 cups **quick-cooking polenta**, found in the Italian or specialty foods aisles

1 head of **escarole**, washed and coarsely chopped

2 tablespoons **butter**

$^1/_2$ cup grated **Parmigiano-Reggiano**, a couple of generous handfuls, plus more to pass at the table

$^1/_2$ cup fresh **flat-leaf parsley** leaves, 2 generous handfuls, chopped

continued

MEALS FOR 6

209

Preheat the oven to 450° F.

Arrange the cauliflower on a rimmed baking sheet, drizzle it generously with EVOO, then season it with salt and pepper, tossing it around to make sure all of it is coated. Roast the cauliflower for 15 minutes, or until it's lightly browned and tender but still has a bit of a bite.

While the cauliflower is roasting, combine 4 cups of the chicken stock and the milk in a sauce pot. Add salt and pepper and bring it up to a simmer, then turn the heat down until you are ready to add the polenta.

Place a large skillet over medium-high heat with the 3 tablespoons of EVOO. Add the fennel, onions, garlic, bell peppers, and red pepper flakes and season them with a little salt and black pepper. Cook, stirring frequently, for about 5 minutes, or until the veggies are approaching being tender. Add the remaining 2 cups of chicken stock and bring it up to a simmer, then continue to cook for 4 or 5 minutes.

Add the roasted cauliflower and the raisins, toss them to combine, and continue to cook them for 3 to 4 minutes, or until the liquids have reduced by half.

Once you've added the cauliflower to the skillet, finish the polenta. Using a whisk, add the polenta to the simmering stock and milk mixture; cook, stirring constantly, for about 5 minutes. Be careful; the closest you'll probably ever come to having hot lava in your kitchen is a pot of bubbling polenta. Once the polenta is cooked, add the chopped escarole to the skillet with the cauliflower and cook it until the escarole wilts, a couple of minutes.

Add the butter and cheese to the polenta, and stir them to melt in. If the polenta thickens too much, add a little more stock or milk to loosen it up.

Add the parsley to the skillet with the cauliflower and combine. To serve, place a helping of the polenta in the bottom of 6 shallow serving dishes and top it with some of the veggie ragù. Serve it along with a little more cheese to pass at the table.

6 SERVINGS

MOVIE MARATHON

GAME PLAN

- Start the mush-rooms for the French bread pizza.

- Make and top the white and puttanesca pizzas.

- While they bake, make the French bread pizza.

- **White Pizza**
- **Really French, French Bread Pizza**
- **Puttanesca Pizza**

Here's a pizza feast to take you through all three versions of *King Kong* on DVD. Invite some friends over to help you eat your way through them all. Even if you have the appetite of a gorilla, you'll need help, just like Faye Wray did. Or, you can make the pizzas one at a time, for movie nights when you're holding just one or two tickets for the sofa.

WHITE PIZZA

1 store-bought **pizza dough** or pick one up from your favorite pizzeria
EVOO (extra-virgin olive oil), for drizzling

2 cups whole or part-skim **ricotta cheese**

2 **garlic cloves**, finely chopped
Handful of fresh **flat-leaf parsley** leaves, finely chopped
Salt and **freshly ground black pepper**

2 cups **shredded mozzarella or Provolone cheese**

1/2 cup fresh **basil**, 10 leaves, shredded

Preheat the oven and a pizza stone, if you use one, to 425° F.

Stretch the dough to form a pie and transfer it to a stone or a pizza pan. Prick the dough with the tines of a fork in several places. Drizzle some EVOO over the dough. Mix the ricotta cheese with the garlic and parsley and season it with salt and pepper. Spread the dough with the ricotta and top it with mozzarella or Provolone. Bake the pizza until the crust is crispy, 20 minutes. Top the white pizza with the shredded basil leaves, cut, and serve.

6 SERVINGS

REALLY FRENCH, FRENCH BREAD PIZZA

- 2 pounds **large white mushrooms**
- 2 tablespoons **EVOO** (extra-virgin olive oil)
- 2 tablespoons **butter**, cut into pieces
- 1 **bay leaf**
- 4 **garlic cloves**, thinly sliced
  Salt and **black pepper**
- 1/3 cup **dry white wine** (eyeball it)
- 2 teaspoons **Dijon mustard**
- 2 teaspoons **Worcestershire sauce** (eyeball it)
- 1 tablespoon chopped fresh **thyme leaves**
- 1 24-inch **crusty baguette**
- 3 cups shredded **Swiss cheese**, such as Gruyère

Wipe the mushrooms clean with a damp paper towel. Slice the mushrooms. Heat a deep skillet with the EVOO and butter over medium heat. When the butter melts into the oil, add the bay leaf, garlic, and mushrooms. Cook until the mushrooms are dark and tender, 12 to 15 minutes. Season the mushrooms with salt and pepper and add the wine. Stir to deglaze the pan, then add the mustard, Worcestershire, and thyme. Turn off the heat. Discard the bay leaf.

Preheat the broiler.

Split the baguette lengthwise and across. Hollow out a bit of the soft insides. Toast the bread lightly under the broiler. Fill the toasted bread evenly with mushrooms, then top it generously with the cheese. Place the bread on a baking sheet. Return the bread to the broiler and melt the cheese until it browns and bubbles. Cut each portion into thirds and serve.

6 SERVINGS

PUTTANESCA PIZZA

2 tablespoons **EVOO** (extra-virgin olive oil)

3 **garlic cloves**, finely chopped

2 tablespoons **anchovy paste** or 6 flat anchovy fillets

$^1/_2$ teaspoon **red pepper flakes**

1 28-ounce can **diced fire-roasted tomatoes**, very well drained

$^1/_2$ cup chopped **good-quality pitted black olives**

Handful of fresh **flat-leaf parsley** leaves, chopped

1 Boboli **thin-crust pizza shell**

2 cups **shredded scamorza cheese** (smoked aged mozzarella)

Preheat the oven to 425° F.

Heat a medium skillet over medium heat. Add the EVOO, garlic, anchovy paste, and red pepper flakes. When the anchovies (if whole) melt into the oil or the garlic is tender, about 2 minutes, add the tomatoes, olives, and parsley. Simmer the sauce for 3 to 4 minutes. Top the pizza crust with the sauce and the cheese. Bake the pizza until the cheese melts and the crust is crisp, about 10 minutes. Cut and serve.

6 SERVINGS

■ ■ ■

MEXICAN AGAIN AND AGAIN

- **Warm Tortilla Chips and Salsas (store-bought)**
- **Grilled Mexican Beef Soup over Rice**
- **Churro Fake-Out**

Start this menu off with warm chips and a varied selection of salsas. Crisp the chips in a low oven and serve them in baskets with mild tomatillo salsa; spicy fresh tomato salsa from the market's refrigerated case; and a hot, smoky chipotle salsa. The soup is spicy but the rice mellows the heat. Finish off the evening with a speedy version of churros, which are like crullers coated in cinnamon and sugar and are delicious dipped in hot chocolate.

GRILLED MEXICAN BEEF SOUP OVER RICE

3 tablespoons **vegetable oil**, plus some for drizzling the steaks

1 tablespoon **butter**

2 cups **long-grain white rice**

Salt and **black pepper**

2 to 2$\frac{1}{2}$ pounds **flank steak**

1 tablespoon **chili powder**, a palmful

1 large **red onion**, thinly sliced

2 **poblano peppers**, seeded and thinly sliced

1 **red bell pepper**, thinly sliced

3 large **garlic cloves**, chopped

1 tablespoon **ground cumin**, a palmful

$\frac{1}{2}$ tablespoon **ground coriander**, $\frac{1}{2}$ palmful

6 cups **chicken stock**

Juice of 2 limes

A generous handful of fresh **cilantro** leaves, chopped
A generous handful of fresh **flat-leaf parsley** leaves, chopped
2 **Hass avocados**, diced
Hot sauce to taste

Preheat an outdoor grill or get a double burner grill pan very hot.

Heat a medium sauce pot over medium-high heat. Add 1 tablespoon of the vegetable oil and the butter; once the butter melts add the rice, season it with salt and pepper, and lightly brown the rice for 1 minute. Add 4 cups of water. Bring the liquid to a boil, then cover the rice and reduce the heat to very low. Cook the rice for 18 minutes, or until it's tender.

Drizzle the flank steak with a little vegetable oil and season with the chili powder and some salt and pepper. Grill the steak for 6 to 7 minutes on each side. Remove the steak to a cutting board and let rest for about 5 minutes, loosely covered with a piece of aluminum foil.

Heat a large soup pot over medium-high heat with the remaining 2 tablespoons of oil. Add the onions, poblano and bell peppers, and the garlic. Season the vegetables with salt, pepper, and the cumin and coriander. Cook them, stirring frequently, for about 3 minutes. Add the chicken stock, cover the pot, and bring it up to a simmer. Remove the lid and simmer the broth for 10 minutes.

To serve, slice the flank steak very thin on a slight angle. Add the lime juice, cilantro, and parsley to the soup. Divide the rice among 6 shallow soup bowls, then ladle some of the broth and veggies over the rice. Top it with sliced steak. Garnish each bowl with some of the diced avocados. Bring the bottle of hot sauce to the table for those who crave the heat.

6 SERVINGS

06

CHURRO FAKE-OUT

1$^1/_2$ cups store-bought **chocolate sauce**
1$^1/_2$ cups store-bought **caramel sauce**
  2 tablespoons **sugar**, 2 palmfuls
  1 teaspoon **ground cinnamon**, $^1/_3$ palmful
  1 tablespoon **cocoa powder**, 1 palmful
  6 small **cinnamon doughnuts**
  2 pints **vanilla bean, cinnamon, or chocolate ice cream**

Warm up both the chocolate sauce and the caramel sauce in the microwave or standing, uncovered, in a pot of hot water on the stovetop. In a bowl, combine the sugar, cinnamon, and cocoa powder. Place each doughnut on a dessert plate or in a bowl. Top the doughnuts with a scoop of ice cream and drizzle with the chocolate and caramel sauces. Sprinkle each serving with some of the sugar mixture.

6 SERVINGS

■ ■ ■

ROSY CHEEKS

- **Chicken Sausage with Sweet Fennel and Gnocchi in a Blushing Cream Sauce**
- **Cucumber, Radicchio, and Radish Salad**
- **Chocolate and Pistachio Ice Cream with Biscotti (store-bought)**

This menu makes me think of rosy-faced, dark-eyed, well-fed children. The blushing sauce, potato-pillow dumplings, and cookies and ice cream will turn the staunchest group into Little Rascals again.

CUCUMBER, RADICCHIO, AND RADISH SALAD

06

1 **shallot**, finely chopped

3 tablespoons **balsamic vinegar** (eyeball it)

Salt and **black pepper**

$^1/_3$ cup **EVOO** (extra-virgin olive oil; eyeball it)

2 **seedless cucumbers**, cut in half lengthwise then sliced into half moons

1 large **head of radicchio**, cored and shredded

10 **radishes**, thinly sliced

Combine the chopped shallot, balsamic, and a little salt and pepper in a salad bowl. In a slow, steady stream, pour in the EVOO while whisking to combine. Add the cucumbers, radicchio, and radishes, and toss them to coat. Taste the salad and adjust the seasoning.

6 SERVINGS

MEALS FOR 6

CHICKEN SAUSAGE WITH SWEET FENNEL AND GNOCCHI IN A BLUSHING CREAM SAUCE

When shopping for the chicken sausages, check the label for heat-and-eat rather than raw sausage; most packaged chicken sausages are of this variety. Also, choose an Italian-inspired flavor.

Salt

3 tablespoons **EVOO** (extra-virgin olive oil)

8 precooked **chicken sausages**, sliced

2 large **onions**, thinly sliced

3 large **garlic cloves**, chopped

1 large **fennel bulb**, cored and thinly sliced

Black pepper

2 tablespoons **tomato paste** (the kind in a squeeze tube stores easily in the refrigerator)

3/4 cup **white wine** (eyeball it)

2 pounds **gnocchi** (Italian potato dumplings; in the refrigerated or frozen foods section of the market)

2 1/2 cups **chicken stock** (eyeball it)

2 ounces **cream cheese** (eyeball it), cut into small pieces

1 cup fresh **flat-leaf parsley** leaves, 4 generous handfuls, chopped

1/2 cup grated **Parmigiano-Reggiano** cheese, a couple generous handfuls, plus some to pass at the table

Bring a large covered pot of water to a boil over high heat to cook the gnocchi. Once the water is boiling add some salt but don't add the gnocchi yet.

Heat the EVOO in a very large skillet over medium-high heat. Add the sliced chicken sausages and brown them for about 5 minutes. Add the onions, garlic, fennel, and a little salt and pepper and continue to cook for 5 more minutes. Scoot the sausages and veggies over to one side of the skillet and add the tomato paste to the pan, spreading it out a bit on the bottom of the skillet. Cook the tomato paste for a minute, then add the white wine and cook it for 1 minute, using a wooden spoon to scrape up any bits on the bottom of the skillet.

At this point, add the gnocchi to the boiling salted water and cook according to the package instructions, about 4 minutes for fresh and 6 minutes for frozen.

Add the chicken stock to the skillet with the sausages and bring it up to a bubble. Add the cream cheese and stir it to combine; simmer for a couple minutes to thicken it.

Drain the gnocchi and add them to the skillet with the sausages, tossing to coat with the sauce. If you don't think your skillet is large enough to accommodate both the sauce and the cooked gnocchi then you can combine the sauce and gnocchi in a serving bowl or in the large pot you cooked the gnocchi in. Add the parsley and cheese, stir them to combine, and serve with more cheese to pass at the table.

6 SERVINGS

■ ■ ■

COUNTRY MILE MENU

- Get the potatoes in the oven.

- Make the salad and dressing while the chicken is in the oven.

- Make the cider sauce and toss the salad.

- Make and assemble the desserts just before serving.

- Cider-Sauced Chicken Breasts
- Roasted Potatoes Tossed in Garlic Butter
- Watercress and Endive Salad
- Warm Blueberries and Vanilla Ice Cream

Where I come from, we'll walk a country mile for apple-anything. In this menu, the bite of apple cider vinegar makes a great flavor partner for the sweet apple cider. The peppery flavor of the watercress and tang of the mustard in the salad make a great companion to the cider-sauced chicken. Bottom line: you are in store for a simply elegant dinner.

WATERCRESS AND ENDIVE SALAD

2 tablespoons **Dijon mustard**

1 large **shallot**, finely minced

3 tablespoons **white wine vinegar**

Salt and **black pepper**

$^{1}/_{2}$ cup **EVOO** (extra-virgin olive oil; eyeball it)

4 large bunches of **watercress**, trimmed of thick stems

3 **Belgian endives**, leaves separated from the cores

In a bowl, combine the mustard, shallots, vinegar, and a little salt and pepper. Whisk the EVOO into the mustard mixture in a slow, steady stream.

Combine the watercress and endive leaves in a salad bowl, pour the dressing over the greens, and toss them to coat.

6 SERVINGS

CIDER-SAUCED CHICKEN BREASTS

3 tablespoons **EVOO** (extra-virgin olive oil; eyeball it)
6 boneless, skinless **chicken breasts**, 6 ounces each
   Salt and **black pepper**
1 large **onion**, finely chopped
6 fresh **thyme sprigs**, leaves removed and coarsely chopped
3 **garlic cloves**, chopped
1 **Gala apple**, peeled, cored, and cut into thin wedges
2 tablespoons **dark brown sugar**
$^1/_2$ cup **apple cider** (eyeball it)
3 tablespoons **apple cider vinegar** (eyeball it)
2 cups **chicken stock** (eyeball it)
3 tablespoons cold **butter**
$^1/_2$ cup fresh **flat-leaf parsley** leaves, 2 generous handfuls, chopped

Preheat the oven to 500° F.

You'll need an extra-large oven-safe skillet that will fit 6 chicken breasts without overcrowding. (If you don't have one that big, use the largest one you have for 4 of the chicken breasts and a medium one for the remaining 2 breasts.) Preheat the skillet over medium-high heat with the EVOO, 3 times around the pan. Season the chicken breasts liberally with salt and pepper, add them to the skillet, and brown them on both sides, about 6 minutes total. Remove the chicken to a baking pan or rimmed baking sheet and transfer them to the oven to cook for 10 minutes more, or until their juices run clear when pierced with a sharp knife.

Return the skillet to the stovetop over medium-high heat and add the onions, thyme, garlic, apples, and brown sugar. (If you used 2 skillets do this step in the larger of the skillets.) Cook, stirring frequently, for 4 to 5 minutes. Add the apple cider and vinegar and cook for about 2 minutes. Add the chicken stock, turn the heat up to high, and simmer until the liquid is reduced by about half, or until it is slightly thickened. Turn the heat off, add the butter and parsley, and stir until the butter is incorporated. Serve the apple cider sauce over the chicken breasts.

6 SERVINGS

ROASTED POTATOES TOSSED IN GARLIC BUTTER

5 **all-purpose potatoes**, scrubbed and dried
4 tablespoons **EVOO** (extra-virgin olive oil; eyeball it)
   Salt and **black pepper**
4 tablespoons (1/2 stick) **butter**
3 **garlic cloves**, chopped
   A generous handful of fresh **flat-leaf parsley** leaves, chopped

Preheat the oven to 500° F.

Cut the unpeeled potatoes in half lengthwise and then again in long, thin wedges; try to get 8 wedges out of each potato. Place them on a rimmed baking sheet and coat the potatoes in a thin layer of EVOO, then season them with some salt and pepper. Toss the potatoes to coat them evenly. Roast the potatoes for 25 minutes, or until they are crisp and golden at the edges. A few minutes before you remove the potatoes from the oven, place a small pot or pan over medium heat with 2 tablespoons of the butter and the garlic, and cook gently for 1 to 2 minutes, just to mellow out the raw garlic flavor. Transfer the garlic butter to a serving bowl and add the roasted potatoes, parsley, and the remaining 2 tablespoons of butter. Toss the potatoes until the butter melts and the potatoes are well coated. Taste and add a little more salt and pepper if you think the potatoes need it.

6 SERVINGS

WARM BLUEBERRIES AND VANILLA ICE CREAM

The rule in my house is the cook is off the hook when it comes to the dishes; it's only fair. Encourage your mate or take the first volunteer up on his or her offer to clear the table once dinner is wrapping up. That way you can throw together this quick dessert.

$^1/_2$ cup **sugar** (eyeball it)
2 pints **blueberries**
   Zest of 1 lemon
2 pints **vanilla bean ice cream**
12 **sugar cookies** or shortbread cookies

In a small sauce pot combine the sugar and enough water to make the sugar look like really wet sand. Place the pot over high heat and cook the mixture until the sugar dissolves. Add the blueberries and lemon zest and continue to cook, stirring, for about 2 minutes, or until a few of the berries start to burst. Serve the warm blueberries over a big scoop of vanilla ice cream. Stick 2 cookies into each serving of ice cream and you're done!

6 SERVINGS

■ ■ ■

GAME PLAN

• Get the chili on.

• Make the peach ice cream topping while the corn cakes cook.

• Assemble the desserts just before serving.

NASCAR MENU

• **Caution-Flag Chili**
• **Flat-Tire Corn and Black Bean Toppers**
• **Fired-Up Peaches and Cream**

I'm not into NASCAR, but I know it has become HUGE. What I *do* like is having another reason to create a new chili recipe. If you're into racing or just a fan of fiery foods, this one is for you! Serve with plenty of cold beer.

CAUTION-FLAG CHILI WITH FLAT-TIRE CORN AND BLACK BEAN TOPPERS

2 tablespoons **EVOO** (extra-virgin olive oil)

2 **poblano peppers**, seeded and thinly sliced

2 pounds **ground sirloin**

1 medium **onion**, chopped

3 to 4 **garlic cloves**, chopped

2 tablespoons **grill seasoning**, such as McCormick's Montreal Steak Seasoning, a couple palmfuls

2 tablespoons **Worcestershire sauce** (eyeball it)

2 **chipotles in adobo**, chopped, plus 1 tablespoon adobo sauce

1/2 cup **steak sauce**, such as Peter Luger or A.1.

1 cup **beer** (2/3 bottle)

1 cup **beef stock**

1 28-ounce can **crushed fire-roasted tomatoes**

1 package **corn muffin mix**, preferably Jiffy, made according to package directions for corn pancakes

1 15.5-ounce can **black beans**, rinsed, drained, and patted dry with paper towels

1/2 tablespoon ground **cumin**, 1/2 palmful

2 **scallions**, finely chopped

Softened **butter**, for greasing a griddle

Heat the EVOO in a medium soup pot over medium-high to high heat. When the oil smokes, add the sliced poblanos and char them for a couple of minutes, then scoot them off to the side of the pan and add the meat. Break up the beef and brown it for a couple of minutes, then add the onions and garlic. Season the meat with the grill seasoning, Worcestershire, chipotles, and adobo sauce. Cook until the onions are tender, 5 to 6 minutes more, then stir in the steak sauce and beer. Cook the beer off for 1 minute, then add the stock and tomatoes and reduce the heat to low.

Prepare the corn pancake batter according to the package instructions. Finely chop the beans in a food processor and stir them into the corn batter. Season the batter with the cumin, and stir in the scallions.

Heat a nonstick griddle pan over medium heat. Butter the griddle, then pour three 3- to 4-inch corn pancakes. Flip the cakes when the bottoms are deeply golden and cook them for another minute or two on the second side. Repeat with the remaining batter to make 6 cakes.

Top each bowlful of the chili with a corn and black bean pancake; these are your flat-tire toppers!

6 SERVINGS

FIRED-UP PEACHES AND CREAM

4 tablespoons ($^1/_2$ stick) **butter**, cut into small pieces

4 medium-ripe **peaches**, sliced

Pinch of ground **cinnamon**

$^1/_4$ cup **brown sugar**

4 shots **whisky**

2 pints **vanilla ice cream**

Whipped cream, from a canister (in the dairy case)

Heat a large skillet over medium heat. Add the butter, and when it melts, add the peaches. Season them with the cinnamon. Turn up the heat to medium high and cook the peaches for 3 minutes, then add the brown sugar and melt it into the butter. Pull the pan off the flame, add the whisky, then return the pan to the stove and dip the skillet to set the whisky aflame, or light it carefully with a kitchen match. When the flame dies out, scoop some ice cream into dishes, top them with peaches and sauce, add some whipped cream, and serve.

6 SERVINGS

TIDBIT

A shot, or jigger, is usually about 1$^1/_2$ ounces, but can be anything from 1 to 2 ounces (2 to 4 tablespoons).

■ ■ ■

POKER NIGHT

- **Texas Hold-Ums (mini chipotle beef burgers)**
- **Fire-Roasted Ketchup**
- **Lucky 7-Layer Dip**

Everyone is watching it on TV, playing it with their friends, betting hands of it online: Poker is *hot!* My hubby and I have a poker table in our apartment but we have no idea how to play. We are *always* bluffing. Mostly, we use the Vegas Room for enjoying cocktails and cigars with friends, but cocktails look cooler with poker chips next to them. Our friends Charlie, Kim, Jon, and Bruce have all threatened to teach us how to play; for now, though, we'll be at the food table, holding mini burgers rather than cards.

TEXAS HOLD-UMS WITH FIRE-ROASTED KETCHUP

- 2 pounds **ground sirloin**
- 1 medium **onion**, peeled and cut in half
- 2 tablespoons **Worcestershire sauce** (eyeball it)
- 2 **chipotles in adobo**, chopped, plus 2 tablespoons of the adobo sauce
- 2 tablespoons **grill seasoning**, such as McCormick's Montreal Steak Seasoning, a couple palmfuls
- 1 tablespoon **EVOO** (extra-virgin olive oil), plus some for drizzling
- 3 **garlic cloves**, finely chopped
- 3 tablespoons **brown sugar**
- 1/4 cup **vinegar**
- 1 15-ounce can **crushed fire-roasted tomatoes**
  Salt and **black pepper**
- 12 1/2-inch-thick slices **smoked cheddar** or sharp cheddar, cut from a brick of cheese, such as Cabot brand (optional)
- 12 small **round rolls**, split (many markets sell mini kaiser rolls, or use dinner rolls in any flavor you like)

continued

MEALS FOR 6

Preheat a grill pan until very hot.

Place the meat in a bowl. Grate half of the onion into the meat using the small holes on a box grater. Chop and reserve the other half of the onion. Add the Worcestershire, chipotles and adobo sauce, and grill seasoning to the meat mixture. Drizzle a little EVOO over the bowl and combine everything. Score the meat into 4 sections. Make 3 mini burgers, each 3 inches wide and 1 inch thick, from each of the 4 sections, for 12 in all.

Heat a small sauce pot over medium heat. Add the tablespoon of EVOO and the garlic. Cook the garlic for 2 to 3 minutes, then add the brown sugar and vinegar. Cook for 2 minutes more and stir in the tomatoes. Season the sauce with salt and pepper and cook it for 5 to 6 minutes more, to thicken a bit.

Grill the mini burgers for 2 to 3 minutes on each side and top them with cheese, if you like, after you turn them.

Place the burgers on buns and top them with raw chopped onions and some of the warm fire-roasted ketchup.

6 SERVINGS

LUCKY 7-LAYER DIP

1 15-ounce can **refried beans**
2 tablespoons **hot sauce**
   EVOO (extra-virgin olive oil), for drizzling
4 **scallions**, cut into 1-inch pieces
1 16- to 18-ounce jar **green chili or tomatillo salsa**
2 tablespoons chopped fresh **cilantro**, a mounded palmful
1 15-ounce can **black beans**
2 teaspoons ground **cumin**, $2/3$ palmful
1 16- to 18-ounce jar **chipotle salsa**
2 cups **sour cream**
   Zest and juice of 1 lime

2 ripe **Hass avocados**

1 small **white onion**, finely chopped

2 **garlic cloves**, finely chopped

Zest and juice of 1 lemon

1 **jalapeño**, seeded and finely chopped

Salt

2 **plum tomatoes**, diced

Pimiento-stuffed jumbo Spanish olives, chopped

Tortilla chips—buy 2 sacks in 2 different colors/varieties

Heat the refried beans in a small nonstick pan over medium heat and season them with the hot sauce. Transfer the beans to a small, deep casserole dish. Scrape the pan clean with a rubber spatula and return it to the heat. Add a little EVOO to the pan and raise the heat to high. When the oil smokes, add the scallions and sear them for 2 to 3 minutes. Add the green salsa to the scallions and heat it through. Stir in the cilantro, then layer the salsa on top of the beans. Return the same pan to the stove, lower the heat to medium, and add the black beans. Heat them through and season them with the cumin. Layer the black beans on top of the green salsa. Top the black beans with a layer of chipotle salsa. Mix the sour cream with the lime zest and juice and spread it over the chipotle salsa. In a bowl, mix the flesh of the avocados with the onions, garlic, lemon zest and juice, jalapeños, and salt to form a chunky guacamole. Spoon it on top of the sour cream. Garnish the dip with a final layer of diced tomatoes and chopped olives. Serve with the chips!

6 SERVINGS

■ ▦ ▧

GAME PLAN

- Mix up the meat-balls and pit-zas and get them in the oven.
- While they bake, make the eggplant roll-ups and yogurt sauce.

LET THE GAMES BEGIN! PARTY

- **Spanakopita Chicken Meatballs**
- **Spicy Cucumber Yogurt Sauce**
- **Hummus-Topped Pit-zas**
- **Grilled Eggplant Roll-ups**
- **Stuffed grape leaves (store-bought)**
- **Salami, olives, and breadsticks (store-bought)**

The Olympics only come around every few years, but there's always a game on *somewhere*. Have some fellow sports spectators over for snacks. Round out this Olympic Party with assorted prepared Mediterranean appetizers, such as store-bought stuffed grape leaves.

SPANAKOPITA CHICKEN MEATBALLS WITH SPICY CUCUMBER YOGURT SAUCE

2	10-ounce boxes frozen **chopped spinach**, defrosted
3/4	cup crumbled **feta cheese**
1	pound **ground chicken**
1	small **onion**, finely chopped
3	**garlic cloves**, finely chopped
1	tablespoon **grill seasoning**, such as McCormick's Montreal Steak Seasoning
	EVOO (extra-virgin olive oil) for liberal drizzling
1 1/2	cups **Greek-style plain yogurt**
1/3	**seedless cucumber**, peeled and chopped
3	tablespoons chopped **fresh dill**
1/2	tablespoon ground **cumin**, 1/2 palmful

$^1/_2$ tablespoon ground **coriander**, $^1/_2$ palmful
   Juice of $^1/_2$ lemon
   Salt

Preheat the oven to 400° F.

Wring out the spinach completely dry. Separate the spinach as you add it to a mixing bowl. Add the feta, chicken, onions, two thirds of the chopped garlic, the grill seasoning, and a liberal drizzle of EVOO to the bowl. Mix the meat with the veggies and feta and form eighteen 1$^1/_2$-inch meatballs. Place the meatballs on a rimmed non-stick baking sheet and bake them for 10 to 12 minutes, until they are golden and the juices run clear.

While the meatballs bake, place the yogurt, remaining chopped garlic, the cucumbers, dill, cumin, coriander, lemon juice, and a little salt in a food processor and process until smooth. Adjust the seasonings and transfer the sauce to a serving bowl. Serve the meatballs with a bowl of the sauce and toothpicks for dipping.

6 SERVINGS

06

TIDBIT

Greek yogurt is widely available and is much thicker and richer than regular yogurt. Substitute plain yogurt if you must, but do try to find the Greek kind.

HUMMUS-TOPPED PIT-ZAS

6 6-inch **pitas**
1 15-ounce can **chickpeas**, drained
2 whole **roasted red peppers**, drained
1 **garlic clove**, crushed from its skin
Juice of $1/2$ lemon
1 tablespoon chopped fresh **rosemary leaves**, from a couple small sprigs
Salt
$1/4$ cup **EVOO** (extra-virgin olive oil; eyeball it)
3 cups **shredded Provolone** or mozzarella cheese, or a combination of the two
Toppings (choose one or all)
6 **anchovies**, chopped
$1/2$ cup **pepperoncini** (pickled hot green peppers), chopped
1 can **artichoke hearts** in water, drained well and chopped
A generous handful of **pitted kalamata olives**, chopped

Handful of fresh **flat-leaf parsley** leaves, chopped

Preheat the oven to 400°F.

Arrange the pitas on baking sheets. In a food processor, combine the chickpeas, roasted red peppers, garlic, lemon juice, rosemary, and salt and turn the processor on. Stream the EVOO into the processor and process the hummus until it's smooth. Spread the hummus on the pitas and top them with the cheese, as you would a pizza. Cover the cheese with toppings of your choice: anchovies, pepperoncini, artichokes, and/or olives. Bake them for 10 to 12 minutes to melt the cheese and crisp the pitas. Cut the pit-zas into wedges and garnish them with the parsley.

6 SERVINGS

GRILLED EGGPLANT ROLL-UPS

1 large, firm **eggplant**
1/2 cup **EVOO** (extra-virgin olive oil; eyeball it)
Grill seasoning, such as McCormick's Montreal Steak Seasoning
2 cups **Alouette** or other soft garlic-and-herb cheese
6 to 8 soft **sun-dried tomatoes**, chopped (tender sun-dried tomatoes are available in small pouches in the produce department)
2 cups **arugula leaves**, chopped
1 cup fresh **basil**, about 20 leaves, chopped

Heat a grill pan over high heat. Thinly slice the eggplant; you should have a minimum of 18 slices. Brush the slices on both sides with the EVOO and season them with grill seasoning. Grill the thin slices to mark and tenderize the eggplant, 2 to 3 minutes on each side. Top each slice of cooked eggplant with a dab of cheese, sprinkle on sun-dried tomatoes and some arugula and basil, then roll them up. The eggplant roll-ups should have a few greens sticking out of each end.

6 SERVINGS

■ ■ ■

06

'TIS THE SEASON

- T-bone Steaks with Chopped Green Garni, and Broiled Tomatoes with Cheese, Olives, and Herbs
- Bacon, Spinach, and Cream Potatoes
- Holiday Parfitini

T-BONE STEAKS WITH CHOPPED GREEN GARNI, AND BROILED TOMATOES WITH CHEESE, OLIVES, AND HERBS

  6   1-inch-thick **T-bone steaks**
$1/4$ cup plus 2 tablespoons **EVOO** (extra-virgin olive oil), plus some for drizzling
  6   vine-ripe **tomatoes**, tops removed, seeds scooped out
      Salt and **black pepper**
  3   slices good-quality **bread**, crusts rimmed, pieces torn
$1/2$ cup pitted **good-quality green or black olives**, a couple handfuls
  3   handfuls fresh **flat-leaf parsley** leaves
      Leaves from 5 to 6 fresh **sage** sprigs
$3/4$ cup grated **Romano cheese**, 3 handfuls
  2   cups **arugula**, chopped
  1   cup fresh **basil**, 20 leaves, shredded or torn
      Juice of $1/2$ lemon

Preheat the oven to 375° F.

Preheat a large griddle or large skillet over high heat. Brush the meat with $1/4$ cup of the EVOO. Sear the steaks for 2 minutes on each side, 3 at a time. Arrange the steaks on a rimmed baking sheet.

When the steaks are all seared off, transfer to the oven and roast for 5 to 6 minutes for medium doneness; subtract or add 2 minutes to that time for medium rare or medium well.

Place the tomatoes on a broiler pan and season with salt and pepper. Combine the bread, olives, parsley, sage, and Romano in a food processor and pulse/grind the mixture. Dress the mixture with some EVOO, salt, and pepper and fill the tomatoes with it.

Dress the chopped arugula and basil with a little lemon juice, a drizzle of EVOO, salt, and pepper.

Remove the steaks and let rest. Switch the broiler on and broil the tomatoes for a couple minutes to brown the cheese and bread crumbs.

Serve the steaks with the greens on top and the broiled stuffed tomatoes alongside.

6 SERVINGS

BACON, SPINACH, AND CREAM POTATOES

3 pounds **Idaho potatoes**, peeled and sliced
Salt
EVOO (extra-virgin olive oil), for drizzling
4 center-cut **bacon** strips, chopped
1 medium **onion**, quartered and thinly sliced
2 10-ounce boxes frozen **chopped spinach**, defrosted and wrung out in a kitchen towel
1 cup **heavy cream**
Black pepper
$^{1}/_{4}$ teaspoon freshly grated or ground **nutmeg** (eyeball it)

Place the potatoes in a pot and cover with water. Bring up to a boil, salt the water, and cook until the potatoes are tender, 12 to 15 minutes.

continued

To a small skillet over medium heat add a little EVOO and the bacon and cook until the bacon is browned, 7 to 8 minutes. Add the onions and cook until soft, 5 minutes more.

Drain the potatoes and place back in the hot pot. Add the bacon and onions and defrosted spinach to the potatoes, and mash to combine, then add the cream. Mash until smooth and season the mixture with salt, pepper, and the nutmeg.

6 SERVINGS

HOLIDAY PARFITINI

1   pint **strawberry ice cream**
6   shots **crème de menthe** liqueur
    Whipped cream, from a canister (in the dairy case)
1   jar **maraschino cherries**
1   can **Pirouette cookies**

Put a scoop of ice cream in the bottom of a martini glass. Pour a shot of crème de menthe over the top. Top with a healthy spray of whipped cream and a cherry. Stick 2 Pirouette cookies in the side to make a festive garnish!

6 SERVINGS

EIGHT IS GREAT BECAUSE EIGHT IS MY LUCKY NUMBER. I AM ALSO BIASED WHERE EIGHTS ARE CONCERNED BECAUSE MY BIRTHDAY IS IN THE EIGHTH MONTH OF THE YEAR. FIGURE EIGHTS ARE ESPECIALLY PRETTY TO LOOK AT AS WELL, BECAUSE THEY ARE EQUALLY BALANCED ON TOP AND BOTTOM, JUST LIKE THESE MENUS, WHICH ARE, YOU GUESSED IT: FOR EIGHT! RESERVATION FOR EIGHT AT EIGHT? NO PROBLEM! JUST GIVE US 30 MINUTES.

BELLY UP TO BRUNCH

• Deviled Frittata
• Heavenly Angel Hair Pasta
• Drunken Citrus Salad

This pairs a mayo-free, warm, spicy take on deviled eggs with a pasta favorite from Trattoria Garga in Florence. The original "Pasta Magnifico," on which the Heavenly Angel Hair pasta is based, is richer, with more cream and liquor. This lighter version is *molto bene* for brunch or a late-night bite. Your pick—it's always brunch time *somewhere.*

DEVILED FRITTATA AND HEAVENLY ANGEL HAIR PASTA

  Salt
1 pound **angel hair pasta**
5 tablespoons **EVOO** (extra-virgin olive oil)
1 medium **onion**, finely chopped
2 **celery ribs** from the heart, with greens, finely chopped
1 teaspoon **sweet paprika**
  Black pepper
2 **garlic cloves**, finely chopped
¼ cup **green olives** with pimiento, finely chopped
1 tablespoon **hot sauce** (eyeball it)
1 rounded teaspoon **Dijon mustard**
16 large **eggs**
1 cup **heavy cream**
  A generous handful of fresh **flat-leaf parsley** leaves, finely chopped
2 **shallots**, thinly sliced
1 nip or 2 healthy shots **cognac**
  Zest of 1 orange

Zest of 1 lemon

3/4 cup grated **Pecorino Romano**, a few generous handfuls

1 cup fresh **basil**, 20 leaves, torn or shredded

Preheat the oven to 400° F.

Bring a large covered pot of water to a boil for the pasta. When it comes to a boil, salt the water, add the pasta, and cook it to al dente, 5 minutes. Before you drain the pasta, measure 2 ladles of starchy cooking water and reserve.

Heat 3 tablespoons of the EVOO, 3 times around the pan, in a large, oven-safe nonstick skillet over medium-low heat. Add the onions and cook them gently for 5 minutes. Do not caramelize the onions, just let them get translucent and sweet. Add the celery and season it with the paprika, salt, and pepper. Stir in the garlic, olives, hot sauce, and mustard. Beat together the eggs and 1/2 cup of the cream (eye-ball it) and pour the mixture into the skillet. Stir in the parsley, then let the eggs settle and form a foundation, as you would for an omelet. Transfer the pan to the oven and bake the frittata until golden, 15 to 17 minutes.

Heat the remaining 2 tablespoons of EVOO in a deep skillet over medium heat. Add the shallots and cook for 5 minutes. Add the cognac, then stir in the remaining 1/2 cup of cream and reduce for 2 minutes. Add the zests and reduce for a minute or so more. Add the reserved pasta cooking water. Toss the drained pasta with the cheese and season it with salt and pepper. Transfer the pasta to a bowl and garnish it with an obscene amount of fresh basil. Yum-o!

8 SERVINGS

DRUNKEN CITRUS SALAD

8 cups drained **citrus salad mix** (orange and grapefruit sections, available in refrigerated section of market; buy 2 quart jars)

2 nips or 4 shots of **gin**

1 tablespoon **lemon zest**

3 tablespoons finely chopped fresh **mint leaves**, plus a couple of sprigs for garnish

Combine all of the salad ingredients and serve it immediately or chill it for up to several hours. Garnish with extra mint sprigs.

8 SERVINGS

■ ■ ■

DINNER FOR EIGHT IS SWIMMINGLY EASY

- **Baked Cod with Stuffing on Top**
- **White Risotto**
- **Asparagus Tips**
- **Lemon Meringue Pie (store-bought—get two pies)**

Fish of any kind is perfect for a 30-Minute Meal, but it's especially great for entertaining, because it is by definition a quick-cooking protein. Cod is the most forgiving of all fish: really hard to screw up, sturdy and forgiving with any cooking method, and still tasty even if served a bit on the dry side. Dinner is swimmingly easy when you serve fish.

ASPARAGUS TIPS

2 bundles of **asparagus**, 1³/₄ to 2 pounds
2 tablespoons **butter**
2 teaspoons **lemon zest**
  Salt

Trim off the top 4 to 5 inches of the asparagus spears and reserve the tough bottoms for soup, if you wish. Add ¹/₂ inch of water to a skillet and bring it to a boil. Reduce the heat to simmer and add the asparagus spears, butter, zest, and salt. Cook until the liquid evaporates, 4 to 5 minutes. Transfer the spears to a serving platter or dinner plates and serve.

8 SERVINGS

■ ■ ■

BAKED COD WITH STUFFING ON TOP AND WHITE RISOTTO

8 cups **chicken stock**

3 tablespoons **EVOO** (extra-virgin olive oil), plus some for drizzling

1 small **onion**, finely chopped

2¹/₂ cups **Arborio rice**

1 cup **dry white wine** (eyeball it)

8 center-cut **cod fillets**, 8 ounces each

Salt and **black pepper**

2 cups **seasoned stuffing mix**, such as Stove Top or Pepperidge Farm

2 small **garlic cloves**, chopped

A generous handful of fresh **flat-leaf parsley** leaves, finely chopped

¹/₂ cup (1 stick) **butter**, softened

1 large **shallot** or ¹/₂ medium onion, minced

1 cup grated **Parmigiano-Reggiano** or Pecorino Romano cheese, 4 generous handfuls

Preheat the oven to 400° F.

Warm the stock in a medium sauce pot over medium-low heat.

Heat the 3 tablespoons of EVOO in a large skillet over medium-high heat. Add the onions and cook for 2 to 3 minutes, then add the rice and cook for 2 minutes more. Add the wine and let it evaporate entirely, stirring occasionally. Add a few ladles of the warm stock. Stir the stock into the rice and cook until it is absorbed, stirring occasionally. Continue to add the stock to the rice, stirring with each addition, as you make the fish.

Pat the cod dry, drizzle it with EVOO, arrange it in a baking pan, and season it with salt and pepper.

Place the stuffing in a large food storage bag. Press out the air and seal the bag, then crush the stuffing into crumbs with a rolling pin. On a cutting board, sprinkle the chopped garlic with some large-flaked salt and smash it to a paste by pressing the heel of your hand against the flat blade of a chef's knife. Combine the paste with some pepper and the parsley. Mix the paste with the softened butter and combine the softened butter thoroughly with the crumbs and the shallots or onions. Top the fish evenly with the buttery crumbs and bake it in the center of the oven for 15 to 18 minutes. If the fish seems slow to firm and the stuffing topping isn't browning, you can switch the oven to broil for the last 2 to 3 minutes and that'll do the job. The rack should remain at the center of the oven.

Add the last of the stock to the risotto and stir until absorbed. The risotto will take 22 minutes, total, and will become very creamy if you stir it frequently as the liquid is added. The stirring process will release the starches that cream the rice. The rice should absorb all of the liquids in that time. If you need a bit of extra liquid, water will do. In the last minute or so of the cooking time, fold in the cheese and turn off the heat.

Serve the fish with the white risotto alongside.

8 SERVINGS

■ ■ ■

MAKE YOUR OWN TAKE-OUT, INDIAN-STYLE

- Lamb Meatballs in Gravy over Jasmine Rice
- Indian-Spiced Roasted Cauliflower
- A Trio of Sorbets: Mango, Coconut, and Lime or Lemon (store-bought)
- Chai Tea (store-bought)

Making your own versions of take-out food can be a fun theme for a get-together. For this Indian meal, I would have *A Passage to India* on the TV on mute and play some fun Indian pop music on the stereo. Later you can move into the Beatles or George Harrison in their Indian-inspired years. Or, rent and pop in a current Bollywood flick for the evening's entertainment to take the theme to its extreme!

LAMB MEATBALLS IN GRAVY OVER JASMINE RICE

5 tablespoons **vegetable or light olive oil**

3 cups **jasmine rice**

Salt and **black pepper**

8 cups **chicken stock**

3-inch piece of **fresh ginger**, peeled and coarsely sliced

5 large **garlic cloves**, crushed away from their skins

1 **serrano or jalapeño pepper**, cut in half lengthwise and seeded

1 large **onion**, quartered

1 cup fresh **flat-leaf parsley** leaves, 4 generous handfuls

1/2 cup fresh **cilantro leaves**, 2 generous handfuls

2 1/2 pounds **ground lamb**

1 tablespoon **ground cumin**, a palmful

¹/₄ teaspoon **ground cloves** or ¹/₂ teaspoon ground cinnamon

¹/₂ tablespoon **ground coriander**, ¹/₂ palmful

3 tablespoons all-purpose **flour**, 2 generous palmfuls

Zest and juice of 2 lemons

5 **scallions**, thinly sliced

1 10-ounce box **frozen peas**

Preheat the oven to 450° F.

Place a large sauce pot over medium-high heat with 2 tablespoons of the oil, 2 times around the pan. Add the rice and some salt and pepper and toss them to coat the rice grains in the oil. Add 5 cups of the chicken stock and 1 cup of water, cover the pot, and bring it up to a boil. Reduce the heat to medium and simmer for 17 to 18 minutes, or until the rice is tender.

In the bowl of a food processor, combine the ginger, garlic, hot pepper, onions, parsley, cilantro, the remaining 3 tablespoons of oil, and salt and pepper. Start by pulsing to break up the mixture, then let 'er rip to grind it up until the ingredients are finely chopped but the sauce is still shy of being smooth. Remove half of the chopped mixture to a mixing bowl; add the ground lamb and use your hands to combine. Roll the mixture into walnut-size balls and place them on a rimmed baking sheet. You can use a couple of soup spoons to help you roll: grab the meat with one spoon, scoot it onto the baking sheet with the other. The meat will look like blobs rather than balls but it will taste just as good. Once you have all the balls or blobs made and arranged on the baking sheet, transfer them to the oven and roast them for 10 to 12 minutes, or until they are browned.

While the lamb is roasting, start the gravy. Place a large skillet over medium-high heat and add the remaining ground mixture from the food processor. Add the cumin, cloves or cinnamon, coriander, and a little salt and pepper. Cook the mixture, stirring frequently, for 2 to 3 minutes. Sprinkle it with the flour and continue to cook it for 1 minute more. Whisk in the remaining 3 cups of chicken stock, bring it up to a bubble, and cook until it's thick, a few minutes. Add the

continued

lemon zest and juice, scallions, peas, and the cooked lamb meatballs; stir to coat the balls in the sauce; and continue to cook them for a few minutes to meld the lamb and sauce flavors together.

When you are ready to serve, fluff the rice with a fork, divide it among your serving plates, and top with meatballs and gravy.

8 SERVINGS, ABOUT 48 MEATBALLS

INDIAN-SPICED ROASTED CAULIFLOWER

1/4 cup **vegetable or light olive oil**
1 tablespoon mild or hot **curry powder**, a palmful
1/2 tablespoon **ground coriander**, 1/2 palmful
  Salt and **black pepper**
11/2 to 2 pounds **cauliflower**, 1 large or 2 small heads, cut into bite-size florets

Preheat the oven to 450° F.

In a bowl, combine the vegetable oil with the curry powder, coriander, and a little salt and pepper. Arrange the cauliflower on a rimmed baking sheet and drizzle it with the oil mixture; toss to coat the cauliflower thoroughly. Transfer the cauliflower to the oven and roast until it's tender, about 15 minutes.

8 SERVINGS

■ ■ ■

GAME PLAN

• Start the pasta water and heat the lemon curd.

• Cook the pasta and assemble the cake while the pasta sauce works.

BUBBA GUMP-STYLE SPAGHETTI SUPPER

- **Shrimp and Gravy with Bucatini**
- **Citrus Ring Cake with Coconut**

I love shrimp and they are great for 30-minute menus for eight because they are so quick-cooking and you don't have to chop them! This entrée combines shrimp with rich, reddish-brown gravy and big fat noodles. It requires no sides or salad because it's made with veggies and topped with greens. Dessert is a great fake-out you'll use time and again when you have no time to spare and guests at the door!

SHRIMP AND GRAVY WITH BUCATINI

Salt

1½ pounds **bucatini** pasta (substitute perciatelli or thick spaghetti if you can't find bucatini)

1 tablespoon **EVOO** (extra-virgin olive oil)

6 slices **bacon**, chopped

4 **garlic cloves**, chopped

4 **celery ribs** from the heart, with leafy tops, finely chopped

1 **red bell pepper**, finely chopped

1 large **onion**, finely chopped

Leaves from 5 to 6 fresh **rosemary** sprigs, finely chopped

Leaves from 5 to 6 fresh **thyme** sprigs, finely chopped

Black pepper

2 rounded tablespoons all-purpose **flour**

2 tablespoons **Worcestershire sauce** (eyeball it)

2 tablespoons **hot sauce** (eyeball it)

1 bottle **dark beer**, such as Negro Modelo

1 28-ounce can crushed **fire-roasted tomatoes**

2 pounds large **shrimp**, peeled, deveined, and tails removed

4 to 5 cups **arugula**, stemmed and chopped

continued

Bring a large covered pot of water to a boil, salt it, and add the pasta. Cook to al dente.

Heat a large, deep skillet over medium-high heat with the EVOO, once around the pan. When the oil is hot, add the bacon and cook it until it's crisp, about 5 minutes. Remove the bacon with a slotted spoon, drain off a little of the fat, keeping a thin layer in the pan, then add the garlic, vegetables, and herbs. Season them with salt and pepper and cook for 7 to 8 minutes. Stir in the flour and cook for 2 more minutes, then stir in the Worcestershire, hot sauce, and beer. Reduce the liquid by half, then add the tomatoes and bring it to a bubble. When the tomatoes are simmering, add the shrimp and cook them for 5 minutes, or until they are just pink and firm. Drain the pasta, toss it with the shrimp and sauce, and adjust the seasonings. Transfer it to a large platter or individual bowls and top it with the chopped arugula.

8 SERVINGS

TIDBIT

Peeling and deveining 2 pounds of shrimp takes time; instead, buy easy peels, which come raw, split down the back, and deveined.

CITRUS RING CAKE WITH COCONUT

2 cups **lemon curd** (found on the jam and jelly aisle of the market)
2 tablespoons **lemon zest**
2 tablespoons **lime zest**
2 tablespoons **orange zest**
1 **angel food cake**, store-bought
2 cups **sweetened shredded coconut**

Place the lemon curd in a small pot with a splash of water and the citrus zests. Heat it over low heat until the curd loosens to a warm lemon sauce.

Using a serrated knife, cut the angel food cake horizontally into 3 layers. Place the bottom layer on a plate and top it with a third of the citrus-infused lemon sauce. Sprinkle with $2/3$ cup of the coconut. Let the sauce cool and set for 2 to 3 minutes. Set the second layer of cake in place and cover it with sauce and coconut. Let it cool and set. Top with the third layer, the remaining sauce and the remaining coconut. Serve.

8 SERVINGS

■ ■ ■

GAME PLAN

- Put up the pasta water.

- Cook the broccoli and cauliflower while the spinach defrosts.

- Assemble the lasagna.

- Finish the veggies while the lasagna is under the broiler.

TWO FRIENDS AND A BABY

- **Spinach-Artichoke Ravioli-Lasagna**
- **Orange-Scented Broccoli and Cauliflower**

All of a sudden, my friends are having babies: my cousins Rich and Amy, my coworker Steve and his sweet wife, Meeri. Welcome Elizabeth and Madeline Grace! Sooooo, what do new parents need? FOOD! They do nothing but tend to the needs of the babes, which is as it should be, but they have no time or energy left for cooking. This is a great dinner, for anyone, but, if you have a friend not in need but rather in new-born, this would be a really cool gift. It takes only 30 minutes to make and it will feed the new parents for a couple of days—unless you decide to steal a portion or two for yourself before giving it away.

SPINACH-ARTICHOKE RAVIOLI-LASAGNA

- 2 10-ounce boxes **frozen chopped spinach**
- 2 tablespoons **butter**, cut into pieces
- 1/4 cup all-purpose **flour**
- 1 quart **milk**
  Freshly grated or ground **nutmeg**
  Salt and **black pepper**
- 2 15-ounce cans **artichoke hearts in water**, drained and thinly sliced
- 4 packages **large fresh ravioli** (cheese, wild mushroom, or spinach varieties)
- 3 cups **ricotta cheese**
- 1 tablespoon **lemon zest**
- 4 **garlic cloves**, minced
- 1 1/2 cups grated **Parmigiano-Reggiano cheese**

Bring a large covered pot of water to a boil for the pasta.

Place the oven rack in the middle of the oven and preheat the broiler.

Defrost the spinach in the microwave for 6 or 7 minutes on high; check the spinach and microwave for another 2 or 3 minutes if not fully defrosted.

While the spinach defrosts, melt the butter in a medium sauce pot over medium heat. Whisk in the flour and cook it for a minute or two, then whisk in the milk. Bring the sauce to a bubble and, as it begins to thicken, drop the heat to low and season it with nutmeg, salt, and pepper to taste. Remove from the heat.

Wring the spinach completely dry in a kitchen towel. Open the towel and separate the clumps of spinach with your fingers. Pile up the sliced artichokes on your cutting board.

TIDBIT

The size of the ravioli will vary a lot depending on the brand, but don't worry, the size doesn't matter, really. If you use small ravs the layers will be more pasta than cheese, and if the ravs are big it will be cheesier.

When the water comes to a boil, salt it, add the ravioli, and cook to al dente, 5 minutes. The ravioli will float to the top when they are close to done. Drain the ravioli.

Warm the ricotta in the microwave for 2 minutes on high. Season it with salt and pepper, the lemon zest, and garlic; cover and reserve it.

Ladle just enough of the white sauce into the bottom of a lasagna dish to coat it lightly. Top the sauce with one third of the ravioli. Top the pasta with half of the ricotta cheese dotted with half of the spinach and artichokes. Thinly cover the veggies with more white sauce, then top it liberally with grated cheese. Repeat these layers, then top your lasagna with the remaining third of the cooked ravioli and the last of the white sauce and grated cheese.

Place the lasagna under the hot broiler until the sauce browns and bubbles, 3 minutes.

8 SERVINGS

ORANGE-SCENTED BROCCOLI AND CAULIFLOWER

1 **navel orange**
1 head of **broccoli**, cut into florets (save those stems for soup!)
1 head of **cauliflower**, cut into florets
  Salt
3 tablespoons **EVOO** (extra-virgin olive oil)
2 **shallots**, thinly sliced
  Handful of fresh **flat-leaf parsley** leaves, finely chopped
  Black pepper

Peel the orange and set the fruit aside. Place the rind in a large skillet with a couple inches of water and add the broccoli and cauliflower florets and salt. Bring to a boil, then cover the skillet and simmer until the vegetables are tender, about 6 minutes. Drain the broccoli and cauliflower; discard the rind. Return the skillet to the heat, add the EVOO, and heat it over medium heat. Add the shallots and cook them until they are soft, 3 to 4 minutes. Add the broccoli and cauliflower and turn them to coat. Squeeze the peeled orange over the pan, add the parsley, and toss the veggies again. Season with salt and pepper.

8 SERVINGS

■ ■ ■

- Get the pasta and porcinis going.

- Start the pasta sauce.

- Start the greens while the tomatoes simmer with the sauce.

EARTHY EATS

- **Three-Mushroom Rigatoni**
- **Wilted Escarole with Garlic, Lemon, and Oil**
- **Ricotta Cheesecake (bakery bought)**

This rigatoni is beefy yet meat-free, so you can entertain vegetarians and carnivores alike with it. The flavor is so hearty even *I* don't ask "Where's the beef?"

THREE-MUSHROOM RIGATONI

	Salt
1¹/₂	pounds **rigatoni**
2	ounces **dried porcini mushrooms**
¹/₄	cup plus 2 tablespoons **EVOO** (extra-virgin olive oil)
4	**portobello mushroom caps**
³/₄	pound **shiitake mushrooms**, stemmed and sliced
4	**garlic cloves**, sliced
1	cup **dry Italian red wine**
	Leaves from 3 to 4 fresh **rosemary** sprigs, finely chopped
	Black pepper
1	28-ounce can **crushed tomatoes** (look for imported Italian San Marzanos)
	A hunk of **Pecorino Romano** cheese, for grating
	Crusty bread, for mopping

Heat a grill pan to high.

Place a large covered pot of water on the stove to boil. Add salt and the rigatoni and cook to al dente.

Place the porcinis in a small pot with about 2 cups of water. Bring the water to a boil, then reduce the heat and simmer until the liquid is reduced by half, 10 minutes.

continued

MEALS FOR 8

While the pasta and porcinis are working, pour about $^1/_4$ cup of the EVOO into a small bowl. Use a pastry brush to coat the portobello mushrooms with EVOO and place them on the hot grill pan. Cook them until they are dark and tender, 7 to 8 minutes, turning once. Transfer them to a plate.

Pour the remaining 2 tablespoons of the EVOO into a large, deep skillet over medium-high heat. Add the shiitakes and cook them for a few minutes, then add the garlic and cook for a couple minutes longer. Add the wine and cook it down for 2 minutes. Halve and slice the grilled portobellos and add them to the shiitakes. Scatter the rosemary into the pan and turn the mushrooms to distribute the herb. Season the mushrooms with salt and pepper. Remove the porcinis from the steeping broth with a slotted spoon and chop them. Stir the mushrooms and a few ladles of the steeping broth into the pan; do not use the very last of it, as any grit from the dried mushrooms will have settled at the bottom of the pot. Stir in the tomatoes and cook for a couple of minutes more to let the flavors combine.

Drain the pasta and return it to the warm pasta pot. Grate some Romano over the pasta and add a few ladles of the mushroom sauce to the pasta. Toss the pasta with the sauce to coat it, then transfer it to a serving platter and top it with the remaining sauce. Pass the cheese at the table for topping, and the bread for mopping. Yum-o!

8 SERVINGS

WILTED ESCAROLE WITH GARLIC, LEMON, AND OIL

1/4 cup **EVOO** (extra-virgin olive oil)

2 **garlic cloves**, crushed from their skins

2 teaspoons **anchovy paste** (eyeball it) or 6 fillets, chopped

8 to 10 cups **escarole**, trimmed, rinsed, and dried, a couple of large heads

1/2 teaspoon **red pepper flakes**

Juice of 1 lemon

Heat the EVOO in a deep skillet over medium-low heat with the garlic and anchovy paste. Cook them together for 3 to 4 minutes to infuse the garlic into the oil. Remove the garlic cloves and stir the oil to mix in the melted anchovies. Raise the heat to medium high. When the oil ripples or begins to waft smoke, add the greens and stir-fry them for 2 to 3 minutes. Season them with red pepper and remove them from the heat. Squeeze the lemon juice over the greens, toss, and serve.

8 SERVINGS

■ ■ ■

GAME PLAN

• Get the veggie
  stew going.

• While the stew
  simmers, cook the
  chickpeas.

• Make the dessert
  sauce and toast
  the cheesy breads.

• Assemble the
  desserts just
  before serving.

MOTHERS WOULD BE PROUD OF THIS HEALTHY EATING

- **Toasted Chickpeas Cacio e Pepe**
- **Giambotta—Eat Your Vegetables Stew**
- **Angel Food Cake with Sorbet Sauce and Berries**

More and more of my friends are eating healthier diets, vegetarians and meat eaters alike. I am, in turn, getting lonelier and lonelier because they are all too healthy to eat with me anymore. I love them, but I for one am not giving up pasta, salt, meat, or cheese any time soon. When my healthy friends do come over, this is what I give them. It's a good meal and it's meat-free. Even if you're not a vegetarian it's good to lay off meat for a night now and then. The next night? I'm eating steak.

TOASTED CHICKPEAS CACIO E PEPE (WITH CHEESE AND PEPPER)

2 15-ounce cans **chickpeas**, rinsed and dried on a clean kitchen towel
1 cup grated **Romano cheese**
2 teaspoons **coarse black pepper**

Place the chickpeas in a skillet and toast them over medium heat for 15 minutes. Top them with the cheese and pepper and let the cheese melt onto the chickpeas, 2 minutes more.

8 SERVINGS

GIAMBOTTA—EAT YOUR VEGETABLES STEW

1/4 cup **EVOO** (extra-virgin olive oil), plus some to drizzle
1 **bay leaf**, fresh or dried
6 **garlic cloves**, 2 cracked from their skins and halved, 4 thinly sliced
2 **onions**, sliced
3 large **Idaho potatoes**, peeled and chopped
1 **eggplant**, chopped
2 medium **zucchini**, chopped
1 **red bell pepper**, seeded and chopped
1 **cubanelle pepper**, seeded and chopped
   Salt and **black pepper**
2 28-ounce cans **fire-roasted diced tomatoes**
2 cups **chicken or vegetable stock**
1 cup fresh **basil**, 20 leaves, torn or chopped
1 loaf **whole-grain crusty bread**, split lengthwise
1 cup grated **Pecorino Romano cheese**

Heat a large soup pot over medium-high heat. Add the 1/4 cup of EVOO, the bay leaf, chopped garlic, and onions and let them sweat while you prepare the rest of the veggies. Work next to the stove and drop as you chop, in this order: potatoes, eggplant, zucchini, and peppers. Season the veggies with salt and black pepper, cover the pot, and cook for 15 minutes, stirring the stew occasionally. Uncover the pot and add the tomatoes and stock and cook for 5 minutes more, to heat through. Turn the heat off and stir in the basil.

While the stew cooks, preheat the broiler. Char the bread under the broiler and rub it with the cracked garlic, then drizzle it with EVOO. Top the bread with the cheese and return it to the broiler for 30 seconds to brown the cheese.

Serve hunks of cheesy whole-grain bread alongside bowlfuls of vegetable stew for mopping.

8 SERVINGS

ANGEL FOOD CAKE WITH SORBET SAUCE AND BERRIES

- 1 pint **lemon sorbet**
- 2 teaspoons **lemon zest**
- 1 pint **blackberries**
- 1 pint **strawberries**, sliced
- 1/2 pint **raspberries**
- 2 store-bought **angel food cakes**

In a small sauce pot, melt the sorbet with the zest over low heat. Stir in the berries. Cut the cake into wedges and pour the berries and sauce over the top.

16 SERVINGS (SO ANGELIC, YOU CAN HAVE 2 SLICES)

GAME PLAN

- Put the pasta water on and get the sausage in the oven.

- Start the sauce, then the peppers and pasta.

- Toss the pasta with the sauce while the cheesy bread toasts.

JUST LIKE MAMA USED TO MAKE

- Spaghetti all'Elsa
- Roasted Sausages, Peppers, and Onions
- Cheesy Bread with Black Pepper
- Cannoli, from a bakery—made by someone else's mama

You may *think* you know how to make spaghetti with sausages, peppers, and onions, but my mama has a few twists that make hers better than yours—or maybe even *your* mama's. Strong words, but just taste!

SPAGHETTI ALL'ELSA

Salt

$1^1/2$ pounds imported Italian dried **spaghetti**

3 tablespoons **EVOO** (extra-virgin olive oil)

3 **garlic cloves**, crushed from their skins

$1/2$ to $3/4$ teaspoon **red pepper flakes**, 2 pinches

1 small **onion**, finely chopped

1 28-ounce can plus 1 14-ounce can **crushed tomatoes** (Italian San Marzanos if available)

Several fresh **basil** leaves, torn or chopped, a handful

4 tablespoons ($1/2$ stick) **butter**, cut into small pieces

1 cup grated **Parmigiano-Reggiano** cheese

Bring a large covered pot of water to a boil and salt it. Add the pasta and cook to al dente, with a bite to it.

continued

MEALS FOR 8

Heat a medium sauce pot over medium-low heat. Add the EVOO and garlic and cook for 5 minutes. The garlic will be soft and light golden. Remove the garlic. Add the red pepper flakes and cook for a minute, then add the onions and cook 5 minutes longer. Add the crushed tomatoes and cook for a minute to reduce. Season the sauce with salt to taste, then stir in the basil and reduce the heat to low. Heads up: reserve $1/2$ cup of the sauce for making the sausage and peppers (recipe follows).

When the pasta is cooked, turn off the heat, drain the pasta, and return it to the still-hot pot. Add the butter to the spaghetti and toss to coat and melt. Add half the red sauce and all of the cheese, working the cheese in a handful at a time as you toss to combine. To serve, use tongs or a meat fork to swirl the pasta into buttery, cheesy mounds to pile onto each plate. Top each portion with spoonfuls of remaining sauce. Whoa, mama!

8 SERVINGS

ROASTED SAUSAGES, PEPPERS, AND ONIONS WITH CHEESY BREAD WITH BLACK PEPPER

- 3 pounds thin **Italian sausages** (the kind sold in coils; each coil will weigh about $1^1/2$ pounds), hot and sweet varieties
- 3 tablespoons **EVOO** (extra-virgin olive oil), plus more for liberal drizzling
- 5 **garlic cloves**, 4 thinly sliced, 1 crushed from its skin
- 2 **red bell peppers**, seeded and sliced $1/2$ inch thick
- 2 **light green cubanelle peppers**, seeded and sliced $1/2$ inch thick
- 1 large **onion**, cut into $1/2$-inch-thick slices
  Salt and **coarse black pepper**
- $1/2$ cup prepared **red pasta sauce**, preferably reserved from Spaghetti all'Elsa on page 261
- 1 loaf of **crusty semolina bread**, split
- 1 cup grated **Parmigiano-Reggiano cheese**
- 2 tablespoons chopped fresh **flat-leaf parsley** leaves, a rounded palmful

Preheat the oven to 425° F.

Place the sausage coils on a rimmed baking sheet and liberally drizzle them with EVOO. Roast them in the oven until the casings are crisp and the juices run clear, somewhere between 15 and 20 minutes. Remove the sausages from the oven; switch on the broiler.

While the sausages roast, heat a skillet over medium heat with the 3 tablespoons of EVOO and the sliced garlic. Simmer for 2 to 3 minutes, then add the peppers and onions to the pan. Season with salt and pepper, turn the heat up a notch, and cook until the vegetables are tender but the peppers still retain their strong colors, 5 to 6 minutes. Thin the red sauce with $1/4$ cup water and add it to the pan. Reduce the heat to a simmer and hold the veggies until the sausages come out of the oven, a couple of minutes. Add any sausage drippings to the pan as well. Place the peppers in a serving bowl and transfer the sausage to a platter.

Toast the semolina loaf under the broiler until golden. Remove from the oven, rub with the cracked garlic, and drizzle liberally with EVOO. Cover the loaf with cheese and lots of black pepper and return it to the broiler to brown the cheese, 1 minute. Scatter the parsley over the bread.

Cut the bread into chunks and arrange around the sausage. Cut the sausage into individual servings. Pile the bread chunks with peppers and onions, then sausages. The bread will soak up the juices as you work your way through the sausages, peppers, and onions.

8 SERVINGS

COUNTRY FARE FOR POST-COUNTY FAIR GATHERINGS

- Mac 'n' Jack Salad
- BBQ Chicken Burgers Topped with Honey Slaw
- Biscuits, Sugared Berries, and Whipped Cream (store-bought)

I grew up in the country, which means I've been to my share of fairs. You can picture the scene: bandstand music, cotton candy, livestock and tractors, whirly-twirling machines that make you dizzy and sick—what fun!

This menu is also tasty after a long day at the office, but it always makes me think of the fairgrounds.

MAC 'N' JACK SALAD

Salt

1 pound **elbow macaroni** or cavatappi (hollow corkscrew pasta)

1 10-ounce **box frozen corn**, defrosted

1 **red bell pepper**, seeded and chopped

1 **red onion**, chopped

4 **celery ribs**, chopped

1 8-ounce brick of **Monterey Pepper Jack** cheese, diced

Black pepper

3 tablespoons **red wine vinegar** (eyeball it)

1/3 cup **EVOO** (extra-virgin olive oil; eyeball it)

1 1/2 cups store-bought **tomatillo salsa** (mild, green) or chipotle salsa (hot, smoky red)

3 tablespoons fresh **cilantro** or flat-leaf parsley leaves, chopped

Bring a large covered pot of water to a boil. Salt it and add the pasta. Cook until al dente.

While the pasta is working, combine the corn, bell peppers, onions, and celery in a bowl with the cheese. Season with salt and pepper.

Drain the pasta and run it under cold water to cool it; drain it well again. Add the pasta to the vegetables and cheese.

Place the vinegar in a small bowl and whisk in the EVOO. Fold in the salsa. Pour the sauce over the salad and toss to coat evenly. Garnish with cilantro or parsley and serve.

8 SERVINGS

BBQ CHICKEN BURGERS TOPPED WITH HONEY SLAW

- 2 tablespoons **butter**, cut into pieces
- 1 medium **red onion**, $1/2$ finely chopped, $1/2$ thinly sliced
- 2 **garlic cloves**, finely chopped
- 3 tablespoons **tomato paste**
- 2 teaspoons **sugar**
- 2 tablespoons **Worcestershire sauce** (eyeball it)
- 1 tablespoon **hot sauce** (eyeball it)
- 2 pounds **ground chicken**
- 2 tablespoons **grill seasoning**, such as McCormick's Montreal Steak Seasoning, a couple of palmfuls
- 5 tablespoons **EVOO** (extra-virgin olive oil)
- 3 tablespoons **honey** (eyeball it)
  Juice of 1 lemon
- 3 rounded tablespoons **sweet pickle relish**
- 4 cups **shredded cabbage mix**
  Salt and **black pepper**
- 8 cornmeal **kaiser rolls**, split

continued

In a small skillet, melt the butter over medium heat. Add the chopped onions, garlic, and tomato paste and sweat them for 5 minutes to soften and sweeten. Sprinkle the mixture with the sugar and transfer to a bowl to cool for 5 minutes. Add the Worcestershire and hot sauce and combine. Add the chicken and grill seasoning and combine well to distribute the flavors evenly. Form the mixture into 8 patties. Wash up.

Heat 1 tablespoon of the EVOO, 1 time around the pan, in a nonstick skillet over medium-high heat. Cook the patties 4 at a time, for 5 minutes on each side.

Combine the honey, lemon juice, and the remaining 4 tablespoons of EVOO in a bowl. Add the relish, cabbage mix, and sliced onions and season with salt and pepper. Toss the slaw to coat.

Serve the burgers on the buns topped with some of the slaw.

8 SERVINGS

GAME PLAN

- Get the soup going.

- While the soup simmers start on the croutons, salad, and dressing.

- Add the tortellini to the soup and toss the salad.

SUPER SOUP AND A SOUPED-UP CAESAR

- **Assorted Antipasti (store-bought)**
- **Sausage and Tortellini Soup**
- **Sweet Orange Caesar Salad**
- **Italian Cookies or Cannoli (bakery bought)**

Let your guests munch on a few store-bought items like mixed olives, cheese, and salamis while you're throwing this dinner together. If your company is impatient for the main course, shave a few more minutes off the soup's cook time by heating up the chicken stock in a separate pot while you start cooking up the sausage. If they can handle the full 30-minute wait, though, don't bother dirtying the extra pot.

SAUSAGE AND TORTELLINI SOUP

  2 tablespoons **EVOO** (extra-virgin olive oil; eyeball it)

  1 pound bulk **sweet Italian sausage**

  2 large **onions**, chopped

  3 **celery ribs**, with green leafy tops, finely chopped

  4 large **garlic cloves**, chopped

  1 small **fennel bulb**, cored and chopped, a handful of the green fronds reserved

  2 large pinches of **red pepper flakes**
    Salt and **black pepper**

  1 28-ounce can **diced tomatoes**

  2 quarts **chicken stock**

  2 9-ounce packages **fresh tortellini** (cheese, spinach, or mushroom)

1¹/₂ cups fresh **basil**, about 25 leaves, chopped

¹/₂ cup fresh **flat-leaf parsley** leaves, about 2 generous handfuls, chopped
    Grated **Parmigiano-Reggiano** cheese, for passing at the table

continued

MEALS FOR 8

Preheat a large soup pot over medium-high heat with 2 tablespoons of the EVOO, 2 times around the pan. Add the sausage to the hot pot and break it up with a wooden spoon into little pieces as it cooks, 3 to 4 minutes. Add the onions, celery, garlic, chopped fennel, red pepper flakes, and a little salt and pepper. Cook, stirring frequently, for 5 minutes. Add the tomatoes and continue to cook for a minute, then add the chicken stock. Put a lid on the pot to bring the soup up to a simmer and cook for 10 minutes. Uncover the pot, add the tortellini, and cook for 5 minutes. Once the pasta is cooked through, add the basil and parsley, then taste and re-season with a little more salt and pepper if you think it needs it. Chop up the reserved fennel fronds, stir them in, and serve. Pass the cheese at the table.

8 SERVINGS

SWEET ORANGE CAESAR SALAD

CROUTONS

3 tablespoons **EVOO** (extra-virgin olive oil; eyeball it)

3 tablespoons **butter**

4 cups cubed **crusty bread**

Salt and **black pepper**

1/2 cup grated **Parmigiano-Reggiano** cheese

SALAD AND DRESSING

2 **oranges**

1 large **garlic clove**, finely chopped

Juice of 1 lemon

1 tablespoon **Worcestershire sauce** (eyeball it)

1 tablespoon **Dijon mustard** (eyeball it)

1 teaspoon **anchovy paste** (look for the kind in the squeeze tube for easy refrigeration)

1/2 cup **EVOO** (extra-virgin olive oil)

2 sacks chopped **romaine lettuce**, 8 to 10 cups

1/2 cup shredded **Parmigiano-Reggiano** cheese, plus a bit more to finish the salad

Salt and **black pepper**

Preheat the oven to 325° F.

For the croutons, combine the EVOO and the butter in a small pot. Place over medium heat and cook until the butter is just barely melted. Place the bread in a large bowl and toss with the oil and butter. Season the bread with salt and pepper and sprinkle with the ½ cup of cheese. Spread the croutons evenly on a rimmed baking sheet and bake until crisp and golden, about 15 minutes. Let them cool.

For the salad, cut the stem end and the opposite end off each orange, stand the oranges on a flat side, and, using a paring knife, cut the peel from each orange in long downward strokes, being sure to also remove the white pith. Cut the oranges into ¼-inch-thick slices, and cut each of those slices in half.

To make the dressing, combine the garlic, lemon juice, Worcestershire sauce, mustard, and anchovy paste in the bowl you made the croutons in. Whisk until the anchovy has completely broken up in the mixture. In a slow, steady stream, whisk in the ½ cup of EVOO.

When you are ready to serve, add the lettuce to the dressing in the bowl and toss to coat evenly. Add the shredded cheese, orange slices, salt, pepper, and the cooled croutons. Toss again. Adjust the seasonings and serve.

8 SERVINGS

■ ■ ■

MARCO "POLLO" MENU

- Italian Chicken Pot Pie from the Boot
- Boozy Berries and Biscuits

What if a pot pie got a Eurail pass and came back home to the States speaking Italian? It might taste something like this; it's one rich meal AND it's a one-pot wonder. For dessert? One good one-pot deserves another! Boozy Berries and Biscuits: are they cocktails or desserts? Your call. My call is YUM-O!

ITALIAN CHICKEN POT PIE FROM THE BOOT

2 tablespoons **EVOO** (extra-virgin olive oil)

3 tablespoons **butter**

1 pound **button mushrooms**, trimmed and halved

1 1-pound bag **frozen pearl onions**, defrosted, then drained on a kitchen towel to remove excess liquid

4 large **garlic cloves**, finely chopped

2 large **carrots**, peeled and thinly sliced

3 **celery ribs**, thinly sliced

1 teaspoon **red pepper flakes**, $^1/_3$ palmful

Salt and **black pepper**

1 24-ounce log prepared plain or flavored **polenta** (on the refrigerator aisle)

1 1-pound ball fresh **mozzarella cheese**

3 tablespoons all-purpose **flour**

1 cup **dry white wine** (eyeball it)

1 quart **chicken stock**

$^1/_2$ cup **heavy cream** or half-and-half

2 cooked **rotisserie chickens**

1 pint **red grape tomatoes**

1 10-ounce box **frozen peas**

TIDBIT

The pot pie can be assembled ahead of time if you like; bake it for 25 minutes, or until browned. It also reheats well.

1 1/2 cups **fresh basil**, about 25 leaves, coarsely chopped or torn

3/4 cup fresh **flat-leaf parsley** leaves, about 3 generous handfuls, chopped

1 cup grated **Parmigiano-Reggiano** cheese, 3 overflowing handfuls

Preheat the broiler. Place the rack at the center position or drop the lower or upper broiler pans as far from the heat source as possible.

Preheat a large pot over medium-high heat with the EVOO, 2 times around the pan. Add the butter and, once it melts, add the mushrooms and cook for 4 to 5 minutes, to give them a little color. Add the pearl onions, garlic, carrots, celery, red pepper flakes, and a little salt and pepper. Cook, stirring occasionally, 5 minutes longer.

While the veggies are cooking, slice the polenta log into 1/4-inch-thick disks. One log should yield 20 to 22 disks. Halve the ball of mozzarella, then slice each half into 1/4-inch-thick half moons and reserve alongside the polenta disks.

Sprinkle the flour into the veggies and stir to combine, then continue to cook for another minute or two. Add the white wine, scraping up any bits on the bottom of the pot with a wooden spoon. Add the chicken stock and cream and bring up to a bubble, then simmer for 10 minutes.

Remove all the meat from the rotisserie chickens, tearing it into large bite-size pieces and discarding the skin. Add the chicken meat to the simmering sauce as you break it up. Once all of the meat is in the pot, add the tomatoes and peas and cook for another 2 minutes. Add the basil and parsley; taste to adjust the seasoning. Transfer the mixture to a large oval or rectangular baking dish, casserole, or lasagna pan. (Disposable pans are fine as well but buy two and double them up for sturdiness and to keep the bottom of the pot pie from scorching.) Shingle the polenta disks and the mozzarella half moons over the top of the chicken and vegetables, distributing the cheese evenly among the polenta. Sprinkle the top of the assembled dish with the grated cheese and transfer to the broiler several inches from the heat. Broil until the polenta is warm and the cheeses have browned.

8 SERVINGS

BOOZY BERRIES AND BISCUITS

- ¹/₂ pint **raspberries**
- ¹/₂ pint **blackberries**
- 2 pints **strawberries**, sliced
- 1 nip (2 ounces) **Frangelico**, Sambuca, or Amaretto—a couple generous shots
- 2 cups **heavy cream** (eyeball it)
- ¹/₄ cup **sugar**
- 2 packages of **anisette toasts,** such as Stella D'oro, cut into large bits with a serrated knife
- 1 3.5-ounce bar **bittersweet chocolate**, such as Ghirardelli (look for it on the baking aisle)

In a bowl, combine the berries with the liqueur of choice. Let the berries sit and macerate while you make dinner. Whip up the cream with the sugar, using a hand mixer, until soft peaks form; reserve the whipped cream in the refrigerator.

Once dinner starts winding down, arrange the bits of anisette toasts in a shallow serving dish with sides. Top with the booze-soaked berries, spreading them over the toasts. If the whipped cream has lost some of its air, give it a quick beat with a whisk. Top the berries with the whipped cream. Using a vegetable peeler, shave curls from the side of the chocolate bar, letting them cover the whipped cream.

8 SERVINGS

■ ■ ■

CITRUS SAMPLER

- **Lime-Grilled Chicken Breasts with Grilled Chili Toasts**
- **Avocado-Orange Salad**
- **Lemon Cookies and Sorbet (store-bought)**

Citrus flavors tie this whole menu together and keep everything tasting light and fresh. Use this cilantro-lime preparation with pork or firm white flaky fish like cod or mahimahi as well as chicken.

LIME-GRILLED CHICKEN BREASTS WITH GRILLED CHILI TOASTS

Zest and juice of 2 limes

1/4 cup **EVOO** (extra-virgin olive oil; eyeball it)

2 large **garlic cloves**, crushed

1 **jalapeño pepper**, halved, seeds removed

1/2 cup fresh **cilantro leaves**, 2 generous handfuls

1 tablespoon **ground cumin**, a palmful

Salt and **black pepper**

8 boneless, skinless **chicken breasts**, 6 ounces each

5 tablespoons softened **butter**

1 tablespoon **chili powder**, a palmful

8 thick slices **crusty, country-style bread**

Preheat the oven to 375° F.

In a blender or food processor, combine the lime zest and juice, EVOO, garlic, jalapeño, cilantro, cumin, salt, and pepper. Puree until smooth; add a splash of water if you have any trouble getting the blender going. Arrange the chicken in a shallow dish, pour the puree over the breasts, and thoroughly coat each piece in the mixture. Marinate for 10 minutes.

Preheat a grill pan over high heat.

continued

Sear the chicken breasts for 2 minutes on each side on the hot grill pan. Transfer them to a baking dish or rimmed baking sheet and place in the oven for 15 minutes.

In a small bowl, combine the softened butter and chili powder. Spread the chili butter on both sides of each bread slice. Lower the heat under the grill pan a little, then char the bread on both sides. Serve alongside the grilled chicken.

8 SERVINGS

OUTDOOR GRILL VERSION

If you are using an outdoor grill, cook the chicken start to finish on it. Char the meat, then lower the heat and set it off to the side to let it finish cooking through.

Add the buttered bread to the grill and grill on each side until lightly marked and the butter is melted. Use the cooler outer edges of the outdoor grill rather than the center.

AVOCADO-ORANGE SALAD

4 **Hass avocados**
  Juice of 1 lime
3 **oranges**
1 small **red onion**, finely chopped
2 bunches of **watercress**, trimmed of thick stems
1 head of **Bibb lettuce**, leaves torn into bite-size pieces
2 tablespoons **Dijon mustard** (eyeball it)
3 tablespoons **red wine vinegar** (eyeball it)
  Hot sauce
  Salt and **black pepper**
$^1/_3$ cup **EVOO** (extra-virgin olive oil; eyeball it)

Halve each avocado, remove the pit, and with a spoon, scoop out the avocado flesh in one piece. Cut each half lengthwise into 5 wedges. Sprinkle the lime juice over the avocado. Transfer the wedges to a large salad bowl.

Cut the stem end and the opposite end off each orange, stand the oranges upright, and, using a paring knife, cut downward to remove the peel from each orange, being sure to also remove the white pith. Cut the oranges into $^1/_4$-inch-thick slices and cut each of those slices in half. Add the orange slices to the avocados along with the red onions, watercress, and Bibb lettuce.

In a small bowl, combine the mustard, red wine vinegar, hot sauce to taste, salt, and black pepper. Whisk to combine, then add the EVOO in a slow, steady stream. Pour the dressing over the salad and fold gently to coat the avocados and oranges.

8 SERVINGS

■ ■ ■

08

• Preheat the grill or grill pan.

• Mix and form the burgers.

• While the burgers grill, cook the couscous and make the salad.

• Grill the pitas.

BURGER NIGHT HITS THE ROAD TO MOROCCO

- Grilled Moroccan-Spiced Turkey Burgers with Mango Chutney Slaw
- Veggie Chickpea and Couscous Salad with Yogurt Dressing

I'm always trying to figure out cool and easy new ways to put turkey burgers together. This one is particularly easy since the dry spices will be doing the heavy lifting. I love inviting a crowd over on burger night. Entertaining with casual food is a great rule to follow: people are more relaxed around relaxed food.

GRILLED MOROCCAN-SPICED TURKEY BURGERS WITH MANGO CHUTNEY SLAW

$3^1/_2$ to 4 pounds **ground turkey breast**

2 tablespoons **ground cumin**, 2 palmfuls

1 teaspoon **ground turmeric**, $^1/_3$ palmful

2 teaspoons **sweet or smoked sweet paprika**, $^2/_3$ palmful

1 tablespoon **ground coriander**, a palmful

1 teaspoon **cayenne pepper**, $^1/_3$ palmful

1 tablespoon **curry powder**, a palmful

1 small **onion**, grated

3 garlic **cloves**, chopped

$^1/_4$ cup fresh **cilantro** or flat-leaf parsley leaves, a handful, chopped

Zest and juice of 1 lemon

Salt and **black pepper**

EVOO (extra-virgin olive oil), for drizzling

$^1/_2$ cup prepared **mango chutney** (find it on the international aisle)

$^3/_4$ cup **plain yogurt** (eyeball it; look for thick, creamy Greek-style yogurt)

1 16-ounce sack of **shredded cabbage mix**
8 **pita breads**, any flavor or variety

Preheat an outdoor grill or grill pan to medium high.

Combine the turkey, cumin, turmeric, paprika, coriander, cayenne, curry powder, onions, garlic, cilantro or parsley, lemon zest, salt, and pepper in a bowl and mix well to distribute the spices. Form the mixture into 8 large patties about 1 inch thick. Drizzle the patties with EVOO and grill them for 6 minutes on each side, or until cooked through.

While the burgers are grilling, chop up the mango chutney, breaking up any large chunks. (This may not be necessary depending on the brand you buy.) Transfer the chutney to a bowl and mix with the lemon juice and yogurt. Add the cabbage mix and a little salt and pepper and toss to combine.

When the turkey burgers are done, put the pitas on the grill and heat on each side just to warm them up. Open up the pocket in each pita, nestle a turkey burger inside each, and spoon in some of the mango chutney slaw.

8 SERVINGS

VEGGIE CHICKPEA AND COUSCOUS SALAD WITH YOGURT DRESSING

4 cups **chicken or vegetable stock**

2¼ cups **couscous**

Salt and **black pepper**

2 tablespoons **EVOO** (extra-virgin olive oil; eyeball it)

1 small **red onion**, thinly sliced

2 **seedless European cucumbers**, cut in half lengthwise, then sliced into half moons

1 **red bell pepper**, chopped

1 cup fresh **flat-leaf parsley** leaves, 4 generous handfuls, chopped

1 pint **grape tomatoes**, halved

2 15-ounce cans **chickpeas**, drained, rinsed, then thoroughly dried

¾ cup **plain yogurt** (look for thick, creamy Greek-style yogurt)

3 tablespoons **red wine vinegar**

2 tablespoons **honey**

Hot sauce

15 fresh **mint** leaves (give or take a leaf), chopped

Bring the stock to a boil. Pour the couscous into a large bowl, add some salt and pepper and the EVOO, and stir with a fork to coat the couscous in the oil. Once the stock is boiling, pour it over the couscous and then wrap the bowl tightly with plastic wrap and let sit for 5 minutes.

While the couscous is steeping, combine the red onions, cucumbers, red bell peppers, parsley, grape tomatoes, chickpeas, salt, and pepper in a large salad bowl. To make the dressing, combine the yogurt, red wine vinegar, honey, a few dashes of hot sauce to taste, the mint, and some salt and pepper. Pour the dressing over the veggies and stir it up.

Fluff the couscous with a fork and add it to the dressed veggies. Toss thoroughly, taste, and adjust the seasonings with more salt and pepper.

8 SERVINGS

- Get the pasta water going.

- While the broccolini roasts, cook the pasta and bread the chops.

- Finish the pasta while the chops cook.

LICK YOUR CHOPS

- **Creamy Pasta with Roasted Broccolini and Red Onion**
- **Breaded Pork Chops**
- **Orange Sherbet with Fruit (store-bought)**

This tasty spread feeds a crowd on the cheap. You can add roasted cauliflower, broccoli, asparagus, or squash to the pasta as well; it's a great way to get picky eaters to embrace their veggies.

CREAMY PASTA WITH ROASTED BROCCOLINI AND RED ONION

Salt

1¹/₂ pounds **cavatappi** (hollow corkscrew pasta, such as Barilla brand)

3 bunches of **broccolini**, ends slightly trimmed

1 large **red onion,** sliced about ¹/₃ inch thick

¹/₄ cup **EVOO** (extra-virgin olive oil; eyeball it), plus some for drizzling

Black pepper

6 large **garlic cloves**, thinly sliced

1 teaspoon **red pepper flakes**

Zest and juice of 2 lemons

¹/₂ cup **heavy cream** or half-and-half (eyeball it)

1 cup grated **Parmigiano-Reggiano** cheese, plus more to pass

Preheat the oven to 450° F.

Bring a large covered pot of water to boil over high heat. Once boiling, add some salt and the pasta and cook to al dente. Right before draining, remove and reserve 1¹/₂ cups of the pasta cooking water.

Once you've got the water going, place the broccolini and sliced red onion on a rimmed baking sheet. Give them a healthy drizzle of EVOO, season with salt and pepper, and toss until they are well coated. Roast until the broccolini ends are crisp and brown and the stalks are tender, about 15 minutes.

continued

Place the pot you cooked the pasta in over medium-high heat with the $^1/_4$ cup of EVOO. Add the garlic and cook until golden; add the red pepper flakes, reserved pasta cooking water, lemon zest and juice, and heavy cream. Bring up to a bubble and cook for a minute or two. Add the pasta and the roasted broccolini and onions. Cook for 1 minute to thicken up the sauce, then turn the heat off, add the cheese, and stir to combine. Serve immediately with more cheese to pass at the table.

8 SERVINGS

BREADED PORK CHOPS

8 boneless **pork loin** chops no more than 1 inch thick
Salt and **black pepper**
$1^1/_2$ cups all-purpose **flour** (eyeball it)
4 **eggs**, beaten
$1^1/_2$ cups **plain bread crumbs** (eyeball it)
1 teaspoon freshly grated or ground **nutmeg** (eyeball it)
$^1/_2$ cup chopped fresh **flat-leaf parsley**, about 2 generous handfuls
Vegetable or light olive oil, for frying
Lemon wedges

Pound the chops between wax paper with a small, heavy skillet to $^1/_2$ inch thickness. Season with salt and pepper. Set up a breading assembly line: a dish with the flour, a shallow dish with the beaten eggs, and a plate with the bread crumbs combined with the nutmeg and parsley. Dip each chop first into the flour, shaking off the excess, then into the eggs, and lastly into the bread crumbs.

Add a thin layer of vegetable or olive oil to a large skillet over medium to medium-high heat. When the oil is hot, add the breaded pork chops. (Cook the chops in 2 batches if necessary.) Cook for 3 to 4 minutes on each side until evenly golden. Sprinkle with a bit more salt while hot. Serve the chops with lemon wedges.

8 SERVINGS

CHINESE CHECKERS

- Orange-Cashew Chicken with Broccoli
- Ginger Noodles
- Coconut Sorbet with Exotic Fruit—mangoes, papayas, and kiwis (store-bought)
- Fortune Cookies and Tea (store-bought—look for fortune cookies on international foods aisle)

Maybe this will sound familiar to you: you go to a Chinese restaurant and order Cashew Chicken. When it comes, you can count the number of cashews you get on one hand. You eat your precious cashews sparingly so as to make them last to the end of your meal. How irritating is that? I say put as many fistfuls of cashews in this dish as you like when you make this orange-flavored version of an old favorite at home. Your friends will hug you for it!

GINGER NOODLES

Salt

1½ pounds **perciatelli** or bucatini pasta—they boil up big!

2 tablespoons **vegetable oil** (eyeball it)

4-inch piece of **fresh ginger**, peeled and grated

3 large **garlic cloves**, chopped

1½ cups **chicken stock**

½ cup **tamari** (dark soy sauce; eyeball it)

6 **scallions**, thinly sliced

Fill your largest pot with water, cover, and bring to a boil over high heat. Once it reaches a boil, add some salt and the pasta and cook to al dente.

continued

Once you've dropped the pasta in the boiling water, preheat a large skillet over medium heat with the oil, 2 times around the pan. Add the ginger and garlic and cook, stirring frequently, for 2 to 3 minutes. Add the chicken stock and tamari and bring up to a simmer. Let it continue to simmer while you wait for the pasta to finish cooking. Drain the pasta thoroughly and add to the skillet. Toss to coat and continue to cook until the pasta has soaked up most of the liquid in the skillet. (If you don't think your skillet is big enough for all the pasta, then transfer the sauce to the pot you cooked the pasta in and combine and cook it in there.) Turn the heat off and add the scallions.

8 SERVINGS

ORANGE-CASHEW CHICKEN WITH BROCCOLI

5 tablespoons **vegetable oil**

7 boneless, skinless **chicken breasts**, 6 ounces each, cut into large bite-size pieces

Salt and **black pepper**

1 large **onion**, thinly sliced

4 large **garlic cloves**, chopped

2 **red bell peppers**, seeded and sliced

1 16-ounce bag of **broccoli florets**

1 rounded teaspoon **red pepper flakes**

1/2 tablespoon **ground coriander**, 1/2 palmful

Zest and juice of 2 oranges

1/2 cup **tamari** (dark soy sauce; eyeball it)

3 tablespoons **honey** (eyeball it)

3 cups **chicken stock**

1 tablespoon **cornstarch**

1, 2, or 3 cups—as many cups of roasted, **unsalted cashews** as you like

1/2 cup fresh **cilantro leaves**, 2 generous handfuls, chopped

Preheat a large, deep skillet over high heat with 3 tablespoons of the oil, 3 times around the pan. Season the chicken with some salt and pepper and brown the meat; brown it in 2 batches if necessary. Once the meat has browned, remove it to a plate and reserve. Return the skillet to the heat and add 2 tablespoons of the remaining oil, the onions, garlic, red bell peppers, broccoli, red pepper flakes, and coriander. Cook, stirring frequently, for 3 to 4 minutes, or until the veggies start to get tender. Add the orange zest and juice, tamari, and honey; stir, scraping up any brown bits on the bottom of the pan. Add the chicken stock and bring up to a simmer, then return the browned chicken to the pan and cook for another 5 minutes, or until the chicken is cooked through. Mix the cornstarch with a little splash of water in a small bowl and add to the pan to thicken up the sauce a bit. Add the cashews—AS MANY AS YOU WANT! Serve the cashew chicken over the ginger noodles and garnish with the chopped cilantro.

8 SERVINGS

• Heat the poaching liquid and start the mushroom ragù.

• Poach the chicken breasts, finish the ragù, and make the salad dressing as they cook.

• Toss the salad just before serving.

PERFECTLY POACHED SUPPER

• **Lemon and Thyme Poached Chicken with a Mushroom-Potato Ragù**
• **Creamy Dijon-Dressed Mixed Greens**
• **Crusty French Bread (store-bought)**
• **Strawberry Pie or Cheesecake (store-bought)**

There's a little bonus to this recipe: poaching the chicken leaves behind some super-fortified, tasty stock. Strain the cooled stock, transfer it to a resealable freezer bag, and label it. Store in the fridge for a few days or freeze your super-stock. Being thrifty can be very tasty!

LEMON AND THYME POACHED CHICKEN WITH A MUSHROOM-POTATO RAGÙ

2 quarts **chicken stock**

4 to 5 **fresh thyme** sprigs

Zest and juice of 2 lemons

5 **garlic cloves**, 3 cracked from their skins, 2 chopped

Freshly ground black pepper

8 boneless, skinless **chicken breasts**, 6 ounces each

3 tablespoons **EVOO** (extra-virgin olive oil; eyeball it)

1 pound **button mushrooms**, halved

1/2 pound **shiitake mushrooms**, stemmed, caps sliced

Salt

1 large **yellow onion**, thinly sliced

3/4 pound **red potatoes**, halved, then thinly sliced into half moons

A couple pinches of **red pepper flakes**

1 pint **grape tomatoes**

1/2 cup fresh **flat-leaf parsley** leaves, 2 generous handfuls, chopped

2 tablespoons **butter**
   Crusty French bread for 8, warmed

Place the chicken stock, thyme, lemon zest, 3 cracked cloves of garlic, and a little freshly ground black pepper in a large soup pot with a tight-fitting lid. Bring to a simmer over high heat. Add the chicken breasts, replace the lid, and bring back to a simmer. Poach the chicken for 15 minutes.

While the stock is coming up to a simmer, heat a large skillet over high heat with the EVOO, 3 times around the pan. Add the mushrooms to the skillet and brown for 7 to 8 minutes. Add the chopped garlic, salt and pepper, the onions, potatoes, and red pepper flakes and cook, stirring frequently, for 7 to 8 minutes more. Add a few ladles, about $1^1/_2$ cups, of the chicken poaching liquid. (You can remove the $1^1/_2$ cups of poaching liquid at any time during the poaching process.) Cook for a couple minutes to reduce the stock, then add the grape tomatoes. The tomatoes will burst and become part of the sauce after 2 or 3 minutes. Add the parsley, butter, and lemon juice and stir until the butter has melted. Turn the heat off.

To serve, transfer the poached chicken breasts from the liquid to a cutting board. Cut each breast into a few slices on a slight angle. Transfer the mushroom-potato ragù to a serving platter and top with the sliced poached chicken. Serve with warm, crusty bread for mopping.

8 SERVINGS

CREAMY DIJON-DRESSED MIXED GREENS

2 tablespoons **Dijon mustard**

2 tablespoons **mayonnaise**

2 tablespoons **white wine vinegar** (eyeball it)

   Salt and **freshly ground black pepper**

3 tablespoons **EVOO** (extra-virgin olive oil; eyeball it)

8 to 10 cups **chopped mixed greens**, 3 12-ounce sacks of any blend

In a large salad bowl, combine the mustard, mayonnaise, vinegar, a little salt, and some freshly ground black pepper. Whisk in the EVOO in a slow, steady stream. Add the greens to the bowl and toss to coat.

8 SERVINGS

■ ■ ■

• Get the rice going and put the prosciutto in the oven.

• Start the soup; while it simmers, make the salad dressing.

• When the soup is ready, assemble the salad.

S-EASY-FOOD SOUPER SUPPER

- **Venetian Seafood Soup with Rice**
- **Tomato and Red Onion Salad with Crispy Prosciutto**
- **Tiramisù (store-bought)**

Venice was a major port of trade and so the spice combinations in Venetian cooking are more unique than anywhere else in Italy. You'll find curry and saffron used more predominantly and in combination with tomatoes and sweet basil. Exotic and good!

VENETIAN SEAFOOD SOUP WITH RICE

3 quarts **chicken stock**

Salt and **black pepper**

1¹/₂ cups **long-grain white rice**

2 tablespoons **EVOO** (extra-virgin olive oil; eyeball it)

2 large **yellow onions**, chopped

3 cups **shredded carrots** (available in pouches in the produce department)

4 **celery ribs**, sliced

¹/₄ teaspoon **saffron threads**, or 1 envelope saffron powder

1 teaspoon **red pepper flakes**

4 **garlic cloves**, chopped

2 heaping tablespoons **tomato paste**

1 cup **dry white wine**

1¹/₂ pounds fresh **halibut**, cut into 2-inch chunks

16 large **shrimp**, peeled, deveined, tails removed

8 **sea scallops**, cut in half

¹/₂ cup fresh **flat-leaf parsley** leaves, a few handfuls, chopped

1 cup fresh **basil**, 20 leaves, shredded

1 **lemon**, cut in wedges

Place a sauce pot with 3 cups of the chicken stock over high heat and bring up to a boil. Add some salt and pepper and the rice. Bring the

continued

liquid back to a boil, place a lid on the pot, and turn the heat down to medium and simmer for 17 to 18 minutes, or until the rice is tender.

Preheat a large soup pot over medium-high heat with the EVOO, 2 times around the pan. Add the onions, carrots, celery, saffron, red pepper flakes, garlic, tomato paste, and a little salt and pepper. Cook, stirring frequently, for 4 to 5 minutes, or until the veggies start to get nice and tender. Add the white wine and bring it up to a bubble, then add the remaining 2 quarts 1 cup of chicken stock; cover the pot to bring it up to a fast bubble. Remove the lid and simmer for 5 minutes. Add the halibut, shrimp, and scallops and simmer gently for 5 more minutes. Stir in the parsley, basil, and cooked rice and serve with lemon wedges.

8 SERVINGS

TOMATO AND RED ONION SALAD WITH CRISPY PROSCIUTTO

- 8 slices **prosciutto di Parma**
- 1 small **red onion**, finely chopped
- 3 tablespoons **red wine vinegar**
  Salt and **black pepper**
- 1/3 cup **EVOO** (extra-virgin olive oil)
- 4 **Roma tomatoes**, thinly sliced
- 1/2 cup fresh **flat-leaf parsley** leaves, coarsely chopped
- 2 heads of **romaine lettuce**, coarsely chopped or torn into bite-size pieces

Preheat the oven to 350° F.

Cut the prosciutto into strips and pull them apart. Arrange them on a baking sheet and bake for 7 to 8 minutes, or until crisp. Cool on the baking sheet.

In a salad bowl, combine the red onions, vinegar, and a little salt and pepper. In a slow, steady stream, whisk in the EVOO. Add the tomatoes, parsley, and lettuce and toss to coat. Top with the crispy prosciutto.

8 SERVINGS

SMALLIDAY GATHERING

- Mix up the martinis.

- Mix up the potato pancakes and assemble the quesadillas.

- While the pancakes and quesadillas cook, make the pomegranate syrup and guacamole.

- Shake the martinis with ice and serve.

- **Pomegranate Martinis**
- **Spicy Sweet Potato Pancakes with Holiday Guacamole**
- **Chicken Quesadilla Pinwheels**
- **Elephant Ears with Warm Caramel Dipping Sauce**

I like to invite people over in small groups and have a few special nights scattered throughout the holiday season rather than kill myself entertaining a huge group on a single big blowout. Celebrate small holidays this year with this Smalliday menu; whether Hanukkah or Christmas is being celebrated, this snack menu has got you and a few friends covered.

CHICKEN QUESADILLA PINWHEELS

4 10- to 12-inch **flour tortillas**
2 cups shredded **Monterey Jack cheese**
1 cup prepared **chipotle salsa**
2 cups chopped **rotisserie chicken meat**, still warm from the store
   or reheated in the microwave

Heat a large skillet over medium heat. Add a flour tortilla, heat it until blistered on one side, then turn it over. Scatter $1/2$ cup of the cheese on top and cook for 1 minute. Remove to a cutting board. Top the tortilla with $1/4$ cup of the salsa, spreading it gently to the edges with the back of a spoon. Top with $1/2$ cup shredded chicken, then roll the tortilla into a log. Let it stand a minute before cutting into $1/2$-inch slices. Make 3 more quesadillas with the remaining ingredients and arrange the pinwheels on a platter.

8 APPETIZER SERVINGS

SPICY SWEET POTATO PANCAKES WITH HOLIDAY GUACAMOLE

Light olive oil or peanut oil, for frying

1 large **Idaho potato**, peeled and shredded

2 medium **sweet potatoes**, peeled and shredded

1 small **onion**, peeled

1 **egg**, beaten

3 tablespoons all-purpose **flour**, cracker meal, or matzo meal

1 tablespoon **chili powder**, a palmful

2 teaspoons **smoked sweet paprika**, $^2/_3$ palmful

2 teaspoons **ground cumin**, $^2/_3$ palmful

2 teaspoons **ground coriander**, $^2/_3$ palmful

Salt

$^3/_4$ cup **pomegranate juice**

2 **Hass avocados**

Juice of 1 lemon

$^1/_2$ medium **red onion**, finely chopped

1 small **garlic clove**, pasted up with some salt

2 **jalapeños**, seeded and finely chopped

Heat about $^1/_3$ cup of the oil over medium to medium-high heat.

Drain the shredded potatoes and sweet potatoes, pressing them down in a colander to get as much moisture out as possible. Place the potatoes in a bowl and, using a box grater, grate the onion directly into the potatoes so that the onion juices fall into the bowl as well. Add the egg and flour or meal to the bowl, then season with the chili powder, paprika, cumin, coriander, and salt. Drop the batter into the hot oil to make $2^1/_2$-inch pancakes. Fry the cakes in batches, adding more oil as needed, until deeply golden on both sides. Drain on paper towels. You will get about 16 pancakes.

Pour the pomegranate juice into a small saucepan. Bring to a boil and cook until it's reduced to a syrup. Cut the avocados in half, all the way around the pit. Remove the pit with a spoon, then scoop the flesh into a bowl. Add the lemon juice, red onions, garlic, jalapeños, and a generous amount of salt. Mash the guacamole until smooth.

Arrange the potato pancakes on a platter and top them with heaping spoonfuls of guacamole. Drizzle with the pomegranate syrup.

8 SERVINGS

POMEGRANATE MARTINIS

1 cup **pomegranate juice**

$^1/_2$ shot **triple sec**

4 shots **vodka**

A splash of **lemon juice**

Chill 2 martini glasses with ice.

Pour the ingredients over ice in a cocktail shaker and shake vigorously to chill the drinks. Strain into the martini glasses and serve.

2 SERVINGS

ELEPHANT EARS WITH WARM CARAMEL DIPPING SAUCE

1 jar **caramel sauce**, any brand

$^1/_4$ teaspoon ground **cinnamon**

2 pinches of **cayenne pepper** or chili powder

1 package **elephant ear or angel wing cookies** (palmiers), such as Stella D'oro brand, at least 12 pieces

Place the sauce in a small pan with a splash of water and warm through over low heat. Stir in the cinnamon and cayenne pepper. When you are ready to serve, pour the sauce into a small serving dish and surround it with cookies for dipping. The sauce can be reheated in a microwave as necessary.

8 SERVINGS

GAME PLAN

- Get the pasta going and toast the pine nuts.

- Start the sauce; while it reduces, make the salad.

- Toss the pasta and sauce with the ricotta and dress the salad.

PRIMA PRIMAVERA SPRING SUPPER

- Sweet Pea and Onion Tortellini with Ricotta
- Bresaola and Prosciutto Salad
- Good, Strong Coffee and Biscotti (store-bought)

Start your spring season off right: with a mailbox full of thank-you notes from your grateful guests! Or, put a little spring into a long winter with this elegant, light menu.

SWEET PEA AND ONION TORTELLINI WITH RICOTTA

1	cup **pine nuts** (pignoli)
2	tablespoons **EVOO** (extra-virgin olive oil; eyeball it)
10	thick slices **pancetta**, chopped
3	**red onions**, chopped
	Salt and **freshly ground black pepper**
5	large **garlic cloves**, finely chopped
2	tablespoons **red wine vinegar** (eyeball it)
2 1/2	cups **chicken stock** (eyeball it)
5	9-ounce packages **fresh cheese, spinach, or mushroom tortellini** (on the refrigerator aisle)
3	10-ounce boxes **frozen peas**
1 1/2	cups **whole-milk ricotta** cheese, at room temperature
1	cup grated **Parmigiano-Reggiano** cheese, plus some to pass at the table
3/4	cup fresh **flat-leaf parsley** leaves, 3 generous handfuls, chopped

Bring a large covered pot of water to a boil over high heat.

Toast the pine nuts in the oven or in a dry skillet over medium heat until fragrant and golden. Transfer to a bowl to cool.

Preheat a large skillet over medium-high heat with the EVOO, 2 times around the pan. Add the pancetta and cook until crispy, 3 to 4 minutes. Once crispy, remove the pancetta from the skillet with a slotted spoon and drain it on a paper-towel-lined plate. Return the skillet to the heat and add the onions, a little salt, and a lot of freshly ground black pepper to the fat in the pan. Cook, stirring frequently, for 7 to 8 minutes, or until the onions just start to brown. Add the garlic and continue to cook for 4 to 5 minutes. Add the vinegar and cook until it evaporates, then add the chicken stock. Bring the liquid to a bubble and cook until reduced by half.

Salt the boiling water, add the tortellini, and cook for 5 minutes. When they have cooked for about 3 minutes, add the peas to the chicken stock.

Place the ricotta cheese in a very large bowl and stir in the onion and pea sauce. Fold in the drained tortellini, crispy pancetta, grated cheese, pine nuts, and parsley. Pass more Parmigiano at the table.

8 SERVINGS

BRESAOLA AND PROSCIUTTO SALAD

16 slices **bresaola**

16 slices **prosciutto di Parma**

8 cups **arugula**, coarsely chopped

1 1/2 cups fresh **basil**, about 25 leaves, coarsely chopped or torn

Juice of 1 lemon

3 tablespoons **EVOO** (extra-virgin olive oil; eyeball it)

Salt and **black pepper**

Arrange alternating slices of the bresaola and the prosciutto on a large platter. Combine the arugula and the basil and mound them in the center of the platter. Squeeze the lemon juice over the platter, drizzle with the EVOO, and season with salt and pepper. Serve.

8 SERVINGS

THANKS

- To all the hungry people who keep me writing and cooking.

- To Starbucks, for all their support with caffeinated beverages.

- To my family and close friends for continuing to inspire.

- To Pam Krauss and her peeps, who continue to brew my babble into books.

- And to Isaboo, my pooch with a discriminating palate, for test-kitchen-tasting so many recipes.

INDEX

INDEX

303

RACHAEL'S ON A ROLL!

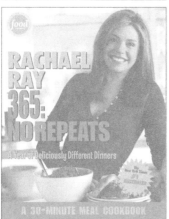